Markt- und Unternehmensentwicklung
Markets and Organisations

Series Editors
Arnold Picot, München, Germany
Ralf Reichwald, Leipzig, Germany
Egon Franck, Zürich, Switzerland
Kathrin M. Möslein, Erlangen-Nürnberg, Germany

Change of institutions, technology and competition drives the interplay of markets and organisations. The scientific series 'Markets and Organisations' addresses a magnitude of related questions, presents theoretic and empirical findings and discusses related concepts and models.

Edited by

Professor Dr. Dres. h. c. Arnold Picot
Ludwig-Maximilians-Universität
München, Deutschland

Professor Dr. Egon Franck
Universität Zürich, Schweiz

Professor Dr. Professor h. c. Dr. h. c.
Ralf Reichwald
HHL Leipzig Graduate School of
Management, Leipzig, Deutschland

Professorin Dr. Kathrin M. Möslein
Friedrich-Alexander-Universität
Erlangen-Nürnberg & HHL
Leipzig, Deutschland

More information about this series at http://www.springer.com/series/12561

Christofer F. Daiberl

Driving Networked Service Productivity

With a foreword by Prof. Dr. Kathrin M. Möslein

 Springer Gabler

Christofer F. Daiberl
FAU Erlangen Nürnberg
Nürnberg, Germany

Dissertation Friedrich-Alexander-Universität Erlangen-Nürnberg, 2019

Markt- und Unternehmensentwicklung Markets and Organisations
ISBN 978-3-658-29579-0   ISBN 978-3-658-29580-6   (eBook)
https://doi.org/10.1007/978-3-658-29580-6

This Springer Gabler imprint is published by the registered company Springer Fachmedien Wiesbaden
GmbH part of Springer Nature.
The registered company address is: Abraham-Lincoln-Str. 46, 65189 Wiesbaden, Germany

Foreword

Improving service productivity is vital for traditional service organizations and servitizing manufacturing firms alike. It addresses the challenge of better utilizing resources in times of rising demand and is connected to economic and social prosperity. However, so far, research mainly focused on the interaction between a single provider and one or more of its customers. This perspective does not do justice to contemporary service delivery which is often characterized by several providers jointly realizing the overall customer journey. Public and private service offerings in industries such as healthcare, e-commerce, mobility, and finance all depend on effective coordination and collaboration among specialized actors who are part of a larger service delivery network.

The work of Christofer F. Daiberl focuses on these interactions and explores how a focal provider can enhance productivity in the context of networked service delivery. Following a pragmatist paradigm, he does not only provide novel and in part surprising insights, but also proposes a research-based approach for decision makers in organizations to identify, analyze and seize productivity improvement opportunities throughout their own service interactions. Moreover, he harnesses his findings to develop design principles that can be applied by scholars and service professionals for their own productivity improvement initiatives.

The thesis has been accepted as a doctoral dissertation in 2019 by the School of Business, Economics and Society at the Friedrich-Alexander-Universität Erlangen-Nürnberg. "Driving networked service productivity" is a truly exciting, thought provoking and very well-organized read providing actual value for academia and industry alike. The author overcomes current conceptual limitations and provides clear managerial guidelines which can be attuned to different service contexts. He stresses the necessity to reflect on the subjective productivity perceptions of all relevant network actors in order to establish mutual beneficial service interactions and ensure sustained operational success. In doing so, the author challenges current beliefs about what it means to be productive in a service context and proposes concise solutions to uncovered problems.

The work deserves a broad dissemination in both the research community and in management practice. It is particularly recommended to scholars and practitioners interested in assessing and driving productivity in a networked service environment. I wish that many readers can harness the insights presented in order to design, implement and improve service offerings from a network perspective, i.e., taking customers, providers, and relevant co-providers into account. As a result, we all could benefit.

Prof. Dr. Kathrin M. Möslein

Preface

This book is the result of my personal journey at the Friedrich-Alexander-Universität Erlangen-Nürnberg, which started in fall 2011 as a master's student in International Business Studies. Soon I began working as a student assistant for the Chair of Information Systems, Innovation & Value Creation. This time truly inspired me to adopt a scientific mindset and fostered my wish to contribute to service research myself. Thus, after finishing my master's studies in 2014, I started working as a research associate at the very same chair and after a challenging, instructive, and exciting time, I received my PHD in 2019. More than seven years in which I not only gained new knowledge and skills but also developed as a person. For me, these outcomes are so much more valuable than the letters on the following pages.

In the last years, some of my colleagues turned into some of my best friends and supervisors turned into mentors. Thanks for your continuous support, the insightful discussions and the good times. You will always have a place in my heart, and I will never forget the good times we shared. Moreover, thanks to my entire family. Thank you for always believing in me and being there for me no matter what. I am very lucky to have you in my life. Finally, thanks to you, Ann Kristin for your infinite patience and continuous support. You gave me the courage to finish this journey – now I am excited to start many new ones with you.

Overview of contents

Part I Introduction: About the research 1

1   Motivation and relevance 3

2   Research questions 9

3   Overall research design 11

4   Structure of the dissertation 15

Part II Foundations: Key concepts of the research 19

1   Objectives and structure 21

2   The concept of service 23

3   Service productivity and its improvement 28

4   Networked service delivery 41

5   Summary and synthesis of key concepts 46

**Part III Systematic literature review: Approaches for improving service
productivity from a network perspective** 49

1   Objectives and structure 51

2   Classification scheme for productivity improvement approaches 53

3   Procedure 55

4   Findings 61

5   Discussion 87

**Part IV Exploratory case study: Proposing the concept of networked service
productivity** 91

1   Objectives and structure 93

2   Method and data 95

3   Findings 108

4   Discussion 122

**Part V Design science research study: Proposing a technique for driving
networked service productivity** 129

1   Objectives and structure 131

2   Theoretical background for design 133

3   Method and data 142

4   Findings 152

5   Discussion 189

Part VI Reflections and conclusion: Driving networked service productivity 195

1   Objectives and structure 197

2   Summary of Parts I-V 199

3   Design principles 209

4   Limitations and directions for future research 215

5   Concluding remarks 220

References 221

Appendix 247

Table of contents

Part I   Introduction: About the research 1

1   Motivation and relevance 3

2   Research questions..9

3   Overall research design...11

4   Structure of the dissertation...15

Part II Foundations: Key concepts of the research 19

1   Objectives and structure..21

2   The concept of service..23

    2.1   Service as a unit of output 23

    2.2   Service as a perspective on value creation 24

    2.3   Service as a particular type of production process 25

3   Service productivity and its improvement...28

    3.1   Dimensions of service productivity 28

    3.2   Models and frameworks of service productivity 29

    3.3   Types of service productivity improvement approaches 34

    3.4   Strategies for improving service productivity..35

    3.5   The service productivity life cycle..38

4   Networked service delivery...41

    4.1   Network-related concepts in service research 41

    4.2   The concept of the service delivery network 43

5   Summary and synthesis of key concepts 46

Part III Systematic literature review: Approaches for improving service

       productivity from a network perspective 49

1   Objectives and structure..51

2   Classification scheme for productivity improvement approaches 53

3   Procedure..55

    3.1   Planning the review...55

    3.2   Conducting the review..56

    3.3   Communication and dissemination 60

4   Findings 61

4.1   Description of core contributions 61

4.2   Thematic overview of approaches 65

    4.2.1 Efficiency-focused approaches: "Doing the things right" from a network
    perspective 65

    4.2.2 Effectiveness-focused approaches: "Doing the right things" from a network
    perspective 69

    4.2.3 Integration approaches: Considering both service efficiency and service
    effectiveness 78

5   Discussion 87

5.1   Theoretical contributions 87

5.2   Implications for practitioners 89

5.3   Implications for the remainder of this dissertation 89

**Part IV Exploratory case study: Proposing the concept of networked service
productivity 91**

1   Objectives and structure 93

2   Method and data 95

2.1   Case study research approach 95

2.2   Research design 96

    2.2.1 Research setting 98

    2.2.2 Data collection and analysis 102

3   Findings 108

3.1   Conceptual model of networked service productivity 108

    3.1.1 Actor's conditions of network membership 110

    3.1.2 Actor's inputs, networked service delivery, and outcomes 111

    3.1.3 Networked service productivity 113

3.2   Drivers of aggregated NSP and related resistances 115

    3.2.1 Compatible conditions of network membership 116

    3.2.2 Commitment to networked service delivery 117

    3.2.3 Network-oriented coordination 118

    3.2.4 Network-oriented processes and surrogates 119

    3.2.5 Mutual learning among network actors 120

4   Discussion 122

4.1   Theoretical contributions 122

4.2   Implications for practitioners 125

4.3 Implications for the remainder of this dissertation.................................127

**Part V Design science research study: Proposing a technique for driving
networked service productivity** **129**

1 Objectives and structure...131

2 Theoretical background for design...133

    2.1 Modeling networked service delivery 133

        2.1.1 Modeling networked service delivery from the customers' point of view....133

        2.1.2 Modeling networked service delivery from an operational point of view 135

    2.2 FMEA-based improvement of service productivity 137

        2.2.1 Background related to FMEA...137

        2.2.2 FMEA-based portfolio approach to service productivity improvement........138

3 Method and data 142

    3.1 Design science research approach 142

    3.2 Research design...143

        3.2.1 Problem and motivation...144

        3.2.2 Objectives of the solution..144

        3.2.3 Design and development 145

        3.2.4 Demonstration and evaluation...145

            3.2.4.1 Evaluation design for the alpha version of NSPIRET.............................. 147

            3.2.4.2 Evaluation design for the beta version of NSPIRET 149

        3.2.5 Communication 151

4 Findings 152

    4.1 Alpha version of NSPIRET: Artifacts and evaluation results.......................152

        4.1.1 Artifact 1: Alpha version of the NSPIRET Navigator.........................153

        4.1.2 Artifact 2: Alpha version of NSPIRET Snapshotting.........................156

        4.1.3 Artifact 3: Alpha version of the NSPIRET Shoutbox.........................157

        4.1.4 Evaluation results..158

            4.1.4.1 Effectiveness of the alpha version 158

            4.1.4.2 Utility of the alpha version... 160

            4.1.4.3 Understandability of the alpha version 161

        4.1.5 Summary of design changes..162

    4.2 Beta version of NSPIRET: Artifacts and evaluation results 163

        4.2.1 Artifact 1: Beta version of the NSPIRET Navigator.........................163

        4.2.2 Artifact 2: Beta version of NSPIRET Snapshotting.........................167

        4.2.3 Artifact 3: Beta version of the NSPIRET Shoutbox 170

          4.2.3.1   *Technical architecture of the beta version of the NSPIRET Shoutbox*......................170

          4.2.3.2   *Main interactions with the beta version of the NSPIRET Shoutbox*......................171

       4.2.4 Evaluation results 175

          4.2.4.1   *Effectiveness of the beta version*...175

          4.2.4.2   *Utility of the beta version* 178

          4.2.4.3   *Understandability of the beta version*...180

          4.2.4.4   *Operational feasibility of the beta version*..182

       4.2.5 Summary of design changes and revised beta version of NSPRIET............183

5   Discussion..189

    5.1   Theoretical contributions..189

    5.2   Implications for practitioners 192

    5.3   Implications for the remainder of this dissertation.....................................194

Part VI Reflections and conclusion: Driving networked service productivity....... 195

1   Objectives and structure 197

2   Summary of Parts I-V...199

    2.1   Summary of Part I 199

    2.2   Summary of Part II...200

    2.3   Summary of Part III..201

    2.4   Summary of Part IV..204

    2.5   Summary of Part V...206

3   Design principles 209

4   Limitations and directions for future research...215

5   Concluding remarks...220

References...**221**

Appendix **247**

Appendix A: Author's work relevant to this dissertation 249

Appendix B: Research proposal for the literature review...251

Appendix C: Review protocol..254

Appendix D: Interview guide for exploratory case study 257

Appendix E: Interview guide for DSR study 261

Appendix F: Feedback tablet positioned at OI-Lab 264

List of figures

Figure 1: Overall research design of this dissertation 14

Figure 2: Overall structure of the dissertation 17

Figure 3: Structure of Part II 22

Figure 4: Service production process and productivity relationships 33

Figure 5: Types of service productivity improvement approaches 35

Figure 6: Service productivity life cycle 40

Figure 7: Service delivery network as a consequence of the customer journey 45

Figure 8: Structure of Part III 52

Figure 9: Scheme for high-level classification of approaches 53

Figure 10: Procedure of the systematic literature review 55

Figure 11: High-level classification of efficiency-focused approaches 65

Figure 12: High-level classification of effectiveness-focused approaches 69

Figure 13: High-level classification of integration approaches 78

Figure 14: Structure of Part IV 94

Figure 15: Three modes of conducting case research 96

Figure 16: Final template for data analysis 106

Figure 17: Conceptual model of networked service productivity 109

Figure 18: Identified drivers and related resistances of aggregated NSP 115

Figure 19: Structure of Part V 132

Figure 20: Portfolios of failure and innovation modes 140

Figure 21: DSR process applied 143

Figure 22: Evaluation episodes of the DSR study 147

Figure 23: Interrelationships of NSPIRET's artifacts 152

Figure 24: Conceptual structure of the alpha version of the NSPIRET Navigator 155

Figure 25: Exemplary snapshot developed in the context of eMobilizer
(anonymized excerpt) 157

Figure 26: Conceptual structure of the beta version of the NSPIRET Navigator 165

Figure 27: Visual notation for modeling networked service delivery 168

Figure 28: Exemplary snapshot for two touchpoints in the context of OI-Lab
(anonymized excerpt) 169

Figure 29: Technical architecture of the beta version of the NSPIRET Shoutbox 170

Figure 30: Sharing of failure modes in the context of OI-Lab 171

Figure 31: Sharing of innovation modes in the context of OI-Lab 172

Figure 32: Exemplary portfolio of failure modes in the context of OI-Lab 173

Figure 33: Exemplary portfolio of innovation modes in the context of OI-Lab 174

Figure 34: Exemplary editing of failure mode and planning of intervention in the context
          of OI-Lab 174

Figure 35: Excerpt of color-coded NSIPRET Snapshot in the context of OI-Lab 186

Figure 36: Revised design of landing page for actors' representatives 187

Figure 37: Sorting and filtering mechanisms in the admin panel of the NSPIRET
          Shoutbox 187

Figure 38: Information included in the admin panel of NSP Shoutbox 188

Figure 39: Positioning of NSPIRET in comparison to other integration approaches
          presented in Part III of this dissertation 190

Figure 40: Structure of Part VI 198

Figure 41: Derivation of design principles 210

List of tables

Table 1: Summary of key concepts of this dissertation 48

Table 2: Outlets considered for the review 57

Table 3: Inclusion and exclusion criteria for the systematic literature review 58

Table 4: Compilation of core contributions 62

Table 5: Qualities of efficiency-focused approaches 68

Table 6: Qualities of effectiveness-focused approaches 76

Table 7: Qualities of integration approaches 85

Table 8: Summary of implications for the remainder of this dissertation 90

Table 9: Comparison of both case settings of networked service delivery 101

Table 10: Primary and secondary data collected for the exploratory case study 104

Table 11: Theoretical relationships for improving aggregated NSP 124

Table 12: Managerial questions and indicators supporting the improvement of aggregated NSP 126

Table 13: Summary of implications for the remainder of this dissertation 128

Table 14: Comparison of failure and innovation modes 139

Table 15: Activities of the alpha version of the NSPIRET Navigator 154

Table 16: Feedback sheet applied in the context of eMobilizer (anonymized excerpt) 158

Table 17: Number of failure and innovation modes identified and interventions in the context of eMobilizer 159

Table 18: Distribution of failure modes across service system elements in the context of eMobilizer 159

Table 19: Distribution of innovation modes across service system elements in the context of eMobilizer 159

Table 20: Design changes to the alpha version of NSPIRET 162

Table 21: Process activities of the beta version of the NSPIRET Navigator 166

Table 22: Number of failure and innovation modes identified and interventions in the context of OI-Lab 175

Table 23: Distribution of failure and innovation modes over the evaluation period in the context of OI-Lab 176

Table 24: Distribution of failure modes across service system elements in the context of OI-Lab 176

Table 25: Distribution of innovation modes across service system elements in the context of OI-Lab *176*

Table 26: Design changes to the beta version of NSPIRET *184*

Table 27: Activities of the revised beta version of the NSPIRET Navigator *185*

Table 28: Theoretical contributions for design and action *191*

Table 29: Practical implications of the artifacts throughout the service productivity life cycle *193*

Table 30: Summary of implications for the remainder of this dissertation *194*

Table 31: Summary of the systematic literature review *203*

Table 32: Summary of the exploratory case study *205*

Table 33: Summary of the DSR study *208*

Table 34: Summary of design principles *214*

List of abbreviations

BPMN	*Business process modeling notation*
C	*Customers*
CEM	*Customer experience modeling*
CEO	*Chief executive officer*
cf.	*confer*
cont.	*continued*
CP	*Co-providers*
CJA	*Customer journey analysis*
CJML	*Customer journey modeling language*
DC	*Design change*
DEA	*Data envelopment analysis*
DSR	*Design science research*
e.g.,	*exempli gratia (lat.); for example*
e-Mobility	*electro mobility*
et. al.	*et alia (lat.); and others*
etc.	*et cetera (lat.); and so on*
EV	*Evaluation*
FEDS	*Framework for evaluation in design science*
FM	*Failure mode*
FMEA	*Failure modes and effects analysis*
FP	*Focal provider*
i.e.,	*id est (lat.); that means*
ICT	*Information and communication technology*
IM	*Innovation mode*
ISB	*Information service blueprint*
KPIs	*Key performance indicators*
MINDS	*Management and interaction design for service*
MSD	*Multilevel service design*
n.d.	*no date*
NSP	*Networked service productivity*
NSPIRET	*Networked service productivity improvement technique*

O	*Objective*
p.	*page*
PCN	*Process-chain-network*
PTN	*Perceptual triadic network*
para.	*Paragraph*
ProMES	*Productivity measurement and enhancement system*
RQ	*Research question*
R&D	*Research and development*
SD	*Service delivery*
SDN	*Service delivery network*
SE	*Service engineering*
SM	*Service management*
UST	*Unified services theory*
VCM	*Value cocreation modeling*
VSA	*Viable systems approach*
WSS	*Work system snapshot*

Abstract

Enhancing the conceptual and operational understanding of how to improve service productivity is of utmost importance for scholars and practitioners alike. Until recently, service research has primarily focused on the dyadic interaction between the customer and a single service provider. However, driven by technological progress and increasing specialization, today services are often delivered by a network of providers. Nevertheless, current models of service productivity and established approaches for its improvement do not reflect upon the networked nature of contemporary service delivery.

Against this backdrop, this dissertation explores *how a focal provider can drive productivity in the context of networked service delivery*. Initially, this research objective is addressed by means of a systematic literature review and an exploratory case study. Whereas the former depicts operational qualities of existing approaches and, in doing so, highlights pitfalls for their practical application, the latter fosters an empirically-derived conceptual understanding for this dissertation. It proposes the concept of networked service productivity (NSP), a new theoretical perspective argued to capture the particularities of contemporary service delivery, and explores its drivers and related resistances.

Findings of both studies are utilized in a design science research process to develop and evaluate the "networked service productivity improvement technique" (NSPIRET). The technique comprises an organized set of artifacts aiming to support a focal provider to systematically and iteratively discover and seize opportunities to enhance NSP for itself, customers, and relevant co-providers. NSPIRET synthesizes and extends approaches from the field of service design, information systems, and engineering. The technique was evaluated in two empirical settings of networked service delivery, demonstrating promising results concerning its effectiveness, utility, understandability, and operational feasibility. Reflecting on the findings of the studies conducted, five design principles are proposed to drive NSP for all relevant network actors. Finally, limitations and directions for future research are presented

Part I

Introduction:

About the research

© Springer Fachmedien Wiesbaden GmbH, part of Springer Nature 2020
C. F. Daiberl, *Driving Networked Service Productivity*, Markt- und
Unternehmensentwicklung Markets and Organisations,
https://doi.org/10.1007/978-3-658-29580-6_1

1   Motivation and relevance[1]

 Enhancing productivity has long been considered a crucial driver to foster competitive advantages (Tangen, 2005) and it is considered fundamental to management science and practice (Djellal & Gallouj, 2013). In the realm of services, Peter F. Drucker, a pioneer of modern management, foresaw in 1991: "The single greatest challenge facing managers in the developed countries of the world is to raise the productivity of knowledge and service workers. This challenge, which will dominate the management agenda for the next several decades, will ultimately determine the competitive performance of companies. Even more, it will determine the very fabric of society and the quality of life in every industrialized nation" (Drucker, 1991, p. 2). Today, scholars, managers as well as policymakers continue to highlight the growing importance of improving service productivity (Klingner, Pravemann, & Becker, 2015; Lehmann, 2019; OECD, 2017; Ostrom, Parasuraman, Bowen, Patricio, & Voss, 2015). In a recent agenda-setting article of the Journal of Service Research, enhancing the conceptual as well as the operational understanding of service productivity was coined as one of the top three research priorities to advance the service field (Ostrom et al., 2015). Traditionally defined as the ratio of service outputs to inputs over a period of time (Johnston & Jones, 2004), increasing service productivity is considered critical as it refers to doing more with limited resources in times of rising demand (Bessant, Lehmann, & Möslein, 2014).

From an economic perspective, driving service productivity is critical for future growth and prosperity. This can be explained by the sheer importance of services for modern economies. The service sector's share of the gross domestic product greatly exceeds the share of the primary and secondary sector for most countries around the world (CIA World Factbook, n.d.). In 2017, for the Group of Seven economies, this share ranged from approximately 69% (i.e., Germany) to approximately 80% (i.e., the United Kingdom) of the respective country's gross domestic product, whereas for the whole

---

[1] A proposal for this dissertation was first presented and discussed at the doctoral colloquium of the EURAM 2017 Conference in Glasgow, Scotland. An overview of the author's work relevant to this dissertation is presented in Appendix A.

world it accounted for approximately 63% of the gross world product (CIA World Factbook, n.d.). Moreover, the service sector accounts for approximately 73% of people in employment in the member states of the Organization for Economic Co-operation and Development (World Bank, n.d.). However, a common finding is that this sector generally lacks behind regarding productivity improvements in comparison to the primary and secondary sector (Maroto-Sánchez, 2012; OECD, 2015). This not only slows down overall economic development but threatens access to service delivery as well. In this sense, it is highlighted that "increasing productivity of services is fundamental to ensure that the one billion people becoming middle class in the next 20 years have adequate provision of services, including health, education, transportation, and government" (Ostrom et al., 2015, p. 140).

From an organizational perspective, striving to optimize service delivery is not only vital for traditional service providers but for servitizing manufacturers as well (Posselt & Roth, 2017). Increasingly, manufacturers overcome a mere product orientation and aim to foster competitive advantages by selling bundles of products and services (Baines et al., 2017; Baines, Lightfoot, Benedettini, & Kay, 2009; Vandermerwe & Rada, 1988). For example, Dutch electronics manufacturer Philips offers light as a service instead of selling lamps. A customer of this service is Amsterdam-Schiphol, which strives to become the most sustainable airport in the world. In a case study it is reported that using the service, the airport can reduce its power consumption by 50% and benefits from 75% longer lifespan of luminaires compared to the previous installment while not having to invest any funds upfront. Moreover, as each luminaire is connected to the internet of things, Philips can continuously monitor operations and can immediately intervene in case any failures occur, optimizing reliability, and reducing maintenance costs for the airport operator (Philips, 2017). Another example is MAN, a German truck company that harnesses digital technologies to collect data of its installed base in order to improve the safety, efficiency, reliability, and sustainability of its vehicles (Baines & Shi, 2014). Hence, these manufacturers not only have to optimize manufacturing processes but also have to ensure that their services are delivered productively.

In this context, Klingner et al. (2015) surveyed 120 German industrial (e.g., machine building industry, metal products) and non-industrial service firms (e.g., consulting, accounting, advertising). The authors found that almost all respondents stressed a constant (21%) or growing (78%) relevance of managing service productivity. Nevertheless, almost 37% of industrial service firms and 28% of non-industrial service firms highlighted that they do not engage in any productivity evaluation at all. This is particularly critical as it was found that independent from the industry, productivity management has a significant effect on corporate success (Klingner et al., 2015).

There are several reasons why companies may find it difficult to drive service productivity. First, an erroneous understanding of the concept of productivity itself can pose challenges in a service context. Being rooted in manufacturing-oriented thinking (i.e., Taylorism and Fordism), service productivity is often narrowly considered as an efficiency-focused concept (Gummesson, 1998). Already in 1972, Levitt talked of a "technocratic hamburger" (p. 44), "french-fried automation" (p. 44), and "mechanized marketing" (p. 45) when demonstrating how ideas from industrial production can be applied to a service setting. In short, Levitt (1972) argues that service managers should think like product manufacturers and carefully plan service operations, invest in technology to save labor and pursue encompassing automation. In doing so, they should reap the same kind of productivity benefits just as product manufacturers did before. Whereas an efficiency-focused approach may be suited to certain scenarios (e.g., fast food), it may be defective in other areas where it has a negative impact on customer experience (e.g., fine dining) and thus reduces performance in the long-term (i.e., number of visitors). Hence, there is a growing consent that, in order to be meaningful, service productivity has to reflect on effectiveness considerations (i.e., the realization of desired results) as well (Bessant et al., 2014; Borchert et al., 2011; Grönroos & Ojasalo, 2004; Yalley & Sekhon, 2014). However, integrating both demands is challenging as improving operational efficiency may reduce service effectiveness and vice versa (Calabrese, 2012; Carlborg, Kindström, & Kowalkowski, 2013; Johnston & Jones, 2004; Rust & Huang, 2012).

Moreover, measuring service productivity is considered difficult (Scerri & Agarwal, 2018; Van Looy, Gemmel, Desmet, Van Dierdonck, & Serneels, 1998; Walsh, Walgenbach, Evanschitzky, & Schaarschmidt, 2016). In this regard, it is unclear how to objectively assess the outputs of intangible service processes (Djellal & Gallouj, 2013; Yalley & Sekhon, 2014). Whereas the unit of output of a production process can generally be depicted in a straightforward manner (e.g., a car, an airplane, a frozen pizza), defining service outputs is a complex issue. As pointed out by Djellal and Gallouj (2013, p. 285): "What is the unit of output of a consulting firm, a bank or a hospital? This does not mean that there is no answer to this question but rather that there are multiple, contradictory answers, each just as legitimate as the others."

A defining characteristic of service processes is that they rely on heterogeneous customer inputs that interactively influence process outputs (Sampson, 2001; Sampson & Froehle, 2006). This issue is highlighted by Sampson and Froehle (2006) who compare two attorneys. Whereas one attorney may win nine out of ten court cases, the other one only wins five out of ten. The question of who is more productive cannot be answered by simply counting court results. The attorney who won more may only take low-risk cases whereas the other one takes over high-risk cases. Thus, the customer inputs strongly influence service outputs but cannot be directly controlled by the provider (Sampson & Froehle, 2006). Similarly, measuring inputs is challenging (Van Looy et al., 1998; Vuorinen, Järvinen, & Lehtinen, 1998; Walsh et al., 2016). For example, it remains unclear how the knowledge applied for realizing a service interaction can be adequately quantified (Biege, Lay, Zanker, & Schmall, 2013).

Furthermore, other actors besides a focal provider and the customer may have a significant influence on service productivity. Driven by technological advances and increasing specialization, many contemporary services are realized by a network of providers each integrating their individual competencies and resources in the course of service delivery (Barile, Lusch, Reynoso, Saviano, & Spohrer, 2016; Field et al., 2018; Jaakkola, Helkkula, & Aarikka-Stenroos, 2015; Pinho, Beirão, Patrício, & Fisk, 2014; Tax, McCutcheon, & Wilkinson, 2013). Smartphones, cloud computing, and the increasing spread of the internet of things represent elements of an ever-growing technological infrastructure fostering many-to-many interactions for connected service delivery (Barile et al., 2016). In this context, one important trend is the rise of intermediary-operated, digital platforms that aim to create mutual value for the customer as well as for a network of service providers (acatech, 2015).

For instance, Hubject offers a so-called eRoaming platform in the context of electro mobility (e-Mobility) in order to overcome fragmented charging solutions throughout

Europe. In the past, users of e-mobility would have to sign an individual contract with a regional charging point operator before being able to charge at the operator's proprietary infrastructure. Via Hubject's platform, the information and communications technology (ICT) systems of the regional operators as well as further service providers (e.g., for payment processing) are connected, allowing e-mobility users to charge their vehicle at any connected charging point without having to conclude an additional contract (acatech, 2015). Whereas this service significantly increases flexibility and comfort for the users of e-mobility, charging point operators can benefit from additional sales due to an increased customer base and ready to use ICT solutions.

Another digital platform connecting complementary service providers in the travel industry is operated by the Hong Kong company handy (Russell, 2016). The company provides branded smartphones that are connected to a digital service platform integrating the service offerings of its local partners. Being distributed for free via partnering hotels, guests receive a fully functional mobile without any roaming fees throughout their trip. Moreover, the platform serves as a travel guide and enables guests to hire hotel specific (e.g., room service, laundry service, wellness treatments) and externally provided services (e.g., online ticketing for entertainment and public transportation, reservations at partnering restaurants, shopping with special promotions based on location). In doing so, handy provides a coordination mechanism integrating various service providers into the overall customer journey at a given travel destination.

Such service delivery networks do not only matter in the context of digital-platform enabled services as almost any service encounter can be considered part of a networked process (Patrício, Fisk, Falcão e Cunha, & Constantine, 2011; Sampson, 2012; Tax et al., 2013). For instance, in the context of healthcare, the treatment of a complex injury may require patients to interact with primary care physicians, healthcare specialists, physical therapists, pharmacies, and insurance companies. (Sampson, 2012; Sampson, Schmidt, Gardner, & Van Orden, 2015). Elderly care can integrate family members, formal caregivers, and socially assistive robots (Čaić, Odekerken-Schröder, & Mahr, 2018). Wealth management services may be realized by a network of certified public accountants, lawyers, investment advisors, chartered life underwriters, and estate planners (Tax et al., 2013). Air travel integrates airport operators, airlines, handling agents, customs and immigration officials, as well as concessionaries (Lehmann, 2019).

In a network context, enhancing service productivity becomes a complex undertaking as it is necessary to reflect on dependencies and multi-sided interactions of actors each having their individual productivity perspective (Daiberl, Roth, & Möslein, 2016a, 2016b, 2016c). Each provider can have a positive or negative influence on customer experiences throughout the connected, overall service (Tax et al., 2013). Moreover, these providers may also have to interact among each other in order to efficiently offer a compelling service experience (Field et al., 2018; Sampson, 2012; Sampson et al., 2015; Tax et al., 2013). Hence, for holistically managing and improving service productivity, it is not enough to focus on dyadic interactions between the customer and a particular service provider. Managers are advised to keep the interdependent processes and activities in mind and strive to enhance service productivity for all relevant network members (Yalley & Sekhon, 2014). In doing so, a focal provider may take the lead role and foster competitive advantages not only by securing the trust and confidence of its customers (Tax et al., 2013) but also by building mutually valuable relationships with other providers (Gummesson, 2008; Quero & Ventrua, 2015).

This dissertation aims to advance both the conceptual and operational understanding of how to drive productivity in the context of networked service delivery. Whereas for service researchers this shall provide a new perspective on service productivity and explore factors as well as systematics for its enhancement, practitioners shall gain guidance for their own productivity improvement initiatives. The remainder of Part I is organized as follows: Next, Chapter 2 translates the overall objective of this dissertation into concrete research questions. Afterward, Chapter 3 introduces the overall research design. Finally, Chapter 4 depicts the structure of this dissertation.

2 Research questions

 The overall objective of this dissertation is to explore *how a focal provider can drive productivity in the context of networked service delivery*. In doing so, constructive knowledge shall be developed supporting organizational practitioners while at the same time presenting contributions to theory (Goldkuhl, 2012; Gregor & Hevner, 2013). This objective is addressed by reviewing existing approaches that can be applied for enhancing service productivity from a network perspective. Scholars from different disciplines have proposed a diverse set of approaches (e.g., Böttcher & Klingner, 2011; Carlborg & Kindström, 2014; Carlborg et al., 2013; Geum, Shin, & Park, 2011; Pritchard, Harrell, DiazGranados, & Guzman, 2008). However, the most common approaches in business practice focus on enhancing service productivity from the perspective of a focal provider and/or the customer (e.g., Klingner et al., 2015). Thus, it is necessary to review existing approaches that may foster productivity enhancement from a network perspective by considering the role of relevant co-providers for delivering the connected, overall service. In doing so, potentials of and barriers for their practical application shall be derived fostering an integrated understanding for both scholars and practitioners. Therefore, the following research question (RQ) is depicted:

RQ1: Which systematic approaches are discussed in service research for the improvement of service productivity from a network perspective and what are their application-oriented qualities?

The second research question addresses the lack of a thorough conceptual understanding concerning networked service productivity, i.e., productivity in the context of networked service delivery. Scholars highlight that the general conception of service productivity is still largely manufacturing-based (e.g., Aspara, Klein, Luo, & Tikkanen, 2017; Rust & Huang, 2012) and lacks behind scientific progress in other areas of service management (Ostrom et al., 2015; Yalley & Sekhon, 2014). Traditional models of service productivity take a provider's point of view (Corsten, 1994). More advanced contributions additionally reflect on the customer's perspective on service productivity (Bartsch, Demmelmair, & Meyer, 2011; Johnston & Jones, 2004; Parasuraman, 2002, 2010). Nevertheless, existing models neglect the networked nature of service delivery and experience – a topic that is of growing interest in service research (Field et al., 2018; Harvey, 2016; Ostrom et al., 2010, 2015; Tax et al., 2013; Verleye et al., 2017). Moreover, apart from a few exemptions (e.g., Grönroos & Ojasalo, 2004; Sekhon et al., 2016) factors for mutually driving service productivity for the different actors involved remain largely unexplored. Therefore, the following question is depicted:

RQ2: How can networked service productivity be conceptualized and what are its drivers and related resistances?

Based on the insights generated by answering the first and second research question, it will be shown that there is a lack of practical approaches that support a focal provider to drive networked service productivity for all relevant network actors. In this context, networked service productivity is established as a subjective, dynamic, and multi-level phenomenon. On the individual level, it is conceptualized as an actor's satisfaction with the perceived effects of networked service delivery at a given time considering its individual resource contributions. These perceptions influence networked service productivity on the aggregated level, which encompasses the collective perceptions of two or more network actors. It is argued that, for sustained operational success, a focal provider should strive to continuously enhance networked service productivity for itself, customers, and all co-providers relevant for realizing networked service delivery. Building on these findings, the third research question is:

RQ3: How can a focal provider systematically and iteratively discover and seize opportunities to enhance networked service productivity for itself, customers, and relevant co-providers?

Having presented the research questions, next the overall research design is introduced.

3   Overall research design

 This chapter introduces the overall research design of this dissertation. A more detailed description of the research methods and data applied is presented in the respective chapters of the following parts. For meeting the overall objective and for answering the research questions detailed in the previous chapter, qualitative research is conducted. Whereas qualitative research is often associated with interpretivism, this research explicitly follows the paradigm of pragmatism integrating an interpretive mode of inquiry (Goldkuhl, 2012). Positioned between pure positivism and interpretivism (Goles & Hirschheim, 2000), the pragmatic ontology can be labeled symbolic realism (Goldkuhl, 2012). Symbolic realism acknowledges that realities exist. However, these realities only acquire human significance when people ascribe meaning to them (Kroll-Smith, Gunter, & Laska, 2000). Empirically, the pragmatic researcher focuses on actions and actively engages in change. In doing so, the focus is on continuous exploration and learning with the goal to create constructive knowledge that is useful for general practice. Therefore, the researcher is not only interested in what is but also in what might be (Goldkuhl, 2012).

Concerning methodology, pragmatism adopts a pluralist attitude, allowing to use any combination of methods considered appropriate for the purpose of the research project (Goles & Hirschheim, 2000). For this research, this base paradigm adapts elements from interpretivism for supportive reasons. Interpretivism acknowledges the existence and continuous reconstruction of subjective meanings in the social world. These meanings have to be interpreted by the researcher in order to use them for theory development (Goldkuhl, 2012). An interpretive mode of inquiry shall support an in-depth understanding of the individual life-worlds of actors and meanings attributed to specific phenomena. Moreover, it acknowledges the co-constructive development of concepts between the researchers and practitioners contributing to the research findings (Goldkuhl, 2012).

Following the combined paradigm detailed above, three research approaches are utilized this research. Initially, the first research question is answered using a (1) *structured literature review* (Tranfield, Denver, & Smart, 2003; Webster & Watson, 2002). Applying a conceptually developed classification scheme, the review identifies and contrasts potentially relevant approaches for enhancing service productivity in the context of networked service delivery. Building on the results of a scoping study, leading service journals, as well as relevant general and operations management journals, are considered for the review. Moreover, the content of the service productivity toolbox developed in the funding priority "productivity of services" of the German Ministry of Education and Research is investigated. The identified approaches are analyzed descriptively and thematically, creating an evidence-informed knowledge base concerning their application-oriented qualities. The findings contribute to the development of constructive knowledge by depicting practical challenges of existing approaches, substantiating the need for establishing a coherent conceptual understanding of networked service productivity, and motivating the development and design of a new productivity improvement approach. Moreover, the findings are utilized for the development of design principles (Gregor, 2006). The latter shall support the creation of new artifacts supporting a focal provider to drive networked service productivity in other contexts than the ones investigated in this work.

For answering the second research question an (2) *exploratory case study* is conducted (Yin, 2014). Case research is selected due to the lack of conceptual clarity concerning productivity in the context of networked service delivery (Ostrom et al., 2015). It is argued that case research enables the investigation of complex phenomena bound by temporal and spatial dimensions in order to elaborate theory (Eisenhardt, 1989). Following a theoretical sampling procedure, two settings of networked service delivery were selected (Glaser & Strauss, 1967). Both case settings are operationally different but considered particularly revelatory concerning the phenomenon of networked service delivery. Whereas the first setting, eMobilizer, was a non-profit digital service platform for private customers, the second setting, OI-Lab is a for-profit research and development (R&D) service for organizational customers. Replicating of findings across both cases should increase confidence in the elaborated theory (Miles, Huberman, & Saldana, 2013; Yin, 2014). Following an abductive approach (Dubois & Gadde, 2002), throughout the case study, existing theoretical themes from the literature on service productivity are combined with themes emerging from the data. All in all, the conceptual understanding developed contributes to the objectives of the final study of this dissertation as well as the development of design principles.

Lastly, a (3) *design science research* (DSR) study is conducted (Hevner, March, Park, & Ram, 2004; Peffers, Tuunanen, Rothenberger, & Chatterjee, 2007). DSR is selected as it enables the researcher to harness different theoretical foundations to develop solutions for environmental contexts that are ill-defined and characterized by complex interactions (Gregor & Hevner, 2013). The DSR study draws on the findings of the systematic literature review and the exploratory case study and synthesizes theoretical contributions from service design, information systems, and engineering. Throughout the DSR process, abductive, deductive, and inductive reasoning is combined. In doing so, a systematic approach supporting a focal provider to identify, evaluate, and implement opportunities for improving service productivity in the context of networked service delivery is developed and evaluated. Finally, insights generated throughout the overall DSR process are discussed in order to develop design principles. The overall research design is summarized in Figure 1. The next chapter details the structure of the dissertation.

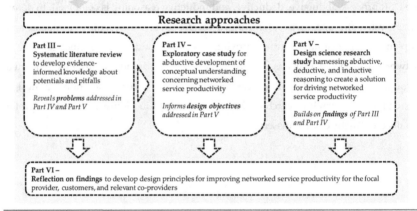

Figure 1: *Overall research design of this dissertation. Own illustration.*

4   Structure of the dissertation

This dissertation is divided into six parts. Part I provides an introduction. Chapter 1 introduces the motivation and relevance of this research. Building on that, Chapter 2 delineates the research objective and research questions. Afterward, Chapter 3 presents the overall research design, before Chapter 4 describes the structure of this dissertation.

Part II develops a coherent understanding of the theoretical concepts applied throughout this dissertation. Initially, Chapter 1 explicates the specific objectives and structure of this part. Next, Chapter 2 demarcates different scholarly perspectives on service productivity in order to derive this dissertation's conceptual understanding. Afterward, Chapter 3 scrutinizes the concept of service productivity and its improvement. In doing so, it provides an overview of its dimensions and related models and frameworks. Moreover, it introduces different types of approaches, strategies, and life cycle phases for systematically improving service productivity. Chapter 4 explicates this dissertation's understanding of networked service delivery. For this purpose, it depicts network-related concepts in service research before the concept of the service delivery network is detailed. Finally, Chapter 5 summarizes the key concepts applied throughout the dissertation.

Part III presents a systematic literature review to foster a better theoretical as well as practical understanding of existing approaches for driving service productivity from a network perspective. The objectives and structure of the literature review are detailed in Chapter 1. Building on the theoretical foundations presented in Part II, Chapter 2 elaborates a multi-criteria classification scheme serving as a high-level analytical framework to compare different approaches for productivity improvement. Next, Chapter 3 summarizes the procedure of the literature review in detail. Subsequently, Chapter 4 presents the identified approaches. In doing so, first, the identified core contributions are described before respective approaches are classified and application-oriented qualities are revealed. Afterward, Chapter 5 discusses the theoretical contributions and implications for practitioners. Lastly, implications for the following parts of this dissertation are specified.

Part IV presents an exploratory case study addressing the lack of a conceptual understanding concerning productivity in the context of networked service delivery. Chapter 1 depicts the goals and structure of the case study undertaken. Chapter 2 initially introduces the case study research approach before it illustrates the research setting followed by the process of data collection and analysis. Afterward, Chapter 3 presents the findings of the case study comprising a new conceptual model of networked service productivity as well as drivers and related resistances. Finally, Chapter 4 discusses the theoretical contributions, practical implications, and implications for the following parts of this dissertation.

Based on the insights generated throughout the literature review and the case study, Part V presents a DSR study in order to develop a systematic approach supporting the improvement of productivity in the context of networked service delivery. Chapter 1 specifies the objectives and structure of the DSR study. Afterward, Chapter 2 presents the theoretical background for design. Chapter 3 summarizes the method and data. For this purpose, initially, the DSR approach is introduced followed by the particular DSR process applied. Chapter 4 presents the findings by detailing both the design and evaluation results of the different artifacts developed. Finally, Chapter 5 discusses both the theoretical contributions and implications for practitioners. Moreover, implications for the overall dissertation are revealed.

Part VI reflects on the previous parts and concludes the dissertation. Again, Chapter 1 introduces the objectives and structure of this part. Chapter 2 recaps the research conducted before. Chapter 3 depicts the design principles developed based on the findings of Part III, IV, and V. Chapter 4 details limitations and directions for future research. Finally, Chapter 5 presents some concluding remarks.

The overall structure is visualized in Figure 2. As illustrated, descriptive icons are used for the following chapters to visually support the reader's journey throughout this dissertation. This representation draws on the customer journey modeling language (Halvorsrud, Kvale, & Følstad, 2016), a tool from service design, which is utilized in the DSR study depicted in Part V. Having presented the structure of this dissertation, the next part introduces the theoretical foundations applied for this research.

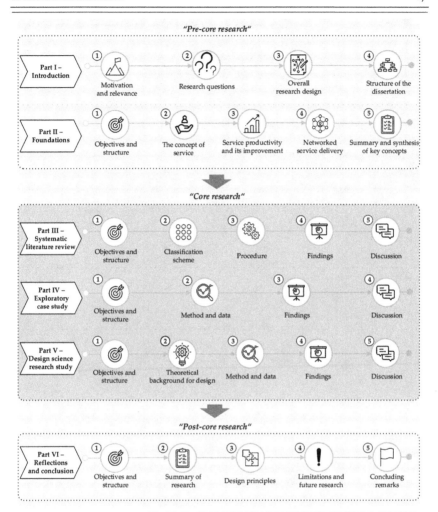

Figure 2: Overall structure of the dissertation. Own illustration.

Part II

Foundations:

Key concepts of the research

© Springer Fachmedien Wiesbaden GmbH, part of Springer Nature 2020
C. F. Daiberl, *Driving Networked Service Productivity*, Markt- und
Unternehmensentwicklung Markets and Organisations,
https://doi.org/10.1007/978-3-658-29580-6_2

Part II

Foundations

Key concepts of theories

1 Objectives and structure

 Part II introduces the key concepts applied throughout the dissertation to answer the research questions depicted in Part I. They serve as the conceptual foundation of the systematic literature review presented in Part III and guide the exploratory case study delineated in Part IV. Moreover, they direct the selection and adaptation of relevant theoretical foundations for the DSR study presented in Part V. All in all, Part II establishes a coherent conceptual understanding that informs the different steps of research conducted in this dissertation and enables the reader to consider the results with respect to this theoretical framing.

The remainder of Part II is organized as follows: Chapter 2 introduces this dissertation's understanding of service and service productivity. For this purpose, the concept of service is defined after comparing different scholarly perspectives. Subsequently, Chapter 3 scrutinizes the concept of service productivity and its improvement. First, it investigates different dimensions of service productivity and compares exemplary conceptual models and frameworks. Next, it defines different types of productivity improvement approaches before highlighting generic productivity improvement strategies. Afterward, it depicts the service productivity life cycle as a model structuring service productivity improvement in the context of dynamic systems. Chapter 4 presents the dissertation's understanding of networked service delivery. Initially, it provides an overview of network-related concepts in service research. Subsequently, the concept of the service delivery network is introduced as the theoretical framing of this research. Finally, Chapter 5 summarizes relevant service productivity and network-related concepts applied in the following parts of this dissertation. Figure 3 displays the structure of Part II.

Figure 3: Structure of Part II. Own illustration.

2 The concept of service

 To explore productivity in the context of networked service delivery, first it is necessary to specify what is meant by service as the concept itself is a widely debated topic. Chapter 2 demarcates different theoretical perspectives and, in doing so, establishes the conceptual understanding of this dissertation.

2.1 Service as a unit of output

Traditionally, goods and services are perceived as two archetypical units of exchangeable outputs (Ng, Parry, Smith, Maull, & Briscoe, 2012; Vargo & Lusch, 2008). Proponents of this understanding highlight that services portray four distinctive characteristics (Lovelock & Gummesson, 2004; Ostrom et al., 2015; Zeithaml, Parasuraman, & Berry, 1985).

The first characteristic, (1) *intangibility*, is also considered to be the most critical differentiator (Bateson, 1979; Edgett & Parkinson, 1993). It refers to the assumption that services, representing marketable patterns of activities, "cannot drop on your foot" (Gummesson, 1987, p. 22). Thus, in contrast to a tangible offering, which can be displayed and demonstrated before purchase, assessing a service's actual quality is only possible after or during consumption, if it is possible at all (Mitchell & Greatorex, 1993; Zeithaml, 1981). The second characteristic, (2) *heterogeneity*, refers to the assumption that it is problematic to standardize services (Edgett & Parkinson, 1993). Being rooted in the nature of human interactions, performance variations may be caused by heterogeneous expectations and needs of the respective service clients as well as constant differences between and within service providers (Edvardsson, Gustafsson, & Roos, 2005; Wilson, Zeithaml, Bitner, & Gremler, 2012). Thirdly, (3) *inseparability* reflects the idea that service production and consumption take place simultaneously as a service's "very act of being created requires the source, whether person or machine, to be present" (Kotler, 1982, cited in Edgett & Parkinson, 1993, pp. 24-25). This implies that the service recipients are integrated into service delivery (Moeller, 2008), and may have to interact with service employees and other customers, who are difficult to control and may influence the service experience significantly

(Carman & Langeard, 1980; Wilson et al., 2012). Finally, (4) *perishability* reflects the idea that services decay in the very instant of their creation (Smith, 1776).

In literature, it is widely discussed if these characteristics are useful for describing services and grasping their true essence (Edvardsson et al., 2005; Lovelock & Gummesson, 2004; Ostrom et al., 2015; Vargo & Lusch, 2004b). Indeed, many services exist that do not fulfill one or more of the proposed characteristics. Among others, services may contain tangible components (Edgett & Parkinson, 1993; Shostack, 1977; Zeithaml et al., 1985) or technology may foster standardization (Carlborg et al., 2013; Edvardsson et al., 2005). In this sense, whereas elements such as superior furnishing and equipment represent crucial aspects of the service expected from a luxury hotel (Lovelock & Gummesson, 2004), specific financial services such as online banking or money withdrawal via automated teller machines are largely standardized (Edvardsson et al., 2005). Due to the conceptual difficulties of the dichotomous view described, many authors increasingly consider service as a perspective on value creation as presented in the next section.

2.2   Service as a perspective on value creation

Another approach in literature is to view service as a perspective on value creation (Edvardsson et al., 2005). This view has become increasingly popular due to the emerging service-dominant logic (Vargo & Lusch, 2004a, 2008, 2017). This logic represents a fundamental break with the traditional focus on discrete transactions of output (i.e., goods or services), which contain value in exchange. In the context of service-dominant logic, service (in the singular) is considered to be the basis of all economic and non-economic transactions and is defined as "the application of resources for the benefit of others" (Vargo & Lusch, 2017, p. 48). In this sense, differentiating between goods and services is redundant (Karpen, Bove, & Lukas, 2012) as "activities render services, things render services" (Gummesson, 1994. p. 78). Considering value creation, it is argued that "the enterprise cannot deliver value, but only offer value propositions" (Vargo & Lusch, 2008. p. 7). Value creation itself is seen as a collaborative and reciprocal process among different entities (i.e., the customer, the firm and third parties), each integrating specific resources (Spohrer, Maglio, Bailey, & Gruhl, 2007; Vargo & Lusch, 2017; Vargo, Maglio, & Akaka, 2008). In this context, the perception of value is "always uniquely and phenomenologically determined by the beneficiary" (Vargo & Lusch, 2008, p. 7). Value is derived in the form of value-in-use and value-in-context, which includes social and cultural dimensions (Chandler & Vargo, 2011; Jacob, Bruns, & Sievert, 2013; Vargo, 2008; Vargo & Lusch, 2017). These considerations can be illustrated when thinking about the value proposition of a car. A customer is only willing to pay the price for it (i.e., value-in-exchange), when he or she derives benefits from its utilization such as mobility or self-expression (i.e., value-in-use). These benefits, however depend on several circumstantial factors (i.e., value-in-context), such as the driver's physical ability to drive, the provision of roads and fuel by third-party providers (Vargo et al., 2008). Moreover, past and imaginary future service experiences play a role (Helkkula, Kelleher, & Pihlstrom, 2012).

Service-dominant logic has received wide academic praise, has been applied in various domains, and is elaborated continuously (Vargo & Lusch, 2017). However, it is also subject to criticism concerning its theoretical soundness as well as its practical relevance (Alter, 2010a; O'Shaughnessy & O'Shaughnessy, 2009, 2011; Sampson, Menor, & Bone, 2010; Schembri, 2006). In this sense, Stauss (2005) not only argues that "a general definition of service that includes virtually everything defines virtually nothing" (p. 222) but also fears that an all-encompassing broadening of the service concept bears the risk of losing service-specific knowledge. Thus, overlooking such particularities on the grounds of a service-dominant perspective may well be considered a Pyrrhic victory (Stauss, 2005). Consequently, for this dissertation, a more differentiated understanding is considered beneficial.

2.3   Service as a particular type of production process

In order to distinguish what a service is and what it is not, this dissertation follows the unified services theory (UST) (Sampson, 2001, 2010; Sampson & Froehle, 2006). According to UST, service can be conceptualized as a special type of production process that relies on customer inputs for its execution. In this context, production processes are understood as "sequences of steps that provide value propositions and therefore warrant compensation" (Sampson, 2010, p. 113). Customers of such processes are "the individuals or entities that determine whether or not the service provider shall be compensated for production" (Sampson, 2001, p. 28). Service providers, in turn, can be considered as actors that provide inputs into service delivery for a particular customer (Sampson, 2012; Sampson & Froehle, 2006). Inputs encompass any tangible or intangible resources that are utilized in a particular production process to achieve a result (Sampson, 2010; Sampson & Froehle, 2006). For example, the customer him- or herself may be included into the production process (e.g., patient at hospital) or the customer may provide his or her physical belongings (e.g., car repair) or information (e.g., legal advisory) for service delivery (Sampson & Froehle, 2006). Customer inputs largely influence the results of the production process. For example, the conditions of the patient affect how well doctors can help.

Essentially, in UST, the presence of individual customer inputs is considered as a necessary and sufficient condition to define a production process as a service process (Sampson & Froehle, 2006). Manufacturing processes, on the contrary, do not involve individual customer inputs and thus must be managed differently. "Services are production processes wherein each customer supplies one or more input components for that customer's unit of production. With non-service processes, groups of customers may contribute ideas to the design of the product, but individual customers' only participation is to select, pay for, and consume the output. All considerations unique to services are founded in this distinction" (Sampson, 2010, p. 112). Following UST, each service provider engages in both service processes and supporting processes that are independent of customer inputs but still necessary for operations. For example, the service processes of a hospital refer to provider-customer interactions like diagnosis and treatment, whereas non-service processes would encompass training and purchase of equipment.

The ideas of UST are largely in line with earlier contributions from German service scholars. In this sense, it is argued that service processes are based on external production factors (i.e., customer inputs) that need to be combined with internal production factors (e.g., assets, commodities) for actual service delivery (Corsten, 1997; Kleinaltenkamp & Haase, 1999; Maleri, 1997). These customer and provider-related factors are combined and form integrative value chains that produce bundles of goods and services (Kleinaltenkamp, 1997).

All in all, building on UST, for this dissertation, service is considered a special type of production process relying on customer inputs for its execution (Sampson & Froehle, 2006). In the following the terms service and service delivery are applied synonymously when referring to such a production process. In this context, the term service delivery is used when the process nature shall be particularly stressed. Having established the conceptual understanding of service for this dissertation, next, the concept of service productivity and its improvement will be explored in greater detail.

3   Service productivity and its improvement

 Chapter 3 scrutinizes the concept of service productivity in greater detail. First, it investigates the dimensions of service productivity before contrasting specific models and frameworks. Subsequently, it defines different types of service productivity improvement approaches and introduces generic strategies for enhancing service productivity. Finally, it depicts the service productivity life cycle as a model that considers the improvement of service productivity in the context of dynamic systems.

3.1   Dimensions of service productivity

Despite being extensively used in everyday language, there is no common understanding of the term productivity. Scholars have proposed various verbal as well as mathematical definitions of productivity (Pritchard, Weaver, & Ashwood, 2012; Tangen, 2005). Often, it is described as the output to input ratio of a production process for a specific period (Chew, 1988; Djellal & Gallouj, 2008; Johnston & Jones, 2004; Parasuraman, 2010). However, this understanding is largely rooted in manufacturing-oriented thinking and it is unclear how to objectively measure service inputs and outputs (Biege et al., 2013; Djellal & Gallouj, 2013; Lehmann, 2019; Yalley & Sekhon, 2014). As described above, a unifying characteristic of service delivery is that it relies on heterogeneous customer inputs that interactively influence process results (Sampson, 2012; Sampson & Froehle, 2006). The evaluation of these outputs is dependent on the individual value system of the recipient under consideration as well as the point of time of the assessment (Djellal & Gallouj, 2013; Sampson, 2010).

Scholars of different fields have explored the concept of service productivity (Lehmann, 2019). Often, service productivity is treated as being synonymous with service efficiency (Aspara et al., 2018; Calabrese, 2012; Rust & Huang, 2012). Addressing the inputs of a production process, efficiency relates to how well the resources are utilized for operations (Tangen, 2005). In other words, efficiency is about "doing the things right" (Drucker, 1974, p. 45). However, to be a meaningful concept, various authors highlight that productivity should also reflect on effectiveness (Bessant et al., 2014; Carlborg et al., 2013; Grönroos & Ojasalo, 2004; Tangen, 2005; Yalley &

Sekhon, 2014). Effectiveness can be defined as "the degree to which desired results are achieved" (Tangen, 2005, p. 41). Hence, effectiveness is about "doing the right things" (Drucker, 1974, p. 45). From a customer's point of view, this is closely related to the concept of service quality (Grönroos & Ojasalo, 2004) whereas from the provider's perspective, it is about meeting operational objectives (Borchert et al., 2011; Pritchard, Harrell, DiazGranados, & Guzman, 2008).

3.2   Models and frameworks of service productivity

For a more in-depth conceptual analysis, various models and frameworks informing the theoretical understanding and practical management of service productivity have been proposed. These contributions can be structured according to three theoretical orientations that overcome industrial productivity thinking (Bartsch et al., 2011). Next, exemplary contributions for each approach are presented.

Proponents of the (1) *service production approach* (e.g., Corsten, 1994; Johnes, 1988) take a provider's perspective and aim to identify specific starting points to analyze service productivity (Bartsch et al., 2011). For instance, Johnes (1988) differentiates three stages of service delivery and three related key result areas. In the first stage (i.e., service production in the narrow sense) inputs are transformed into intermediate outputs (e.g., the kitchen of a hotel transforms food supply into daily menus). In the second stage (i.e., consumer take-up) a proportion of the intermediate output is sold (e.g., sold menus). Finally, in the third stage (i.e., impact on consumers), the output is transformed into outcomes (consumer experiences such as dissipation of hunger, comfort, social contact) (Jones, 1988). According to the author, productivity focuses on the first stage taking into consideration the ratio of the intermediate outputs and the inputs required for production. The second stage addresses capacity management and the third stage quality management. In doing so, this early model highlights that for sustained operational success it is not enough to solely focus on service productivity (in a narrow sense) but to consider the related concepts of capacity and quality as well (Bartsch et al., 2011; Jones, 1988).

Next, proponents of the (2) *customer integration approach* (e.g., Fitzsimmons, 1985; Johnston & Jones, 2004; Lovelock & Young, 1979; Parasuraman, 2002, 2010) consider the management of customer involvement throughout service delivery as a key issue for service productivity (Bartsch et al., 2011). In this context, it is highlighted that both the customer and the provider have their individual productivity perspectives (Anitsal & Schumann, 2007; Johnston & Jones, 2004; Parasuraman, 2002, 2010). For example, Johnston and Jones (2004) distinguish between operational and customer productivity. In this context, operational productivity addresses a function of the ratio of operational outputs (e.g., revenues, customers served, used resources) to operational inputs (e.g., materials, equipment, costs, and staff). Customer productivity, on the other hand, refers to a function of the ratio of customer outputs (e.g., experience, emotions, and value) to customer related inputs (e.g., time, effort, and costs). The authors stress that both concepts are interrelated as service operations and customer experience overlap. Thus, changes in operational productivity may have a positive or negative effect on customer productivity. For instance, increasing the flow and pushing customers faster through service delivery (e.g., a medical consultation) may improve service productivity from a provider's perspective while at the same time reducing customer productivity (Johnston & Jones, 2004).

Lastly, contributions falling under the (3) *service marketing approach* (e.g., Chase & Haynes, 2000; Grönroos & Ojasalo, 2004; Vuorinen, Järvinen, & Lehtinen, 1998; Yalley & Sekhon, 2014) stress the interdependence of service productivity and quality (Bartsch et al., 2011). In doing so, they dismiss the constant quality assumption of industrial management, i.e., the idea that an altered configuration of inputs has no impact on quality (Grönroos & Ojasalo, 2004). Thus, different models have been developed that integrate customer perceived quality as an integral component of service productivity (Bartsch et al., 2011). A key contribution of this stream is the service productivity model of Grönroos & Ojasalo (2004), which is summarized next.

Grönroos and Ojasalo (2004) consider service delivery as an interactive production process integrating inputs from both the provider and the customer. Thus, service delivery cannot be standardized and different effects of customer integration have to be considered. Based on this understanding, the authors conceptualize service productivity as a function of (1) *internal efficiency*, (2) *external efficiency*, and (3) *capacity efficiency*. In this sense, internal efficiency (or cost efficiency) refers to how efficiently the service provider transforms inputs to outputs. External efficiency (or effectiveness), on the other hand, reflects on service quality, i.e., how well the customer perceives the output. The provider's image mediates this perception. Lastly, as services cannot be stored in advance, capacity efficiency addresses how effectively a provider's capacity for delivering services is utilized. Moreover, Grönroos and Ojasalo (2004) stress that service productivity is a learning experience. Both providers and customers learn how to avoid problems and mistakes. Based on such learning relationships, internal, external, and capacity efficiency (and thus service productivity) can be improved over time. The authors admit that it is unclear how these efficiencies can be quantified, thus they suggest that the "only theoretically correct and practically relevant approach to measuring service productivity seems to base productivity calculations on financial measures"(Grönroos & Ojasalo, 2004, p. 421). Therefore, Grönroos and Ojasalo (2004) highlight that service productivity measures the ratio of revenues from a given service divided by the costs of producing this service.

Notwithstanding the encompassing theoretical contribution of Grönroos and Ojasalo (2004), one can easily think about examples where financial calculations for defining service productivity may be impossible or misleading. For instance, many public services (e.g., primary education, police, or fire brigade) have other goals than maximizing profits for the provider. Moreover, for many commercial services an exclusive focus on the financial results for the provider is prone to deliver negative results for the customer in the short run and possibly for the provider and society in the long run (e.g., healthcare or banking). Hence, in general, it is possible to identify various purposeful indicators for service productivity (Djellal & Gallouj, 2008) as managing productivity is dependent on its conceptual understanding and the specific organizational context (Pritchard, Weaver, & Ashwood, 2012). Furthermore, Grönroos & Ojasalo (2004) still consider a ratio of total productivity. In doing so, the authors stress that effectiveness relates to the perception of service outputs by the customer. However, they do not reflect on the efficiency of service delivery for the customer.

More recently, Yalley and Sekhon (2014) synthesized theoretical advances in service research into a new framework depicted in Figure 4. Similar to Grönroos and Ojasalo (2004) the authors distinguish between producer and customer related inputs that are combined and transformed in the course of service delivery. In this context, inputs are considered to include operand and operant resources (Constantin & Lusch, 1994).

Whereas operand resources are typically physical (e.g., people, money, machines, and materials), operant resources are intangible (e.g., individual skills, knowledge, information, and technology). Operant resources are applied to perform an operation on operand resources in order to derive an effect (Constantin & Lusch, 1994). Both operand and operant resources are considered to be dynamic. According to Constantin and Lusch (1994), resources "are not, they become . . . they are not static, but expand and contract in response to human wants and human culture that can convert 'neutral stuff' and resistances into want-satisfying resources" (p. 41). Yalley and Sekhon (2014) stress that the quantity and quality of operand and operant resources required are defined by the particular transformation process under consideration and affect service efficiency and effectiveness. Additionally, technological readiness (i.e., ability to use service-related technology) as well as co-production readiness (i.e., ability to provide required inputs) and value co-creation readiness (i.e., ability to co-create value) of both entities are considered fundamental for successfully transforming inputs into service outcomes (Yalley & Sekhon, 2014).

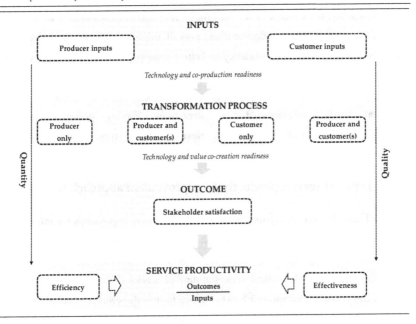

Figure 4: Service production process and productivity relationships. Illustration based on Yalley & Sekhon (2014)

Due to the conceptual and methodological difficulties of measuring service outputs the authors stress that is favorable to focus on service outcomes. Following Pena (2011), service outcomes encompass both the direct effects as well as the long-term, indirect results of service delivery. Yalley and Sekhon (2014) argue that service outcomes can be measured by assessing stakeholder satisfaction. The latter refers to how well an organization meets the expectations of its stakeholders (Berrone, Surroca, & Tribó, 2007).

Yalley and Sekhon (2014) highlight several important aspects not considered before. They tap the ideas of resource management (Constantin & Lusch, 1994) and shed light on the importance of direct and indirect outcomes for all stakeholders affected by service delivery. In doing so, the authors propose a differentiated understanding of what it means to be productive (Yalley & Sekhon, 2014). Still, their model takes a dyadic perspective and does not reflect on the networked nature of contemporary service delivery.

To summarize, the concept of service productivity has been researched by various authors. Whereas different understandings prevail, there is an increasing agreement that it should encompass both efficiency and effectiveness dimensions. It is highlighted that service productivity can be understood as a broad, multisided concept, which ultimately affects the satisfaction of particular stakeholders. Still, existing models solely focus on dyadic provider-customer interactions. Having presented diverse perspectives on service productivity, next, different types of productivity improvement approaches, strategies, and phases are introduced.

3.3 Types of service productivity improvement approaches

Scholars from different disciplines have proposed various approaches for improving service productivity. In order to distinguish between the different contributions, it is important to initially define different types of service productivity improvement approaches. Given the theoretical understanding of service delivery as a special kind of production process (Sampson & Froehle, 2006), for this dissertation, definitions from business process improvement literature are applied (Dale, 2003; McQuater, Scurr, Dale, & Hillman, 1995; van der Wiele, van Iwaarden, Dale, & Williams, 2006). In general, an approach can be defined as a "way of dealing with a situation or problem" (Oxford-Dictionaries, n.d., para. 1). In this sense, a tool can be considered as the least complex approach. It can be defined as a practical method, skill, mean, or mechanism that can be applied to a specific task (McQuater et al., 1995). A tool has a narrow focus and can be applied on its own (e.g., a flowchart or a cause and effect diagram). Techniques on the other hand, have a wider scope and typically integrate several tools (e.g., failure mode and effects analysis, benchmarking, or statistical process control). For this purpose, they rely on specific procedures and infrastructures (van der Wiele et al., 2006). Consequently, techniques are more complex than single tools and require a higher level of intellectual effort for being applied effectively (Dale, 2003; McQuater et al., 1995).

Moreover, there exist systems as well as strategic approaches for process improvements that are enacted for a longer period of time and integrate other tools and techniques.[2] In this regard, according to van der Wiele et al. (2006), systems represent formalized instructions and procedures that direct and control certain operations on a continuous basis (e.g., performance measurement system). Certain systems are used in all strategic approaches (e.g., lean management or Six Sigma). Strategic approaches follow certain core concepts (e.g., customer orientation, or process control and improvement) and require a strategic decision by management, the commitment of organizational resources over an extended period of time, and dedication to learning (e.g., training of personnel) (van der Wiele et al., 2006). The interconnections of the different types of approaches are represented in Figure 5. Choosing an appropriate approach is dependent on the particular service productivity strategy applied. These strategies are introduced next.

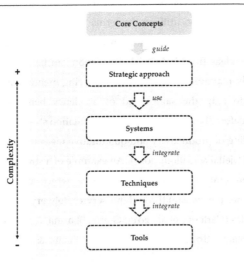

Figure 5: *Types of service productivity improvement approaches. Illustration based on Dale (2003), McQuater et al. (1995), and van der Wiele et al. (2006).*

3.4 Strategies for improving service productivity

[2] Van der Wiele et al. (2006) do not explicitly differentiate between strategic approaches and non-strategic approaches. For them, all approaches integrate systems, techniques, and tools. For this dissertation the adjective "strategic" is added when referring to such a complex approach that is purposefully enacted over an extended period of time by top-management.

Djellal and Gallouj (2013) distinguish three groups of generic service productivity strategies. These strategies differ in terms of the inherent focus on efficiency (i.e., productivity in a strict sense) as well as the rationale and operationalization of productivity enhancement:

(1) *Assimilation strategies* focus on efficiency. In doing so, they aim to minimize service-specific characteristics (i.e., their intangible, interactive and subjective nature) in order to apply approaches from industrial management. In this sense, assimilation can be considered synonym to industrialization (Djellal & Gallouj, 2013). Inspired by the Fordist production model, factory-like thinking is typically considered beneficial, thus management should invest in standardization, technology, and automation etc. (Bartsch et al., 2011; Djellal & Gallouj, 2013). In this context, an early contribution is provided by Levitt (1972) who utilized the terms "technocratic hamburger" (p. 44), "french-fried automation" (p. 44), and "mechanized marketing" (p. 45) when demonstrating how ideas from industrial production can be applied to a fast food restaurant. Carefully planning operations and replacing manual labor should enable service managers to reap the same kind of efficiency benefits just as product manufacturers did before (Levitt, 1972). Hence, assimilation strategies rather address a narrow understanding of productivity and quantitative measurement of conventional indicators prevails (Djellal & Gallouj, 2013). An example of a strategic approach in line with an assimilation strategy would be lean service, which aims to minimize non-value-adding activities (i.e., waste) throughout service delivery by harnessing a set of operational principles (Carlborg et al., 2013; Gupta, Sharma, & Sunder M., 2016; Liker & Morgan, 2006; Staats, Brunner, & Upton, 2011; Staats & Upton, 2011). Besides encompassing standardization, lean service is based on defining value from the customer's perspective, precisely defining the value stream, ensuring flow, applying pull instead of push as well as striving for perfection (Carlborg et al., 2013).[3] For its operationalization, a comprehensive set of tools has been developed (Bicheno, 2008), and various studies have explored both potentials as well as challenges of its

---

[3] Whereas the ideas behind lean service are strongly rooted in manufacturing, it is acknowledged that lean service can overcome a mere efficiency focus (Carlborg et al., 2013). For instance, in case variation of demand is rather low, the concept of lean service can also foster effectiveness for the customers (Carlborg et al., 2013).

implementation (e.g., Bateman, Hines, & Davidson, 2014; Hadid, Mansouri, & Gallear, 2016; Matthias & Brown, 2016; Radnor & Osborne, 2013; Syltevik, Karamperidis, Antony, & Taheri, 2018).

(2) *Demarcation strategies* focus on effectiveness and aim to enhance service outcomes by considering the particularities of service delivery. Rather than industrializing services, organizations following a demarcation approach adopt approaches that rationalize service processes (Djellal & Gallouj, 2013). In this context, cognitive rationalization refers to the identification of standard cases, contracts, or solutions (i.e., typification), the establishment of problem-solving approaches (i.e., formalization) and the automated response to difficulties (i.e., individual or organizational routines) (Djellal & Gallouj, 2013; Gadrey, 1994). Thus, cognitive rationalization may drive productivity by reducing inputs based on harnessing learnings and establishing organizational capabilities. However, the primary performance assessment is not based on optimizing efficiency. Rather, measurement is based on multiple criteria (Djellal & Gallouj, 2013). An exemplary approach which can be applied in line with a demarcation strategy is the so-called productivity measurement and enhancement system (ProMES). ProMES is an evidence-based productivity improvement system originally developed by the organizational psychologist Robert D. Pritchard (1990). ProMES is primarily designed to increase the productivity of an organization based on enhancing personnel's motivation. The underlying assumption is that higher levels of motivation would lead service employees to improve their work strategies and align their efforts with organizational objectives. This shall be achieved by a structured and participatory process of interventions, systematically quantifying objectives, providing feedback for goal attainment, and mutual learning (Pritchard & Ashwood, 2008; Pritchard et al., 2012). ProMES has been applied in various industrial and service settings, demonstrating promising results for systematically enhancing organizational effectiveness (Pritchard et al., 2008).

(3) *Integration strategies* aim to synthesize efficiency and effectiveness considerations. Hence, firms engage in both, industrialization as well as rationalization of processes in order to enhance service efficiency and effectiveness (Djellal & Gallouj, 2013). In this context, integration strategies demand a multi-criteria assessment of performance that overcomes a narrow (i.e., efficiency-focused) productivity understanding seeing it just

as one component of overall service performance. Hence, a performance regime is enacted replacing a narrow productivity or effectiveness regime (Djellal & Gallouj, 2013). An example in line with an integration strategy is the failure modes and effects analysis- (FMEA-) based portfolio approach to service productivity improvement proposed by Geum, Shin, et al. (2011). Building on a broad understanding of service productivity, the authors adopt and modify traditional FMEA, which is commonly used in engineering, to enhance both efficiency and effectiveness of service delivery. For this purpose, initially, the service process is delineated in the form of a traditional flowchart to depict the different service steps. Based on this, sub-processes are analyzed to identify, evaluate, and eliminate critical failures reducing service productivity (i.e., prevent potential loss). Moreover, the process is analyzed to identify and assess opportunities to innovate future service delivery in order to enhance service productivity (i.e., create new value). Evaluation is conducted using a formalized portfolio approach to overcome the limitations of traditional FMEA-based ratings. So far, there is limited empirical evidence on how well this approach works in practice. Nevertheless, Geum et al. (2011) present a flexible and structured systematic to integrate both efficiency and effectiveness considerations for service productivity improvements.

This dissertation builds upon the differentiation of Djellal and Gallouj (2013) introduced above but adopts a less exclusive categorization. In the following, it will be distinguished between (1) *efficiency-focused approaches*, (2) *effectiveness-focused approaches*, and (3) *integration approaches*. Efficiency-focused approaches primarily aim to improve resource utilization for service delivery but do not necessarily have their origins in production. Effectiveness-focused approaches primarily aim to improve service outcomes but do not necessarily apply cognitive rationalization. Lastly, integration approaches integrate both considerations in a certain manner. Besides being in line with a particular strategy, each approach informs one or more phases of the service productivity life cycle. The latter is introduced in the next subsection.

3.5   The service productivity life cycle

Janeschek, Hottum, Kicherer, and Bienzeisler (2013) propose the service productivity life cycle depicted in Figure 6. The model shall foster a better understanding of how to measure and improve service productivity in the context of open and dynamic systems (Janeschek et al., 2013). Focusing on the service portfolio of a focal provider, the authors claim that service productivity can be enhanced throughout three interdependent phases:

The (1) *service engineering phase* addresses the systematic creation of new or improved service value propositions with the goal to foster service productivity at later stages.[4] For that, among others, approaches can foster in-depth insights concerning customer requirements, create an appropriate process and interface design as well as support the allocation of resources taking their respective characteristics into account. Throughout service engineering, the customer's productivity perspective can be included by integrating him or her into respective activities (Janeschek et al., 2013).

Throughout the (2) *service delivery phase* the service is offered to customers. Thus, this phase is characterized by multisided service interactions between one or more service providers and one or more customers. Approaches can help to analyze actual service interactions as they may provide important opportunities for productivity enhancement. For example, service-related skills and qualification of service-providing individuals need to be considered for potential productivity gains. Another critical aspect is to improve information flows between the entities involved in service delivery. By exploring customer requirements and expectations throughout delivery, important opportunities for re-engineering service processes may be discovered (Janeschek et al., 2013).

Finally, throughout the (3) *service management phase* certain approaches can help to monitor productivity on an aggregated level utilizing key performance indicators (KPIs). In doing so, the service provider can judge performance based on quantitatively assessing certain input and output factors of service delivery. In case pre-defined goals of a given period are not met, interventions can be conducted in order to enhance productivity (Janeschek et al., 2013).

---

[4] According to Bullinger et al. (2003) service engineering can be understood as a technical discipline, transferring systematic approaches from product development for the development of innovative services. For this dissertation service engineering shall not only address the usage of approaches from product development but include service-specific approaches as well.

Janeschek et al. (2013) argue that there is no defined starting point within this life cycle. Each phase can trigger changes in other phases. For example, whereas the discovery of unsatisfactory KPIs in the service management phase may initiate the re-engineering of existing services, the development of new services may require considering new KPIs. All in all, the model provides a conceptual structure to reflect on productivity enhancement as a cyclic process that may address different life cycle phases and can be supported by various practical approaches.

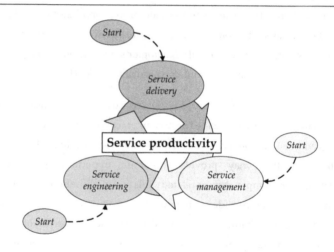

Figure 6: Service productivity life cycle. Illustration based on Janeschek, Hottum, Kicherer, & Bienzeisler (2013).

Having introduced the concept of service productivity and having presented different types of approaches, strategies, and phases for its improvement, the next chapter will establish this dissertation's understanding of networked service delivery.

4 Networked service delivery

 Chapter 4 establishes this dissertation's theoretical understanding of networked service delivery. First, it introduces and demarcates relevant network-related concepts in service research. Afterward, it depicts the concept of the service delivery network that serves as the theoretical foundation for the following parts of this dissertation.

4.1 Network-related concepts in service research

In the past, service research mainly focused on the interactions between one provider and its customers (Field et al., 2018; Ostrom et al., 2015; Tax et al., 2013). In this context, the service encounter is considered as the "dyadic interaction between a customer and a service provider" (Suprenant & Solomon, 1987, p. 87). However, as highlighted in Part I, scholars increasingly advocate a network perspective for service research as it is argued to provide a richer and more realistic picture of contemporary service delivery that is strongly dependent on collaboration among various entities (Barile et al., 2016; Field et al., 2018; Verleye et al., 2017).

In order to overcome a dyadic perspective on service research, different network-related concepts have been proposed. According to network theory, a network can be conceived as a set of nodes (i.e., actors such as providers and customers) that are linked by ties (Borgatti & Halgin, 2011). Nodes can be persons, teams, organizations etc. (Borgatti & Foster, 2003) and ties can be of state-type (kinship ties, role-based types, cognitive or affective ties) or event-type (e.g., interactions, transactions) and enable or prevent some kind of flow (e.g., information, money, goods) between nodes (Borgatti & Halgin, 2011).

Explicitly or implicitly building upon these ideas, scholars have investigated various service network-related concepts (e.g., Alexander, Teller, & Roggeveen, 2016; Ekman, Raggio, & Thompson, 2016; Gummesson, 2008; Scerri & Agarwal, 2018; Verleye et al., 2017). Whereas all of these concepts focus on the role of multi-sided service interactions, different conceptual understandings prevail. Addressing the complexity of emerging service theory and contemporary service practice, Barile et al. (2016) aim to lift the level of analysis in service research and propose to consider service networks as a particular unit of analysis intertwined with the concepts of service systems and service ecosystems. Following Maglio et al. (2006), the authors consider a service system as a dynamic configuration of physical and non-physical resources (e.g., people, technology, information) connected internally and externally via value propositions. Actors of these service systems (e.g., people, organizations, or machinery) form interconnected service networks (Barile et al., 2016). As an example, the authors portray the homestay network Airbnb that is realized by connecting people and private property or the company Uber operating a transportation network of mostly privately owned cars. Lastly, service networks are integrated into larger and dynamic service ecosystems (Vargo & Lusch, 2011), which can be defined as "relatively self-contained, self-adjusting system[s] of resource integrating actors, connected by shared institutional logics and mutual value creation through their service exchanges" (Barile et al., 2016, p. 660). Examples include Apple's, Google's or ALIBABA's ecosystem connecting and advancing networks of suppliers and customers (Barile et al., 2016).

Notwithstanding the theoretical relevance of this multi-layered view, the proposed understanding poses challenges for operationally analyzing and improving service productivity. It remains unclear where to draw the boundaries for each service system, network, or ecosystem and which actors and interactions should be considered for improving productivity for the different actors of the service network.

Taking a service operations perspective, recently, Field et al. (2018) proposed to investigate the concept of the service supply network as a key theme for future research. Building upon Sampson et al. (2015) they refer to such a network as "the set of entities that participate directly or indirectly in the realization of a service outcome" (Field et al., 2018, p. 57). Thus, the service delivery process can be considered as the reference point to draw the boundaries of a service supply network. However, following the definition presented above, such networks may be very large and complex as various suppliers may indirectly participate in the realization of a particular service outcome (Tax et al., 2013). For example, the producer of medical equipment indirectly participates in the realization of a successful surgery or the producer of car tires indirectly contributes to a smooth transportation experience. Given the definition above, it remains somewhat unclear which actors to include or exclude into a particular service supply network. Thus, this dissertation follows a related but more focused conceptual foundation, which is described next.

4.2   The concept of the service delivery network

Tax et al. (2013) build upon network theory (Borgatti & Foster, 2003; Borgatti & Halgin, 2011) and propose the concept of the service delivery network defined as "two or more actors that, in the eyes of the customer, are responsible for the provision of a connected, overall service" (Tax et al., 2013, p. 457). Whereas Tax et al. (2013) do not explicitly define their understanding of a network actor, their use of the term implies that they mean social actors (i.e., persons or organizations)[5]. The concept of the service delivery network integrates the customer experience approach stressing the importance of understanding the overall customer journey, i.e., "all activities and events related to the delivery of a service from a customer's perspective" (Zomerdijk & Voss, 2010, p. 74). In line with this understanding, throughout the customer journey, the customer becomes the focal node of a potentially unique network connecting different actors for service delivery (Tax et al., 2013). In network terms, the customer is the center of an ego network, whereas the actors perceived by the customer to be responsible for service delivery are known as alters (Borgatti & Foster, 2003).

This dissertation builds upon this concept as it provides a pragmatic way to decide upon the subset of actors for analyzing and improving service delivery. However, in line with Sampson (2015), relevant providers are not limited to "just those agencies with which the customer interacts directly" (Tax et al., 2013, p. 460) in case direct interactions are understood as "people are interacting with people in some way" (Sampson, 2012, p. 187). For this dissertation, providers also encompass actors with whom the customer interacts via a surrogate in the course of the customer journey. Such surrogates encompass belongings and information of the interaction partner (Sampson, 2012). An example would be a customer using the online portal of his or her bank or a doctor analyzing the blood of a patient using specific diagnostic devices. All in all, the customer journey then is realized by a set of direct (i.e., person to person) and

---

[5] For an extended understanding of the term actor see Storbacka, Brodie, Böhmann, Maglio, & Nenonen (2016)

surrogate interactions (i.e., acting on belongings and information of another entity) between the customer and a network of co-providers in order to achieve the customer's desired goals (Sampson, 2012; Sampson et al., 2015; Tax et al., 2013). Customers can be both, organizations as well as individuals (Tax et al., 2013). In this context, other customers may also take the role of a co-provider in case they contribute to overall service delivery (e.g., fellow students in an education program).

Voorhees et al. (2017) argue that the customer journey can be separated into pre-core service, core service, and post-core service periods (Voorhees et al., 2017). From a service delivery network perspective, throughout the pre-core service period, a particular customer interacts with one or more providers, for instance to share and review related information, and to initiate core-service delivery (Voorhees et al., 2017). Next, the core service period encompasses interactions between the customer and one or more providers for delivering the primary service. These interactions address the fulfillment of a specific customer need, which represents the customer's main motivation for choosing the service under consideration (Voorhees et al., 2017). Finally, in the post-core service period, the customer assesses service results and certain providers may re-engage with the customer in order to develop long-term relationships or initiate future service delivery (Voorhees et al., 2017). Throughout these periods, it may be necessary that the different providers interact with each other and coordinate the connected, overall service (Tax et al., 2013). As indicated in Figure 7, interactions throughout the different periods of the customer journey lead to a potentially unique service delivery network for each customer. Note that following this understanding, the service delivery network represents a subset of the service supply network. Whereas the latter includes all actors that directly or indirectly contribute to service outcomes, the former only includes the actors that the customer interacts with directly or via a surrogate. Thus, it does not include suppliers of providers who are responsible for service delivery from the customer's point of view.

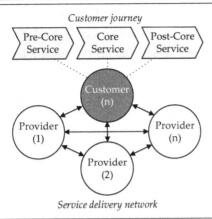

Customer journey

Service delivery network

Figure 7: *Service delivery network as a consequence of the customer journey. Own illustration.*

Applying such a network perspective for managing service delivery throughout the overall customer journey sheds light on various operational and relational issues that otherwise might remain unconsidered. Among others, for any focal provider within a service delivery network managerial questions may arise concerning the customer's role in choosing co-providers, the coordination of network actors throughout the customer journey, the commonality among service delivery networks, as well as the planning of processes according to the demands of the anticipated clientele (Tax et al., 2013) and other co-providers. Insights and decisions concerning any of these questions may significantly influence service productivity for the customer as well as the other network members. Next, Chapter 4 summarizes and synthesizes the relevant concepts for this dissertation.

5   Summary and synthesis of key concepts

 Chapter 5 briefly summarizes the key concepts introduced in Chapters 1 to 4. In doing so, it synthesizes the concepts depicted above to establish a coherent theoretical understanding that is applied throughout the following parts of this dissertation.

It was stressed that this dissertation takes a process perspective on the service concept. More specifically, service delivery is specified as a special type of production process that relies on individual customer inputs for execution (Sampson & Froehle, 2006). Customers are considered as actors (individuals or entities) that decide upon the monetary or non-monetary compensation of one or more (co-)providers (Sampson, 2012; Sampson & Froehle, 2006; Tax et al., 2013). In this regard, it was highlighted that fellow customers can also be co-providers themselves (e.g., fellow students in an education program) (Tax et al., 2013). Inputs of customers and providers encompass both tangible and intangible resources. Typically, the former represent operand resources, i.e., physical resources like people, machines, or materials (Constantin & Lusch, 1994). The latter, on the other hand, refer to operant resources that are applied to perform an operation on operand resources. Examples include individual skills, knowledge, information, and technology (Constantin & Lusch, 1994). Throughout service delivery, inputs are transformed into outputs and outcomes. In this context, it is argued that the concept of output is underpinned by classical or neo-classical economic theories and can be understood as the tangible results of a transformation process (Yalley & Sekhon, 2014). Outcomes, on the other hand, refer to the direct and indirect effects of the transformation process (Pena, 2011; Yalley & Sekhon, 2014). It is proposed that focusing on outcomes instead of outputs better addresses the particularities of service delivery and thus should be considered for managing service productivity (Yalley & Sekhon, 2014).

Service productivity is defined as a context-specific performance measure. It was highlighted that there is no common understanding and scholars have applied this term when focusing on efficiency and/or effectiveness of service delivery (Djellal & Gallouj, 2013; Grönroos & Ojasalo, 2004). Whereas efficiency refers to how well resources are utilized throughout a transformation process, effectiveness addresses the degree of goal attainment (Tangen, 2005). Nevertheless, there is an increasing consent that, for being a meaningful concept, it should include both dimensions (Bessant et al., 2014; Yalley & Sekhon, 2014). Moreover, it was highlighted that scholars have proposed several approaches for improving service productivity. In this regard, these approaches refer to tools, techniques, systems, or strategic approaches (van der Wiele et al., 2006) that aim to enhance efficiency and/or effectiveness of service delivery (Djellal & Gallouj, 2013) by informing one or more phases of the service productivity life cycle. This life cycle can be divided into a service engineering, service delivery, and service management phase (Janeschek et al., 2013).

Finally, several network-related concepts were introduced. A network was defined as a set of nodes (e.g., actors) that are linked by ties (e.g., interactions) that enable or prevent some kind of flow (e.g., money, goods, information) (Borgatti & Halgin, 2011). Building on this understanding, a service delivery network was defined as two or more providers that, from the customer's point of view, are responsible for overall service delivery (Tax et al., 2013). It was highlighted that the concept of the service delivery network integrates the customer experience approach, stressing the importance of understanding the overall customer journey. The latter refers to all service-related activities and occurrences from the customer's point of view (Zomerdijk & Voss, 2010). In this regard, it was highlighted that the customer journey can be separated into a pre-core, core, and post-core period. A summary of these concepts is presented in Table 1.

Table 1: Summary of key concepts of this dissertation.

Concept	Description	Main references	Presented in
Service (delivery)	A special type of production process relying on individual customer inputs	Sampson & Froehle (2006)	Chapter 2.1
Customers	Actors that decide if a provider shall be compensated for service delivery	Sampson (2012); Sampson & Froehle (2006)	Chapter 2.1
(Co-)Providers	Actors that provide inputs into service delivery for a particular customer; interact with customers directly or via a surrogate; can include fellow customers	Tax et al. (2013); Sampson (2012)	Chapter 2.1 Chapter 3.2
Inputs	Operand (typically tangible) and operant (typically intangible) resources applied to service delivery	Sampson (2012); Sampson & Froehle (2006); Constantin & Lusch (1994)	Chapter 2.1 Chapter 2.2
Outputs	Typically tangible results of service delivery (quantitative nature)	Sampson & Froehle (2006); Yalley & Sekhon (2014)	Chapter 2.1 Chapter 2.2
Outcomes	Direct and indirect effects of service delivery (qualitative nature)	Yalley & Sekhon (2014); Pena (2011)	Chapter 2.3
Service productivity	Context-specific performance measure; Focuses on efficiency and/or effectiveness of service delivery	Grönroos & Ojasalo (2004); Tangen (2005); Yalley & Sekhon (2014)	Chapter 2.3
Efficiency	How well resources are utilized throughout a production process	Tangen (2005)	Chapter 2.2
Effectiveness	The degree to which a production process achieves desired outputs/outcomes	Tangen (2005)	Chapter 2.2
Service productivity improvement approach	Tool, technique, system, or strategic approach that aims to enhance service efficiency and/or effectiveness for one or more actors throughout one or more phases of the service productivity life cycle	Djellal & Gallouj (2013); Janeschek et al. (2013); Van der Wiele et al. (2006)	Chapter 2.3
Network	A set of nodes that are connected by ties that enable or prevent flow	Borgatti & Halgin (2001)	Chapter 3.1
Service delivery network	Two or more providers that, from the point of view of the customer, are responsible for overall, networked service delivery	Tax et al., (2013)	Chapter 3.2
Customer journey	All service-related activities and occurrences from the customer's point of view; can be divided into pre-core service, core service, and post-core service periods	Zomerdijk & Voss (2010); Voorhees et al. (2017)	Chapter 3.2

Part III

Systematic literature review:

Approaches for improving service productivity from a network perspective

© Springer Fachmedien Wiesbaden GmbH, part of Springer Nature 2020
C. F. Daiberl, *Driving Networked Service Productivity*, Markt- und
Unternehmensentwicklung Markets and Organisations,
https://doi.org/10.1007/978-3-658-29580-6_3

1 Objectives and structure[6]

 This dissertation explores *how a focal provider can drive productivity in the context of networked service delivery.* Part III aims to support this goal by contributing to a better theoretical as well as practical understanding about existing approaches for driving service productivity from a network perspective. As highlighted before, scholars from different disciplines have proposed diverse approaches aiming to enhance service productivity (e.g., Böttcher & Klingner, 2011; Carlborg & Kindström, 2014; Carlborg et al., 2013; Geum, Shin, & Park, 2011; Pritchard, Harrell, DiazGranados, & Guzman, 2008). However, most established approaches applied for improving productivity in the context of industrial and non-industrial services take a monadic or dyadic perspective (e.g., Klingner et al., 2015). Hence, in organizational practice, potentials to improve service productivity throughout the connected, overall service and establish mutually beneficial interactions with relevant co-providers may remain untapped.

In order to foster an integrated understanding for both scholars and practitioners, Part III has the objective to systematically identify and assess approaches that can inform the improvement of service productivity from a network perspective. In doing so, a structured comparison between the different approaches concerning their application-oriented qualities shall be enabled. All in all, this part answers the first research question of the dissertation:

RQ1: Which systematic approaches are discussed in service research for the improvement of service productivity from a network perspective and what are their application-oriented qualities?

Part III is organized as follows: Chapter 2 illustrates the classification scheme developed to foster a high-level comparison between different productivity improvement approaches. Subsequently, Chapter 3 describes the procedure of the systematic literature review. In doing so, the different activities for planning and

---

[6] Part III of this dissertation builds upon and extends a conference contribution presented and discussed at the 26th Annual RESER Conference in Naples, Italy (i.e., Daiberl et al., 2016a).

conducting the review as well as communicating and disseminating the findings are depicted. Afterward, Chapter 4 presents the findings of the literature review. For this purpose, first, core-contributions are described, followed by the thematic overview of the efficiency-focused approaches, effectiveness-focused approaches, and integration approaches. Finally, Chapter 5 discusses the results of Part III by highlighting contributions to theory and implications for practitioners. Moreover, implications for the remainder of this dissertation are derived. Figure 8 summarizes the structure of Part III.

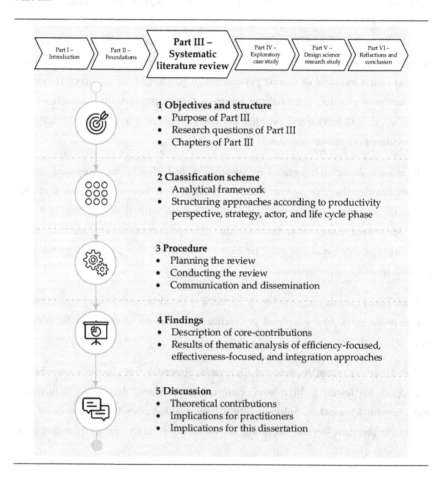

Figure 8: Structure of Part III. Own illustration.

2   Classification scheme for productivity improvement approaches

The classification scheme depicted in Figure 9 was developed in line with the conceptual understanding presented in Part II. It serves as a high-level analytical framework to compare different approaches for productivity improvement. Throughout the literature review, it was used as a scheme for selecting and thematically structuring the results presented in Chapter 3.

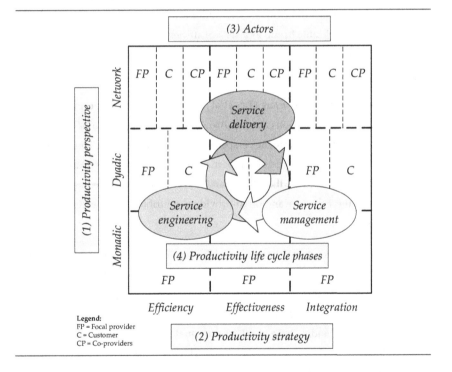

Figure 9: Scheme for high-level classification of approaches. Own illustration.

Following the classification scheme, each approach (i.e., tool, technique, system, or strategic approach) for enhancing service productivity can basically be classified according to four criteria: The first criterion is concerned about the (1) *productivity perspective* (Ostrom et al., 2015). Approaches taking a monadic perspective merely strive to enhance service productivity from the point of view of a particular focal provider (FP), i.e., the provider who would apply the approach under consideration. In doing so, these approaches mainly address the focal providers' internal processes and activities. Other approaches consider service productivity in the context of dyadic interactions with customers (C) or take a network perspective by acknowledging the influence of further co-providers (CP) as well.

Next, the (2) *productivity strategy* serves as the second criterion for classification (Djellal & Gallouj, 2013). As discussed in Section 2.3 of Part II, the productivity strategy affects the specific productivity dimensions addressed by a particular approach. Each approach may be applicable to enhance service efficiency and/or service effectiveness for one or more actors involved in service delivery (Grönroos & Ojasalo, 2004; Yalley & Sekhon, 2014).

The particular network (3) *actors* (Tax et al., 2013) targeted by a specific approach represents the third classification criterion. As highlighted above, monadic approaches reflect upon service delivery from the perspective of the focal provider. Thus, their goal is to enhance service productivity for this particular actor. Approaches taking a dyadic and network perspective, on the other hand, may also strive to enhance service productivity for the customer and/or co-providers contributing resources to overall service delivery.

Lastly, each approach may be suited to drive service productivity throughout one or more (4) *service productivity life cycle phases* (Janeschek et al., 2013). Thus, an approach may provide a systematic for (re-)designing a service delivery process (i.e., service engineering phase), provide guidelines how to develop and/or use KPIs (i.e., service management phase), and/or help to reflect on actual service interactions in order to drive productivity (i.e., service delivery phase). Having introduced the theory-based classification scheme of this literature review, next, the procedure is explicated. As highlighted above, the review is only concerned with the approaches addressing a network perspective (i.e., the top row of the classification scheme).

3 Procedure

The literature review followed the overall procedure of Tranfield, Denver, and Smart (2003) and harnessed the advice of Webster and Watson (2002) as well as Wickham and Woods (2005). In the following, the different phases of the literature review presented in Figure 10 are described in detail.

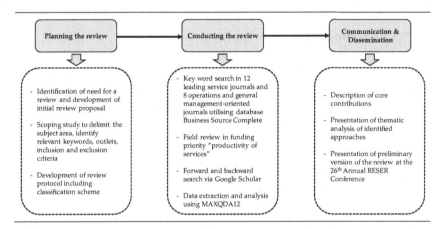

Figure 10: Procedure of the systematic literature review. Own illustration.

3.1 Planning the review

First, the need for a systematic review was identified and an initial proposal was developed (see Appendix B). The latter was created together with a fellow senior researcher and included the overall objectives of the study, the intended outlet and method, as well as the expected results. Afterward, a scoping study was conducted in order to delimit the subject area, identify relevant keywords, outlets, as well as inclusion and exclusion criteria for the main search (Tranfield et al., 2003). Building on the insights derived by the scoping study and discussions with two senior scholars who are experts in the field of service research, a review protocol was developed (see Appendix C). Unlike in other disciplines (e.g., medicine), in management research, the level of formality and standardization of such protocols is rather low in order to foster the exploration and discovery of new ideas (Tranfield et al., 2003). In line with the suggestions of Tranfield et al. (2003), the review protocol of this study contained a brief conceptual discussion of the research problem and arguments for its significance. Next, the review protocol summarized the objectives and intended audience, the preliminary set of keywords, the sample of outlets, a short description of the search strategy and a list of inclusion as well as exclusion criteria derived throughout the scoping study. Moreover, the review protocol included the high-level classification scheme introduced in Chapter 2, to support the organization of the literature review (Cooper, 1988; Webster & Watson, 2002).

3.2　Conducting the review

In the second phase, the systematic literature review was conducted. For keyword search a broad set of often interchangeably used terms identified in the scoping study was applied to capture as many potentially relevant articles as possible. Several sets of keywords were combined with the term service to limit results to the most promising contributions. Truncation (*) was used to ensure that different word endings are considered (e.g., effective* to include effectiveness and effectivity). For keywords, the term *servic** was combined with three network-related terms (*net**, *syste**, *tria**), seven productivity-related terms (*productiv**, *effectiv**, *efficienc**, *qual**, *perfor**, *experienc**, *valu**), twelve improvement-related terms (*enhanc**, *improv**, *increas**, *optimi**, *manag**, *desig**, *enginee**, *innovat**, *develo**, *driv**, *rais**, *gai**) and ten systematic-related terms (*metho**, *tool, system, approach, instrument, procedure, framework, technique, process, strategy*). For each set of keywords, at least one of these terms had to be found in the title or the abstract of a study.

Following Webster and Watson (2002), the major contributions are likely to be found within the leading journals of a particular research field. As this dissertation aims to contribute to service research, as shown in Table 2, all leading, peer-reviewed, service-specific journals were considered for the keyword search. Additionally, seven non-service-specific, production and general management-oriented journals were included as they were discovered throughout the scoping study to potentially contain relevant contributions concerning the topic of service productivity. In order to ensure that high quality evidence is investigated, VHB JOURQUAL ranking was applied and journals were only considered if they were ranked A-C in VHB JOURQUAL3.

Table 2: Outlets considered for the review.

Outlets	VHB Ranking
Leading service journals:	
Journal of Retailing; Journal of Service Research; Manufacturing & Service Operations Management	A
International Journal of Service Industry Management (before 2009)/Journal of Service Management (since 2009)	B
Service Science; Journal of Retailing and Consumer Services; Journal of Services Marketing; Journal of Financial Services Research; Managing Service Quality (before 2015)/ Journal of Service Theory and Practice (since 2015); Service Industries Journal; International Journal of Retail & Distribution Management; International Review of Retail; Distribution and Consumer Research	C
General and operations management-oriented journals:	
Production and Operations Management; Journal of Operations Management; International Journal of Operations & Production Management; Journal of Business Research; European Management Journal; Journal of Productivity and Performance Management; Benchmarking: An International Journal; Journal of Business & Industrial Marketing	A-C

For 18 of the 20 journals considered, it was possible to utilize the database Business Source Complete (via EBSCOhost) for keyword search. However, the journal of Service Theory and Practice (since 2015 successor of Managing Service Quality) and the journal Service Science had to be manually screened as, at the point of writing, both were not listed in Business Source Complete. This procedure led to 1178 potentially relevant contributions. Next, following the previously developed inclusion and exclusion criteria depicted in Table 3, titles and abstracts were screened leading to 17 core contributions describing 16 different approaches that can be applied for productivity improvement in the context of networked service delivery.

Moreover, the approaches for productivity management published in the so-called "service productivity toolbox" were considered.[7] The toolbox represents a collection of best practice approaches, which were either used, reflected upon, or developed in the context of the funding priority "productivity of services" of the German Ministry of

---

[7] In December 2017, the toolbox could be found on the website www.service-productivity.de.

Education and Research. The latter comprised 33 sponsored research projects with a funding volume of 41,54 million EUR and lasted from August 2009 to September 2015. Thus, it presents a database of approaches considered practically relevant by the participating institutions.

Table 3: Inclusion and exclusion criteria for the systematic literature review.

Inclusion & exclusion criteria for core contributions
• Approaches should have a managerial focus and not focus on a macro-economic perspective on service productivity
• Approaches should present a systematic that informs the improvement of service efficiency and/or effectiveness from a network perspective (i.e., consider the role of the customer and two or more providers for service delivery)
• Approaches should be applicable to different settings of networked service delivery and not only present a solution to very specific domains (e.g., optimization of call-center networks)
• Contributions should be application-oriented (i.e., describe how to apply a particular approach)
• Contributions should be written in English or German language and published in scientific outlets

For reviewing the productivity toolbox, first, all 35 approaches summarized in the toolbox were screened using the same inclusion and exclusion criteria presented above.[8] In case the approach seemed potentially relevant, author information provided in the summary was used to look for related scientific contributions. However, only two approaches (i.e., modularization and the service system snapshot) explicitly took a network perspective. In both cases, no additional core contributions could be discovered by the end of December 2017.

Having identified a set of core-contributions, next, backward and forward search was conducted (Webster & Watson, 2002). In this context, backward search refers to reviewing citations of the core-contribution to identify articles that were published before but need to be considered. Forward search, on the other hand, refers to identifying articles that cite the previously identified core-contributions (Webster & Watson, 2002). The search was conducted via Google Scholar. In doing so, the goal was

---

[8] These approaches can be found when filtering for "methods" in the toolbox.

to identify further core contributions as well as related contributions. The latter are fundamental to a particular core-contribution as they describe building blocks for developing an approach proposed by a particular core-contribution or address its evaluation and/or advancement. In both cases, only the primary sources cited in the core-contribution specifically detailing the building block adopted by the core-contribution or citing the core-contribution were considered. In this context, related contributions describing particular research methods were included as long as they were highlighted as an integral part for carrying out the approach described in the respective core-contribution and a source was referenced. Following this procedure, all in all, 2 new core contributions and 62 related contributions were identified.

As proposed by Wickham and Woods (2005), in order to foster efficient and effective analysis, key information was extracted using computer-aided qualitative data analysis software. Such programs facilitate the organization and analysis of review data by electronic storage, search, and retrieval functionalities. Moreover, they possess functionalities for streamlined disaggregation of data into analytical categories (i.e., coding), supporting the efficiency and depths of exploration (Wickham & Woods, 2005). For this study, the software MAXQDA12 was applied and coding had the goal to foster both a descriptive and a thematic analysis of the contributions identified (Tranfield et al., 2003). The descriptive analysis should foster a better general understanding of the identified sample of approaches and related scholarly research. For this purpose, the coding scheme encompassed the following categories: the (1) *main reference*, the (2) *discipline* of the authors, the (3) *outlet* and (4) *name* of the approach, the (5) *research method* conducted, as well as the nature of (6) *demonstration and evaluation*. The latter reflects upon how the approach under consideration was illustrated and how its performance was assessed. Both steps may either be conducted artificially and/or naturalistically (Venable, Pries-Heje, & Baskerville, 2016). Throughout a purely artificial demonstration and evaluation, artifacts are not applied to any reality (i.e., real users, real systems, real tasks) (Sonnenberg & vom Brocke, 2012). Naturalistic demonstration and evaluation, on the other hand, are more interpretive in nature and explore the evaluand's performance in the real world (Venable et al., 2016). Finally, for descriptive analysis, the (7) *empirical field* where the research was conducted as well as the (8) *application domain* for future usage of the respective productivity improvement approach were considered.

In contrast to the descriptive analysis undertaken, thematic analysis focused on gaining in-depth insights concerning the application-oriented qualities of the identified approaches. The focus on qualities has been demonstrated to reveal nuanced insights when comparing related approaches for context-dependent problem solving (e.g., Edvardsson, Kristensson, Magnusson, & Sundström, 2012). For this purpose, initially, the approaches were thematically structured according to the following criteria of the classification theme: their (9) *productivity strategy* as well as the (10) *actors* and (11) *productivity life cycle phases* affected.[9] Subsequently, the approaches were analyzed according to their (12) *type*, (13) *main logic* for productivity improvement, (14) *application requirements*, (15) *application results* as well as the (16) *reporting and measurement* of the information generated. Finally, the degree of (17) *practicability* was assessed. The latter represents a subjective evaluation concerning how detailed operational activities for carrying out the respective approach in a real-world context were described and how well the approaches already demonstrated successful empirical application.

3.3   Communication and dissemination

In the third phase, the findings of the systematic literature review are communicated and disseminated (Tranfield et al., 2003). As highlighted before, a preliminary version of this review was presented at the 26th Annual RESER Conference of the European Association for Research on Services in Naples, Italy (i.e., Daiberl et al., 2016a). This review included articles until the end of June 2016 and included 15 approaches for systematically enhancing service productivity from a network perspective. The findings of the updated version including articles until December 2017 are presented in the following chapter.

---

[9] Note that the criterion *productivity perspective* is not applied for thematic analysis as approaches were only selected if they take a network perspective.

4 Findings

 This chapter presents the findings of the literature review. For that, initially, the core contributions are described. Afterward, the results of the thematic analysis are presented to deepen the qualitative understanding of the different approaches identified.

4.1 Description of core contributions

As described above, 19 core contributions describing 18 approaches informing the systematic improvement of service productivity from a network perspective could be identified. A descriptive compilation of these contributions is presented in Table 4. The earliest core contribution was published in 1999 whereas the most recent one was published in 2017. Approaches were either developed or discussed by scholars from the disciplines of engineering (6/19), information systems and marketing (each 4/19), operations management (3/19), and innovation management (2/19).

Core contributions were published in seven of the twenty journals reviewed. The majority of the core contributions was published in the Journal of Service Research (5/19), followed the International Journal of Service Industry Management/Journal of Service Management, Service Science, and Managing Service Quality/Journal of Service Theory and Practice (each 3/19). Additionally, a contribution in another Journal (i.e., International Journal of Research in Marketing) and one book chapter were identified via backward search. Most commonly, scholars conducted qualitative research (8/19), followed by quantitative (4/19) and conceptual studies (4/19). Several authors mixed qualitative and quantitative research methods (3/19). Most of the core contributions demonstrated the respective productivity improvement approach in a naturalistic setting (14/19). However, only a minority indicated specific evaluation criteria assessed using real-world data (7/19). Approaches were applied in various empirical fields, with healthcare as the most prominent one (5/14), followed by municipal and multi-media services (each 2/14). Whereas most of the approaches are generic as they can be applied to any case of networked service delivery (14/19), five approaches pose certain limitations to the application domain. The next section presents the findings of the thematic analysis.

Table 4: *Compilation of core contributions.*

#	Main Reference	Discipline	Outlet	Name	Research approach	Demonstration and evaluation	Empirical field	Application domain
1	Badinelli et al. (2012)	Operations management	Journal of Service Management	Fuzzy-modeling based on VSA	Conceptual paper	Artificial demonstration; no formal evaluation	N.A.	Generic
2	Böttcher & Klingner (2011)	Information systems	J. of Business & Industrial Marketing	Modularization	Qualitative; field study	Naturalistic demonstration and evaluation	Industry; IT-service	Generic
3	Govind et al. (2008)	Marketing	Int. Journal of Research in Marketing	Resource allocation modeling	Quantitative; optimization	Naturalistic demonstration; artificial evaluation	Healthcare	Locally distributed service delivery networks
4	Gustafsson et al. (1999)	Marketing	Int. Journal of Service Industry Management	Customer focused service development	Qualitative; case study	Naturalistic demonstration; no formal evaluation	Aviation	Generic
5	Halvorsrud et al. (2016)	Innovation management	Journal of Service Theory and Practice	Customer journey analysis	Qualitative; design science research	Naturalistic demonstration and evaluation	Telecom	Generic
6	Hammerschmidt et al. (2012)	Marketing	Journal of Service Research	DEA-based benchmarking	Mixed methods; field experiment	Naturalistic demonstration and evaluation	Healthcare	Service delivery networks coordinated by network hubs

Table 4 (cont.): Compilation of core contributions.

#	Main Reference	Discipline	Outlet	Name	Research approach	Demonstration and evaluation	Empirical field	Application domain
7	Hsu (2011)	Engineering	Service Science	Hyper-networking	Conceptual paper	Artificial demonstration; no formal evaluation	N.A.	Internet-based service delivery networks
8	Kieliszewski, Maglio, & Cefkin (2012)	Engineering	European Management Journal	Service system analysis	Quantitative; case scenario	Rather artificial demonstration and evaluation	Municipal service	Generic
9	Lessard (2015)	Information systems	Service Science	Modeling value co-creation	Qualitative; case study	Naturalistic demonstration; artificial evaluation	Municipal service; education	Generic
10	Lim & Kim (2014)	Engineering	Service Science	Information service blueprint	Qualitative; case study	Naturalistic demonstration; rather artificial evaluation	Automotive; IT; healthcare	Information-intensive service delivery networks
11	Meyer, Jekowsky, & Crance (2007)	Innovation management	Managing Service Quality	Modularization	Qualitative; case study	Naturalistic demonstration and evaluation	Healthcare	Generic
12	Milton & Johnson (2012)	Information systems	Managing Service Quality	BPMN	Conceptual; illustrative comparison	Artificial demonstration and evaluation	N.A.	Generic

Table 4 (cont.): Compilation of core contributions.

#	Main Reference	Discipline	Outlet	Name	Research approach	Demonstration and evaluation	Empirical field	Application domain
13	Patrício et al. (2011)	Engineering	Journal of Service Research	Multilevel service design	Mixed; design research	Naturalistic demonstration and evaluation	Retail; banking	Generic
14	Pullman & Thompson (2003)	Operations management	Journal of Service Research	Simulation-based capacity-demand integration	Mixed; simulation	Naturalistic demonstration; rather artificial evaluation	Tourism	Location constrained service delivery networks
15	Sampson (2012)	Operations management	Journal of Service Research	PCN Analysis	Conceptual; illustrative examples	Artificial demonstration and evaluation	N.A.	Generic
16	Svensson (2002)	Marketing	Journal of Services Marketing	Perceptual triadic network method	Quantitative; survey	Naturalistic demonstration; no formal evaluation	Various fields	Triadic service delivery networks
17	Tan et al. (2011)	Information systems	Service System Implementation (book chapter)	E³-value & e³-control	Quantitative; case study	Naturalistic demonstration and evaluation	Logistics	Generic
18	Teixeira et al. (2012)	Engineering	Journal of Service Management	Customer experience modeling	Qualitative; grounded theory	Naturalistic demonstration; artificial evaluation	Multi-media service	Generic
19	Teixeira et al. (2017)	Engineering	Journal of Service Research	Management and interaction design method	Qualitative; design science research	Naturalistic demonstration and evaluation	Multi-media service; healthcare	Tech.-based service delivery networks

4.2   Thematic overview of approaches

As described above, all in all, the systematic literature review identified 18 approaches for improving service productivity from a network perspective. In the following, the different approaches are presented in greater detail. Initially, efficiency-focused approaches are presented followed by effectiveness-focused approaches. Finally, approaches integrating both considerations are depicted.

4.2.1   Efficiency-focused approaches: "Doing the things right" from a network perspective

All in all, three efficiency-focused approaches were identified. Using the high-level classification scheme presented in Chapter 2, these approaches are depicted in Figure 11. In the following, their application-oriented qualities are delineated.

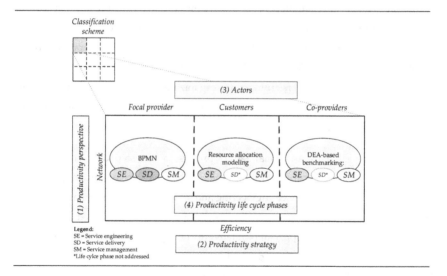

Figure 11: High-level classification of efficiency-focused approaches. Own illustration.

A well-known tool that can be applied to inform efficiency improvements from a network perspective is the business process modeling notation (BPMN), which is also considered as the de-facto standard for modeling organizational processes (Fetke, 2008;

Kazemzadeh, Milton, & Johnson, 2015b; Milton & Johnson, 2012). BPMN informs the overall service productivity life cycle of a particular focal provider by providing a notation for standardized engineering, executing, and control of service delivery. At its core, BPMN is a comprehensive tool that allows describing even complex processes using a wide range of concepts and symbols (Milton & Johnson, 2012). Whereas in the past, BPMN (Version 1.2) was mainly concerned about visualizing processes from one provider's point of view, it has been extended to represent complex, networked processes as well (Version 2.0). For each actor, BPMN contains an individual swimlane depicting the actor's activities from the start to the end of a certain business process (Chinosi & Trombetta, 2012; Milton & Johnson, 2012). In order to derive quantified and productivity relevant insights (e.g., cycle time, costs) BPMN models can be simulated and support the execution and monitoring of business processes using different software solutions (Chinosi & Trombetta, 2012). Whereas BPMN overcomes the dyadic focus of traditional service blueprinting (Kazemzadeh et al., 2015b), it does not consider co-productive steps that simultaneously involve multiple actors (Sampson et al., 2015). Moreover, it does not define any concepts concerning qualitative service outcomes (e.g., customer value) and does not reflect on the objectives and expectations of network actors (Kazemzadeh et al., 2015b). Hence, it is largely efficiency-oriented, enabling to gain insights concerning inter-organizational process configuration to optimize resource utilization concerning efficiency-related KPIs (e.g., idealized time and costs for process cycles).

Hammerschmidt, Falk and Staat (2012) propose a two-step data envelopment analysis (DEA)-based benchmarking technique that can drive efficiency for co-providers throughout the service engineering and service management phase. In a first step (i.e., diagnosing), DEA (Charnes, Cooper, & Rhodes, 1978) is applied to calculate efficiency scores of service providers relative to best performers. For this purpose, Hammerschmidt et al. (2012) adopt the bootstrapping procedure to test the heterogeneity in the sample (Dyson et al., 2001; Simar & Wilson, 1998), conduct a monte carlo simulation for sample size-corrected efficiency scores (Zhang & Bartels, 1998) and a superefficiency analysis for eliminating outliers (Banker & Chang, 2006; Simar, 2003). As a result of this procedure, efficiency gaps are identified that are addressed in the second step (i.e., therapy). Inspired by detailing endeavors in the context of life-sciences

(Chintagunta & Desiraju, 2005; Manchanda, Rossi, & Chintagunta, 2004; Narayanan, Manchanda, & Chintagunta, 2005), network improvement calls are enacted. For this purpose, an actor taking the role of a network hub (e.g., health maintenance organization as the focal provider of a healthcare delivery network) informs the co-providers of the service network about their individual benchmarking results with respect to current resource consumption in comparison to optimal consumption of similar providers. Next, specific improvement initiatives are proposed (i.e., reduction of overspendings concerning different practice styles). For that, the focal provider allocates individual efficiency targets that are inspired by best performers and shares guidelines how to reach them as well as relevant network-focused information (e.g., potential savings on an aggregated network level if individual providers improve efficiency). This approach has been evaluated successfully in a real-world scenario (Hammerschmidt et al., 2012). However, for the focal provider, its application is dependent on extensive collaboration of co-providers.

Whereas DEA-based benchmarking described above focuses on network providers' efficiency, Govind, Chatterjee, & Mittal (2008) propose a resource allocation modeling framework in order to enhance efficiency for the customer. The authors harness publicly available data (i.e., disease incidence, location and capacity of hospitals in a greater region, socio-economic and demographic data) and apply autoregressive, moving average with exogenous inputs modeling (Box, Jenkins, & Reinsel, 1994), and universal kriging (Marshall, 1991) to calculate the optimal resource allocation (i.e., bed capacity) within a regional network of hospitals in order to enhance timely access to health care. In this way, the authors identify discrepancies between supply and demand with respect to different disease groups. This informs service management of individual providers about possibilities for enhancing customer efficiencies (i.e., travel time) and gives them the opportunity to re-engineer their services accordingly. Whereas the approach was developed in a healthcare setting it is argued to be suitable to optimize resource allocation (i.e., service engineering phase) in any retail service network (Govind et al., 2008). This technique seems promising to enhance customer efficiency in terms of timely access to a particular provider of a larger service network. However, it does not provide any insights for improving productivity when multiple providers collaborate throughout a particular customer journey. Furthermore, it does not detail how to implement optimization results.

Table 5 summarizes the qualities of the identified efficiency-focused approaches. Next, identified approaches contributing to an effectiveness strategy are presented.

Table 5: Qualities of efficiency-focused approaches.

Approach (Type)	Main logic	Application requirements	Application results	Reporting and measurement	Practicability
BPMN (Tool)	Improving efficiency for focal provider and co-providers by process integration, standardiza-tion, and automation	Description of process elements; performance data; BPMN-software for simulation, execution, and monitoring	Visualization of networked process; possible efficiency evaluations based on simulation results; automated process execution and monitoring	Visual model of networked service delivery; context specific KPIs	High; de-facto standard for business process modeling
DEA-based bench-marking (Technique)	Improving efficiency for co-providers by imitative learning based on sharing of best practices and bench-marking	Performance data of co-providers; software for calculations; position as network hub and trustful relationship with co-providers	Identification of providers' relative efficiencies and resource utilization patterns; detailing of better resource utilization	Efficiency scores; personal detailing calls	Rather high; detailed description of activities and real-world application
Resource allocation modeling (Tool)	Improving efficiency for customers by optimizing resource allocations within the network	Provider, customer, and environmental data; software for calculation	Information about optimal resource allocation within a service network regarding different quantifiable factors	Optimization results	Medium; description of activities and real-world application; specific questionnaires applied unclear

4.2.2   Effectiveness-focused approaches: "Doing the right things" from a network perspective

As depicted in Figure 12, eight of the eighteen approaches identified focus on enhancing service effectiveness for one or more network actors. Next, their application-oriented qualities are presented in greater detail.

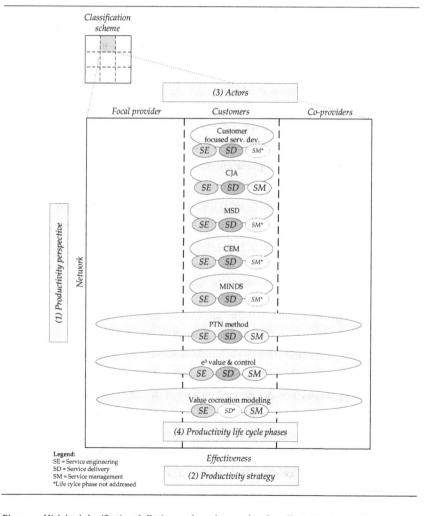

Figure 12: *High-level classification of effectiveness-focused approaches. Own illustration.*

An early strategic approach to enhance customers' effectiveness throughout the service engineering and service delivery phase is presented by Gustafsson, Ekdahl, and Edvardsson (1999). The authors explain how SAS (i.e., Scandinavian Airlines) systematically engaged in customer focused service development by analyzing customer experiences throughout the total customer journey (i.e., from check-in to baggage claim). Whereas the authors do not specifically address service delivery networks, they describe the customer journey as containing interactions with other service providers (e.g., airports, shops, hotels) that can inform service innovation opportunities for a focal provider (i.e., SAS). In order to improve the holistic customer experience, it is considered essential to deeply understand their needs, service systems, values, behaviors, and quality perceptions. For this purpose, SAS analyzed actual interactions using in-depth interviews and extensive video data collected at airports in order to identify clusters of customer behavior throughout the travel journey. These insights were used to inspire a systematic, customer-oriented service development process throughout the service engineering phase. Harnessing a set of design principles (i.e., give the passengers control, make the process transparent, and empower the staff) and service blueprinting (Shostack, 1984) the company could develop new solutions that improve customers' effectiveness throughout the total, networked customer journey. By continuously updating video recordings, it is argued that the company may engage in a continuous learning and innovation process that ensures customer orientation in the long run (Gustafsson et al., 1999).

A more recent journey-centered technique is the so-called customer journey analysis (CJA) proposed by Halvorsrud, Kvale, and Følstad (2016). The authors argue that, for the identification and elimination of performance gaps, it is critical to analyze actual service delivery and compare it to planned service delivery. CJA builds upon the customer journey framework that is based on a set of design principles and contains a coherent terminology and visual notation. CJA adopts a case study approach (Yin, 2014) to qualitatively analyze and improve customer experiences throughout the overall service productivity life cycle. All in all, CJA comprises five phases: In the first phase, the setting of service delivery is analyzed. In the second phase, the planned customer journey is depicted from the perspective of the service providers with the help of interviews, walkthroughs of customer-oriented material, as well as mystery shopping (van der Wiele, Hesselink, & van Iwaarden, 2005). Moreover, workshops with experts on system architecture and operations and representatives of co-providers are carried out involving tools like service blueprinting (Bitner, Ostrom, & Morgan, 2008) or general process analysis (Lillrank, 2009). Third, customers are recruited and data are collected. For this purpose, initially, interviews are conducted in order to gain insights with respect to customer expectations. After that, customer self-record events using a diary approach (Wheeler & Reis, 1991). Diary data are complemented with process data from back-end systems and discussed throughout a debriefing interview. In the fourth phase, the collected data is utilized to model actual customer journeys and identify deviations from the planned journey. Lastly, in the fifth phase, the goal is to identify patterns of deviation across the informants. Background information and prioritized issues are shared with decision makers together with suggestions on how to solve respective problems (Halvorsrud, Kvale, et al., 2016). The authors describe how the approach was applied in the context of a mobile and fixed-broadband service involving several co-providers. The authors do not detail how results were shared with respective co-providers. However, it is argued that CJA helped to identify operational problems informing the focal provider about critical issues and required modifications to improve service effectiveness from the customers' point of view (Halvorsrud, Kvale, et al., 2016).

Multilevel service design (MSD) focuses on improving the fulfillment of customer needs throughout the service engineering and service delivery phase. Taking a holistic system thinking perspective, MSD aims to enhance service outcomes for the customers by systematically transferring high-level, network-oriented decisions into low-level interaction design. Building on the conceptual foundations of service science, MSD develops new or improved service offerings at three hierarchical levels: the firm's service concept (addressing the value constellation experience), the firm's service system (addressing the service experience), and the service encounter (addressing the service encounter experience) (Patrício et al., 2011). At each level, activities are carried out by a multidisciplinary team and build on qualitative customer insights generated, for instance, by in-depth interviews, focus groups, observations, usability testing, or walkthroughs (Preece, Roger, & Sharp, 2002). These qualitative insights can be supplemented with quantitative methods to assess the global customer experience or specific aspects of it (Patrício et al., 2011). MSD follows the analysis-synthesis bridge model, postulating that in order to derive a preferred future it is necessary to initially investigate the current situation (Dubberly, Evenson, & Robinson, 2008). In this context, models are understood to bridge between analysis (i.e., the current problematic situation) and synthesis (the envisaged solution). The starting point of MSD studying a customer's value constellation experience and modeling a firm's service offering in the context of a customer's larger value network. Afterward, the customer's service experience is analyzed and the firm's service system is depicted using service system architecture and service system navigation models. Finally, the service encounter experience is investigated leading to insights for the design of so-called service experience blueprints (Patrício, Falcão e Cunha, & Fisk, 2009; Patrício, Fisk, & Falcão e Cunha, 2008). However, these blueprints still take a dyadic perspective, i.e., focus on interactions between the customer and one provider. Thus, the influence of interactions with co-providers on the service experience is neglected (Sampson et al., 2015).

The different levels of MSD are also applied in the context of customer experience modeling (CEM) (Teixeira et al., 2012). CEM is a multidisciplinary technique integrating MSD with human activity modeling from the field of interaction design (Constantine, 2009) to inform potential improvements of customer experiences "as a whole, through the integrated view of activities, actors, artifacts, and technological systems" (Teixeira et al., 2012, p. 372). Following a grounded theory approach (Charmaz, 2006; Corbing & Strauss, 2008), in CEM an in-depth customer study is conducted using techniques like contextual inquiry (Beyer & Holtzblatt, 1997) to elucidate customer experience requirements describing the qualities a customer desires of a particular service experience (e.g., reliability, engagement, speed). These qualities are mapped for the different activities, artifacts, technological systems, and actors involved at the value constellation (i.e., network) experience level, the service experience level, and the service encounter experience level. In case one contextual element is not connected to a specific experience requirement, there is an opportunity to improve the customer experience at the respective level by building new linkages (Teixeira et al., 2012). Thus, CEM can be used as a supportive analytical technique for analyzing service delivery and inform service engineering about potential experience improvements at the network, organizational, and interaction level.

A second approach that strongly relies on MSD is the so-called Management and Interaction Design for Service (MINDS) method (Teixeira et al., 2017). This approach aims to integrate the management perspective and interaction design perspective for interdisciplinary service design that leverages technology, fosters service innovation, and enhances service effectiveness (Teixeira et al., 2017). For this purpose, for designing the service concept (i.e., the first level of MSD), the customer value constellation model is visually extended by delineating customer activities following the human activity modeling notation (Constantine, 2009) and complemented with affinity diagrams (Beyer & Holtzblatt, 1997). These diagrams shall structure brainstorming by the design team to create new service ideas taking the value network into consideration. Next, for designing the service system (i.e., the second level of MSD), service system navigation from the management perspective is combined with storyboards from the interaction design perspective that visually illustrate the intended customer experience and technology usage. Moreover, scenarios are developed in order to provide a more compelling storytelling of storyboards (Carroll, 2000). Combining service system navigation with scenario-based storyboards shall help the design team to operationally orchestrate service delivery while gaining a visual understanding of the customer experience created by the service system (Teixeira et al., 2017). Finally, for designing particular service encounters (i.e., the third level of MSD), the service experience blueprint is combined with wireframes (Garrett, 2011) and sketches (Buxton, 2007) of the technological interfaces utilized. In doing so, frontstage and backstage activities as well as visual aspects of the technological interfaces for the respective service encounter are detailed (Teixeira et al., 2017). The authors evaluated MINDS in the context of media and healthcare and argue that it provides an improvement over existing approaches for service design as it fosters a seamless service experience across different service encounters and technologies. However, like MSD and CEM, MINDS primarily considers the role of co-providers for designing the service concept and does not consider how to model and improve the effectiveness of networked service delivery on the service encounter level.

An effectiveness-focused contribution informing the overall service productivity life cycle is described by Svensson (2002). The author presents the perceptual triadic network (PTN) method in order to quantitatively evaluate service quality in triadic service encounters. Using questionnaires adopting dimensions and items from the well-known SERVQUAL questionnaire (Parasuraman, Zeithaml, & Berry, 1988), the balance, level, and quality of triadic service quality are assessed using particular attitude measurement formulae. In case any of the resulting scores fall below a recommended level, it is interpreted as a weakness of the well-being of a specific triadic network. Moreover, service management can evaluate sub-values for each dyad making up the aggregated score for a specific triad. In doing so, weak connections can be identified and screened out by adapting respective interactions with the goal to foster long-term competitive advantages (Svensson, 2002). In this context, it is argued that the related perceptual bi-directionality method (Svensson, 2001) can be applied to gain a more in-depth understanding of particular dyads. Whereas Svensson (2002) indicates that the PTN method has been successfully applied to analyze different triadic networks both in industry and service firms, the author does not present the particular questionnaires used and thus limits reusability of the PTN method by practitioners.

Other contributions aim to drive effectiveness throughout the service productivity life cycle by gaining insights based on modeling value co-creation. For this purpose, Tan, Hofman, Gordijn, and Hulstijn (2011) combine a set of related and software supported modeling approaches. The authors present a framework based on the modeling language e³ value (Gordijn & Akkermans, 2003) to model and analyze value co-creation in a network of actors and e³ control (Gordijn & Tan, 2005; Kartseva, Gordijn, & Tan, 2005; Kartseva, Hulstijn, Gordijn, & Tan, 2010) to safeguard long-term (financial) effectiveness for the actors involved. Following this framework, initially, a value model is developed that depicts the exchange of value objects (i.e., services, products, money, or experiences) throughout the service network. Additionally, profitability sheets allow to conduct cost-benefits analyses for each actor involved (Tan et al., 2011). Whereas the value model presents the ideal situation as it assumes that all actors in a given network behave correctly and engage in reciprocal exchanges (e.g., money for service), e³ control is applied on a process level to sustainably safeguard actors interests (Tan et al., 2011). For that, weak points of the existing (ideal) model are analyzed and corrective measures are proposed such as new governance or control mechanisms. The latter changes current processes and may require new actors. Thus, e³ value is applied again in order to ensure effectiveness for all existing and new network actors (Tan et al., 2011).

Beyond the focus on financial value, value cocreation modeling (VCM) fosters the development (i.e., service engineering) and indicator-based assessment (i.e., service management) of value co-creation, particularly in the context of knowledge-intensive business services (Lessard, 2015). For that purpose, VCM initially draws on distributed intentionality, an agent-oriented, semi-formal modeling approach, in order to analyze strategic relationships among network actors for goal attainment (Yu, 2002, 2009). This understanding is enriched by harnessing value network analysis, allowing to structure value exchanges of tangible and intangible deliverables as well as to analyze their impact on affected network actors using analytical tables (Allee, 2008). Moreover, business intelligence modeling is adapted to incorporate indicators evaluating goal attainment and measuring the results of sub-processes (Horkoff et al., 2012). In doing so, VCM provides a comprehensive systematic to visualize interdependencies among network actors and assess the alignment of network actors' high-level interests, perceived benefits, value propositions, organized resources, and articulated deliverables. Moreover, it enables the assessment concerning the successful integration of service results, which is essential for actual value perception (Lessard, 2015). All in all, VCM can foster service effectiveness for network actors by depicting misalignments as well as barriers to operational integration of service results inspiring correctional activities (Lessard, 2015). Nevertheless, VCM does not portray any guidelines for practitioners how these insights can be translated into improved service offerings.

Table 6 presents a compilation of the qualities of the identified effectiveness focused approaches. Subsequently, the next subsection depicts the identified integration approaches.

Table 6: Qualities of effectiveness-focused approaches.

Approach (Type)	Main logic	Application requirements	Application results	Reporting and measurement	Practicability
Customer focused service development *(Strategic approach)*	Improving effectiveness for customers by better fulfilling their needs	Expertise in qualitative research; access and technology to observe customers	New service concepts that enhance the customer experience throughout networked service delivery	Collection of extensive qualitative data: interviews, video records, observation protocols etc.	Medium; general description of activities and real-world application
CJA *(Technique)*	Improving effectiveness for customers by mitigating deviations from planned customer journey	Expertise in qualitative research; customer participation for diary study	Understanding of deviation patterns; suggestions for improvement	Visual models of planned and actual customer journey; documentation of experiences	Rather high; detailed description of activities and real-world application
MSD *(Technique)*	Improving effectiveness for customer by enhancing value constellation, service, and, service encounter experience	Multidisciplinary design team; expertise in qualitative/ quantitative research; in-depth customer understanding	New or improved service concepts at three hierarchical levels; grounded in an understanding of the overall network	Visual models of value constellation, service system navigation, and service experience	High; detailed description of activities and different real-world applications
CEM *(Technique)*	Improving effectiveness for customers by better fulfilling customer experience requirements	See MSD	Identification of opportunities for experience improvement at different experience levels	Visual model of customer experience	Medium; general description of activities and real-world application

Table 6 (cont.): Qualities of effectiveness-focused approaches.

Approach (Type)	Main logic	Application requirements	Application results	Reporting and measurement	Practicability
MINDS (Technique)	See MSD	See MSD	See MSD; extended with insights for interaction design	See MSD; extended with affinity diagrams/ storyboards, scenarios and wireframes/ sketches	Rather high; detailed description of activities and different real-world applications
PTN-method (Tool)	Improving effectiveness for all actors of a triadic service network by eliminating defective interactions	Expertise in quantitative research; adopted SERVQUAL question-naires for different network actors; participation of actors	Identification of weak links within the triadic service network	Quantitative scores of the balance, level, and quality of triadic service quality	Rather low; general description of activities and indication of real-world applications; specific questionnaires unclear
e³ value & e³ control (Technique)	Improving effectiveness for all actors by improving network configuration and safeguarding of interests	Description of process elements; performance data; ICT and e³ value software	Visualization of value exchanges; cost-benefit analysis; proposal of new governance and control mechanisms	Diagrams; profitability sheets	Rather high; description of activities and real-world applications; supporting material and software available
Value coreation modeling (Technique)	Improving effectiveness for network actors by better aligning interests and managing resource integration	Description of actors' goals, value propositions, resources, deliverables; expertise in qualitative research	Multilevel and multi-perspective view of value creation; understand-ing relationships and misalign-ments among network actors	Visual model of resource integration; analytical tables	Rather low; general description of activities and different real-world applications; details of data collection and analysis unclear

4.2.3   Integration approaches: Considering both service efficiency and service effectiveness

Seven of the eighteen approaches identified were classified as integrating efficiency and effectiveness considerations. They are depicted in Figure 13 and their application-oriented qualities are described in the following.

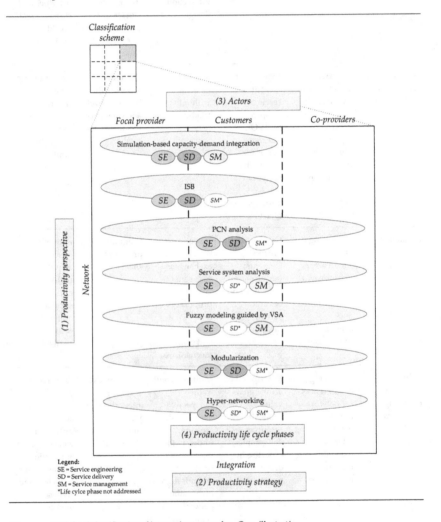

Figure 13: *High-level classification of integration approaches. Own illustration.*

Pullman and Thompson (2003) integrate efficiency and effectiveness considerations for the focal provider and the customers of location-constrained service delivery networks where capacity and demand can be shifted proactively. For this purpose, the authors present simulation-based capacity-demand integration, which can drive productivity throughout all life cycle phases. The authors demonstrate this technique in the context of a ski resort that includes multiple services such as ski lifts, shops, and restaurants. The authors propose a mathematical integrative profitability model, which is implemented by combining a simulation model with a conjoint-analysis-based optimal product design model. The former considers the impact of different capacity-demand strategies (i.e., pricing, customer class variation, information provision, capacity extension, capacity upgrades) on customer waiting times. For applying the simulation model, an extensive set of primary data (e.g., cycle times and waiting statistics, travel times between lifts, expected industry growth, feasible capacity improvements) as well as secondary data (i.e., historical data concerning snowfall and snow depth at the resort) is collected. For this purpose, observations on site, interviews with management and selected customers as well as a survey among customers are conducted. Using this data, simulations for different capacity-demand strategy combinations are run leading to insights concerning minimum peak wait times. Afterward, pre-selected attributes that affect customer service choice (e.g., other facilities on site, distance from home, type of runs on site, price etc.) are assessed using a survey. Building on these insights an aggregated model is estimated using LOGIT (Ben-Akiva & Lerman, 1991) and the customer's utility function is derived. Finally, using service prices, management's cost assumptions, attributes of competing networks, and other data derived before, expected market share and expected profit for different combinations of capacity-demand strategies are estimated. Pullman and Thompson's (2003) approach enables evidence-based forecasting, however, it is complex, demands access to a large amount of data, and does not foster the exploration of new customer demands. Moreover, it does not integrate the productivity perspective of co-providers who cannot be directly controlled by the focal provider.

Next, different flowcharting-based approaches have been identified that take a network perspective and aim to foster both efficiency and effectiveness improvements throughout the service engineering and service delivery phase. The information service blueprint (ISB) modifies traditional service blueprinting (Shostack, 1982, 1984) to reveal improvement opportunities for contemporary information intensive services (Lim & Kim, 2014). The latter represent a broad range of services where customer value is primarily created through information interactions, such as online learning, mobile map applications, or remote diagnostics of machinery (Lim & Kim, 2014). ISB is a structured representation detailing operational elements of the information-intensive service including the co-providers necessary for its delivery. Blueprinting using ISB follows three phases. In the first phase, the scope of blueprinting is defined and the rows of the visualization are customized. In the second phase, blueprinting takes place. In doing so, the customers' actions, the information exchanged, the elements of the information delivery system, and information production system as well as the relevant co-providers are identified and visualized. Additionally, different steps for accomplishing the customer's goal in the context of information-intensive service delivery are depicted building on the universal job map (Bettencourt & Ulwick, 2008). Lastly, in the third phase, the blueprint is reviewed and improvement opportunities are analyzed. Based on the insights of three case studies in the field of the automotive, IT, and healthcare industry, it is claimed that this representation can help to analyze the focal provider's efficiency of information production, delivery, and partnerships with co-providers. Moreover, reflecting on the different steps of goal-fulfillment can foster improvements of service effectiveness from the customers' point of view (Lim & Kim, 2014).

Whereas an ISB focuses on the perspective of the focal provider and the customers of networked service delivery, process-chain-network (PCN) analysis can be applied to detail and improve interactions between all network actors (Sampson, 2012; Sampson et al., 2015). PCN analysis presents a flowcharting-based technique for service engineering and service delivery that harnesses so-called PCN diagrams to identify the value proposition of a networked service, assess performance characteristics, and foster process improvements (Sampson, 2012; Sampson et al., 2015). A PCN diagram allows to systematically visualize the nature of interactions between the focal provider, customers' and co-providers. In doing so, it overcomes the limitations of a traditional service blueprint that focuses on the provider-customer dyad. Moreover, in contrast to other network-oriented flowcharting tools such as BPMN, it allows portraying co-

productive steps that simultaneously integrate various process actors (Sampson et al.,
2015). Based on this documentation, service designers can analyze process steps
concerning benefits and costs and apply different operational principles for
systematically improving efficiency and/or effectiveness of interactions (Sampson,
2012). However, so far, contributions on PCN either compare it to other flowcharting
approaches, demonstrate illustrative examples, or apply this technique for generating
ex-post theory (Kazemzadeh, Milton, & Johnson, 2015a; Kazemzadeh et al., 2015b;
Sampson, 2012; Sampson et al., 2015). Hence it remains unclear how to proactively
implement multi-actor process improvements using PCN analysis in a real business
scenario.

Service system analysis is a more recent simulation technique based on composite
modeling to evaluate the expected outcomes of interventions and reconfigurations
within a complex service system (Kieliszewski et al., 2012). For this purpose, it adopts
the dedicated IT-platform Smarter Planet Platform for Analysis and Simulation of
Health for loosely coupled modeling (Tan et al., 2012). Using the platform, a composite
model is built that integrates data from different component models (e.g., a specific
geographic model, demographic model, migration model, transportation model). In
doing so, it is possible to simulate and examine what-if scenarios with modified roles
and relationships among the customers and the different service providers. As a result,
promising scenarios can be identified that drive the efficiency and effectiveness of
value creation for the different network actors (Kieliszewski et al., 2012). Thus, service
system analysis can inform the service engineering and service management phase by
simulating and comparing the results of possible alternatives prior to actual
implementation. Whereas the general principles behind service system analysis are
demonstrated in a case scenario focusing on a public service, there still exist technical
and social challenges for actual implementation. First, the identification, integration,
and modeling of data of large and complex systems remain highly challenging tasks.
Second, it remains unclear how to foster mutual understanding and complementary
objectives of diverse stakeholders in the service system to operationally take advantage
of the simulation results (Kieliszewski et al., 2012).

Another modeling-based technique potentially applicable to enhancing both the
efficiency and effectiveness in the context of networked service delivery is proposed by

Badinelli et al. (2012). The authors describe fuzzy modeling (Badinelli, 2012; Liu & Lin, 2006; Ross, Booker, & Parkinson, 2002; Tsoukalas & Uhrig, 1997) guided by the viable systems approach (VSA) (Golinelli, 2010) to inform rational decision making based on understanding complex interactions among the heterogeneous actors involved in service delivery. Building on Beer's (1972) viable system model, VSA stresses that each service system has the ultimate goal of survival. For this purpose, it is highlighted that heterogeneous perspectives need to be directed toward a common and shared goal (Badinelli et al., 2012). Specifying a goal of a service system allows identifying necessary resources and with that respective resource integrating actors (i.e., the focal provider, customers and co-providers) for the system's effective functioning. The latter shall be supported by adopting multi-criteria decision support systems that foster actors' satisfaction through mutual win-win interactions. The perspective of VSA is operationalized by applying fuzzy modeling. For that, initially, the network of actors, resources, processes, and decisions is depicted. Subsequently, fuzzy modeling is applied to construct membership functions concerning inputs, outputs, and value of a service process. Based on that understanding, an adaptive fuzzy logic controller can be developed, allowing for continuous learning and adaptation of a system's resource offerings to better meet the needs of its customers (Badinelli et al., 2012). Whereas this technique has the potential to support service engineering and management by taking into consideration the complexity of multisided interactions, detailed guidelines for its application and empirical support for its successful operationalization are missing.

Next, several authors have proposed to use some form of service modularization in order to foster both, the efficiency and effectiveness of service delivery in a networked context (Böttcher & Klingner, 2011; De Blok, Meijboom, Luijkx, Schols, & Schroeder, 2014; Meyer et al., 2007). According to Böttcher and Klingner (2011) service modularization is related to the idea of mass customization (Pine, 1999) and is widely used in industry for enhancing productivity (Klingner et al., 2015). Adopting the ideas of modularization in industrial engineering (Baldwin & Clark, 1997; Starr, 1965) as well as software engineering (Sametinger, 1997), the goal of service modularization is to offer standardized service modules (i.e., sub-processes with a specific functionalities) that can be combined with other modules according to individual customer demands (Böttcher & Klingner, 2011). In doing so, efficiency (e.g., reduced effort for pricing and resource allocation, reuse of modules fostering economies of scale) and effectiveness (custom-tailored service for each customer) considerations can be integrated (Böttcher & Klingner, 2011) throughout the service engineering and service delivery phase. Once specific architectures, interfaces and standards are considered, it is assumed that complex portfolios of heterogeneous service modules offered by different service providers can be managed efficiently and effectively (Böttcher & Klingner, 2011; De Blok et al., 2014). Typically, service modularization is realized with IT-support. In this context, Böttcher and Klingner (2011) provide a method for a formal description of service modules particularly in the business to business domain taking into consideration their logical and temporal-interdependencies. Meyer, Jekowsky, & Crane (2007) propose to utilize a modular platform design for improving networked service delivery in the context of healthcare. The authors build on the foundations of product platforms (Meyer & DeTore, 1999; Meyer & Leonard, 1997), and synthesize ideas of medical case management to depict an integrated, IT-based case management platform for a particular healthcare delivery network. The authors could identify distinct subsystems (i.e., modules) of networked service delivery and argue that these subsystems and interfaces between them could be better orchestrated using a dedicated platform. As a consequence, continuous care involving several co-providers (e.g., primary physicians, physical therapists, surgeons, insurance companies) would be improved. It is argued that the platform-based approach would allow to establish and monitor network-wide performance measures and harness cost savings while at the same time improve customer satisfaction by providing better clinical pathways (Meyer et al., 2007). All in all, service modularity may present a powerful strategic approach to foster productivity in network settings. Nevertheless, dedicated research on this topic is scant, thus it remains unclear how to successfully implement modularity in multi-provider settings (Brax, Bax, Hsuan, & Voss, 2017).

Finally, hyper-networking is proposed as a generic strategy to drive mutual value co-creation among stakeholders of digitally connected services, while at the same time harnessing economies of scale (Chan & Hsu, 2009; Hsu, 2011). A hyper-network consists of a digital connections infrastructure (i.e., the physical internet) on top of which individual users and organizations have built countless layered and interrelated networks to fulfill their individual objectives (Chan & Hsu, 2009). Like hyperlinks connect content on the web, hyper-networks connect a multitude of customers and providers throughout their life cycles to efficiently address individual needs (Hsu, 2011). Hyper-networking (i.e., the strategic creation and utilization of such multisided linkages) is based on the digital connections scaling model (Hsu & Spohrer, 2009). The latter claims that digitization reduces both cycle times and transaction costs of connecting network entities for collaborative value creation. Moreover, scaling of these connections allows reducing the marginal and average costs for individual service delivery (Hsu & Spohrer, 2009). Thus, Hsu (2011) argues that in order to operationally foster efficiency and effectiveness in the networked delivery of digital services, firms should employ open and scalable information systems allowing to integrate, share, and reuse external actors and resources. For that purpose, they should develop or use common societal cyberinfrastructure (i.e., open source, open technologies), use common enterprise information systems, and integrate or connect these systems among the providers of the service network (Hsu, 2011). Whereas Hsu (2011) illustrates the operational success of hyper-networking in various cases (ex-post) and proposes a framework for developing respective information systems, empirical results and analysis beyond the field of e-commerce are missing.

A compilation of undergirding qualities of the effectiveness-focused approaches discussed above is presented in Table 7. Having presented the thematic overview of the identified approaches, the next chapter discusses the findings of the systematic literature review.

Table 7: Qualities of integration approaches.

Approach	Main logic	Application requirements	Application results	Reporting and measurement	Practicability
Simulation-based capacity-demand integration *(Technique)*	Improving efficiency and effectiveness for focal provider and customers due to optimized capacity-demand management	Data for integrative profitability model, operations simulation model, and conjoint analysis	Forecasted market-share and profit for different capacity-demand strategies	Simulation results; forecasted KPIS	Medium; detailed description of activities and real-world application; no implementation of results
Inf. service blueprint *(Tool)*	Improving efficiency for focal provider due to better process design; improving effectiveness for customers due to better meeting their goals	Data for the description of customers' goals and process elements of the information intensive service delivery	Identification of opportunities for enhancing information intensive service delivery	Visual model of information intensive service delivery; description of jobs to be done	Medium; detailed description of activities; indication of different real-world applications; details of data collection and analysis unclear
PCN analysis *(Technique)*	Improving efficiency and effectiveness for all actors by systematically re-configuring network interactions	Description of value proposition, interactions; performance characteristics; environmental conditions	Identification of possibilities to re-configure interactions; principle-based assessment of consequences	Visual model of process chain network; depiction of performance characteristics	Rather low; general description of activities; ex-post demonstration of real-world application
Service system analysis *(Technique)*	Improving efficiency and effectiveness for all actors due to simulation-based re-configuration of actors' roles/ relationships	Relevant data for component models; supporting IT-platform	Projections of efficiency and effectiveness consequences for network actors for different what-if scenarios	Simulation results: forecasted KPIS	Low; general description of activities; hypothetical real-world application described

Table 7 (cont.): Qualities of integration approaches.

Approach	Main logic	Application requirements	Application results	Reporting and measurement	Practicability
Fuzzy modeling guided by VSA *(Technique)*	Improving effectiveness for customers and efficiency for all actors due to continuous learning and adaptions of resources	Description of goals; setting up fuzzy controller as feedback control system	Decision making support for resource allocation throughout networked service delivery	Fuzzy models and controller	Low; general description of activities; illustrative example indicated
Modular-ization *(Strategic approach)*	Improving effectiveness for customers due to individual service; improving efficiency for providers due to reduced efforts, complexity, and reuse of modules	Clear description of modules architecture, interfaces and standards; IT support	Catalogue of standardized service modules that can be combined via defined interfaces	Service catalogues; IT-based descriptions	Low; general description of ideas and supporting approaches; implementa-tion in network setting unclear
Hyper-networking *(Strategic approach)*	Improving efficiency and effectiveness for all actors due to digitization, economies of scale, reuse of external resources	Open and scalable IT-infrastructure	Scaling and quality improve-ments in the context of digital services	Not specified	Low; general description of activities; ex-post demonstration of real-world applications

5   Discussion

 This chapter discusses the theoretical contributions and practical implications of the systematic literature review as well as the implications for the following parts of this dissertation. Limitations of the review and possibilities for future research are presented in Part VI.

5.1   Theoretical contributions

The systematic literature review answers the first research question of this dissertation: *Which systematic approaches are discussed in service research for the improvement of service productivity from a network perspective and what are their application-oriented qualities?* By answering this question, the review contributes to the theoretical understanding of improving service productivity from a network perspective. First, a high-level classification scheme for analyzing existing approaches for enhancing service productivity was developed. The scheme is theoretically anchored in recent conceptual developments in service productivity research. It is proposed that approaches for enhancing service productivity can basically be classified according to four criteria: the (1) *productivity perspective* (Ostrom et al., 2015), the (2) *productivity strategy* (Djellal & Gallouj, 2013), the (3) *actors* (Tax et al., 2013), and the (4) *service productivity life cycle phases* affected (Janeschek et al., 2013). Following Gregor's (2006) taxonomy of theory types, the classification scheme can be considered as a theory for analysis. Such theories describe what is without trying to explain causality or foster predictive generalization. Moreover, they can be applied to inform the development of prescriptive knowledge (Gregor, 2006). The scheme will be applied in Part VI to position the new approach in relation to the existing ones identified in the review.

Second, the systematic review and comparison of different approaches for driving networked service productivity provides an integrative assessment with respect to this largely unexplored field. It was demonstrated that there exist various approaches that potentially can inspire service productivity improvements from a network perspective. Being proposed by scholars from different disciplines, approaches are rooted in heterogeneous conceptual foundations and follow particular logics for improving service efficiency and/or effectiveness. Whereas all approaches could be classified using the scheme presented above, qualitatively they are very different and are applicable for particular operational purposes. In this regard, each approach identified and explained above relates to certain network-related concepts. However, reflecting on their description in the core-contributions identified, none of the approaches was built based on a coherent conceptual understanding of productivity in the context of networked service delivery. This observation is in line with previous claims stressing the importance of further conceptual work in this respect (Ostrom et al., 2015).

Moreover, it was found that efficiency-focused approaches and several effectiveness-focused approaches identified demonstrated a rather high degree of practicability. Authors provided a detailed description of activities for their execution and compelling accounts of their successful empirical application. However, applied on their own, these approaches largely neglect the interdependencies of service efficiency and effectiveness, which is found critical for successfully managing productivity in the long run (Bessant et al., 2014; Tangen, 2005). To a certain degree, this issue is considered by the integration approaches identified. However, most of them demonstrated a low degree of practicability. In fact, the five integration approaches addressing the focal provider, customers, and co-providers of networked service delivery (i.e., PCN analysis, service system analysis, fuzzy modeling guided by the CSA, modularization, and hyper-networking) lacked clear guidelines and/or empirical evaluations. Moreover, none of these approaches addresses all phases of the service productivity life cycle. Thus, for holistic productivity management, they need to be complemented with other approaches, which remains challenging due to the lack of common concepts and principles.

All in all, besides the conceptual pitfalls with respect to productivity in the context of networked service delivery, the review reveals a lack of practical approaches that follow an integration strategy and aim to enhance productivity for the focal provider, customers, and co-providers of networked service delivery throughout the overall service productivity life cycle. Given the increasing prevalence of connected service offerings depending on sustained collaboration and collective performance (e.g., Gummesson, 2007; Hillebrand et al., 2015; Verleye et al., 2017), these issues can be considered highly problematic and should be addressed in future research.

5.2   Implications for practitioners

For practitioners, the classification scheme proposed and the findings of the review may foster reflection about their own initiatives for managing service productivity. In this respect, the classification scheme may raise practitioners' awareness of the different productivity perspectives, strategies, affected actors, and life cycle phases in the context of their own productivity improvement initiatives. The identified approaches can serve as an evidence-informed and actionable knowledge base potentially relevant for different contexts of networked service delivery.

The review enables practitioners to map and compare approaches adopted by their organizations with the ones identified. In doing so, they may explore unutilized opportunities for productivity improvement throughout the service engineering, service delivery, and service management phase. Furthermore, practitioners may harness the insights presented for their own development activities. The review may inspire the (dis-)integration of different approaches established in organizational practice to better analyze and improve service productivity for the different network actors contributing resources to networked service delivery.

5.3   Implications for the remainder of this dissertation

The findings of the systematic literature review inform Parts IV, V, and VI of this dissertation as summarized in Table 8. With respect to Part IV, as highlighted above, scholars from different fields have proposed heterogeneous approaches for improving service productivity in the context of networked service delivery. However, none of these approaches was built on a coherent model of productivity in such a context substantiating the need for establishing such an understanding (Ostrom et al. 2015). This problem is addressed in Part IV of this dissertation by developing a conceptual model describing respective factors, drivers, and related resistances. Afterward, in Part V, a new technique is developed and evaluated that addresses the identified lack of practical approaches that follow an integration strategy and aim to enhance productivity for the different network actors throughout the overall service productivity life cycle. Finally, the insights generated by the systematic literature review inform the development of design principles in Part VI.

Table 8: Summary of implications for the remainder of this dissertation.

Insight	Implications for this dissertation
Identified approaches were not built on a coherent conceptual model of productivity in the context of networked service delivery	Part IV: Development of a corresponding conceptual model
There is a lack of practical approaches following an integration strategy and aiming to enhance productivity for the focal provider, customers, and co-providers throughout the overall service productivity life cycle	Part V: Development of a corresponding technique
There exist several approaches that can be applied to enhance service productivity from a network perspective; identified approaches address different productivity-related criteria and are characterized by heterogeneous application-oriented qualities	Part VI: Importance to gain complementary information and to harness synergies with established productivity improvement initiatives; in-depth understanding of contextual requirements and established initiatives as boundary conditions

Part IV

Exploratory case study:

Proposing the concept of networked service productivity

© Springer Fachmedien Wiesbaden GmbH, part of Springer Nature 2020
C. F. Daiberl, *Driving Networked Service Productivity*, Markt- und
Unternehmensentwicklung Markets and Organisations,
https://doi.org/10.1007/978-3-658-29580-6_4

1   Objectives and structure[10]

 This dissertation has the overall goal to explore *how a focal provider can drive productivity in the context of networked service delivery*. Part IV supports this goal by enhancing the conceptual understanding in this regard. In Part II it was stressed that advanced conceptual models depict service productivity from a dyadic perspective (Bartsch et al., 2011). In doing so, they reflect upon provider-customer interactions and elucidate implications for managing service productivity (e.g., Grönroos & Ojasalo, 2004; Parasuraman, 2010; Yalley & Sekhon, 2014). So far, these models neglect the role of co-providers and thus are not suited to depict the particularities of contemporary, networked service delivery. Consequently, dedicated work addressing this issue is considered a key priority for service research (Ostrom et al., 2015). The lack of coherent conceptual productivity models taking a network perspective was also revealed in Part III. None of the approaches identified was built on a model describing the content and influencing factors of productivity within service delivery networks. Thus, for this dissertation it is critical to establish conceptual clarity concerning what it means to be productive in a networked service setting.

Therefore, Part IV has the objective to empirically explore networked service productivity, i.e., service productivity in the context of networked service delivery. After having established a conceptual understanding, the second objective of this part is to explore its drivers and related resistances. So far, apart from a few exemptions (e.g., Grönroos & Ojasalo, 2004; Sekhon et al., 2016) factors for mutually driving productivity for the different actors contributing resources to networked service delivery remain largely unexplored. All in all, this part answers the following research question:

RQ2: How can networked service productivity be conceptualized and what are its drivers and related resistances?

---

[10] Part IV of this dissertation builds upon and extends conference contributions presented and discussed at the EurOMA Conference 2016 in Trondheim, Norway (Daiberl, Roth, & Möslein, 2016b) and the KSS Workshop 2016 in Karlsruhe, Germany (Daiberl, Roth, & Möslein, 2016c). An adapted version is currently prepared to be submitted to a service management-oriented journal.

The structure of Part IV is organized as follows: Subsequent to this introductory chapter, Chapter 2 presents the method and data. In doing so, first, case study research is introduced. Subsequently, the two research settings are presented and the procedure for data collection and analysis is depicted. Afterward, Chapter 3 presents the conceptual model derived followed by the drivers and related resistances identified. Next, Chapter 4 discusses the theoretical contributions and practical implications. Furthermore, it discusses the implications of the findings for this dissertation. The structure of Part IV is summarized in Figure 14.

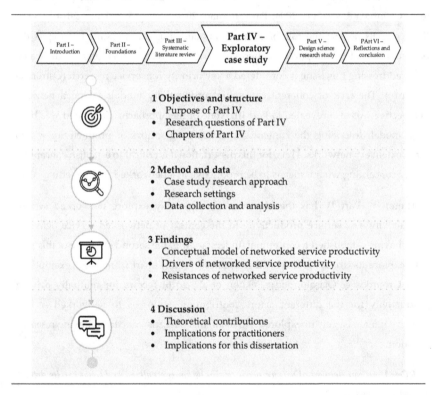

Figure 14: Structure of Part IV. Own illustration.

2   Method and data

 This chapter details the method and data of the empirical study conducted for exploring productivity in the context of networked service delivery. In the next section, case study research is introduced as the overall research approach. Afterward, the research design of the conducted case study is described in detail.

2.1   Case study research approach

To explore productivity in the context of networked service delivery, case study research was conducted. Yin (2014) defines a case study as "an empirical inquiry that investigates a contemporary phenomenon (the 'case') in depth and within a real-world context, especially when the boundaries between phenomenon and context may not be clearly evident" (p. 16). Case study research applies to different paradigms of research, copes with complex situations and a lack of control of behavioral events (Yin, 2014). It is argued that it is particularly suited when the research aims to explore phenomena in messy environments bound by temporal and spatial dimensions (Eisenhardt & Graebner, 2007; Yin, 2014).

Case study research may adopt a qualitative or quantitative orientation (Ketokivi & Choi, 2014; Yin, 2014). The former investigates concepts regarding their context-specific meanings whereas the latter examines them according to criteria like amount, frequency, or intensity (Ketokivi & Choi, 2014). Moreover, Ketokivi and Choi (2014) argue that case research strives for meeting the duality criterion of being situationally grounded as well as aiming for a sense of generality. The first criterion reflects the necessity of taking situational idiosyncrasies into consideration throughout data collection. The second criterion stresses that the researcher should strive "to transcend the empirical context and seek broader theoretical understanding through abstraction" (Ketokivi & Choi, 2014, p. 234). Thus, generality does not focus on generalization of the findings to other empirical contexts but considers the importance or interestingness with respect to the overall theoretical implications (Ketokivi & Choi, 2014).

Whereas the design of a particular case study can take various forms and follow different recommendations (e.g., Dubois & Gadde, 2002; Eisenhardt, 1989; Voss, Tsikriktsis, & Frohlich, 2002; Yin, 2014) in general, as represented in Figure 15, three modes of conducting case research can be distinguished: Theory generation (inductive research), theory testing (deductive research) and theory elaboration (abductive research) (Costa, Lucas Soares, & Pinho de Sousa, 2017; Ketokivi & Choi, 2014).

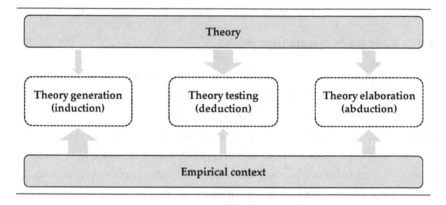

Figure 15: Three modes of conducting case research. Adapted from Costa et al. (2017) and Ketokivi and Choi (2014).

Whereas inductive case research (e.g., Eisenhardt, 1989) derives theoretical explanation from empirical exploration, deductive case research (e.g., Walker & Weber, 1984; Yin, 2014) develops hypotheses from a contextualized theory and subsequently tests them following the duality criterion specified above (Ketokivi & Choi, 2014). Finally, abductive case research (e.g., Dubois & Gadde, 2002) identifies particular theoretical foundations for approaching a particular research problem. However, the context does not yet allow for theory testing research. Thus, the goal is to iteratively elaborate respective theory in light of the empirical evidence (Ketokivi & Choi, 2014). Having introduced the case study research approach, next the research design of the conducted case study is depicted.

2.2   Research design

As highlighted in Part I, this dissertation adopts a pragmatist stance integrating an interpretive mode of inquiry. In line with this paradigm, the case study followed a qualitative orientation and explored productivity in the context of networked service delivery (i.e., the case) in two empirical settings. Therefore, it can be considered as a multiple, embedded case design (Yin, 2014). In both case settings, the focus was on the individual perceptions of network actors as the units of analysis and themes and patterns were identified using abductive reasoning (Ketokivi & Choi, 2014). In doing so, existing literature on service productivity fostered a priori theoretical understanding that was iteratively elaborated throughout the research process (Dubois & Gadde, 2002). Whereas case study research is often described as a linear process, it is acknowledged that this case study contained intertwined activities. This is in line with arguments of Dubois and Gadde (2002, p. 555): "A standardized conceptualization of the research process as consisting of a number of planned subsequent 'phases' does not reflect the potential uses and advantages of case research. Instead, we have found that the researcher, by constantly going 'back and forth' from one type of research activity to another and between empirical observation and theory, is able to expand his understanding of both theory and empirical phenomena".

Both case settings of networked service delivery were selected following a theoretical sampling strategy (Glaser & Strauss, 1967). They were chosen as they represent operationally different but particularly revelatory settings of networked service delivery. In both case settings, the author of this dissertation engaged with practitioners, customers, and fellow researchers over an extended period of time in the context of collaborative, funded research projects (Van de Ven & Johnson, 2006). Both projects were not explicitly focusing on the topic of service productivity, however, over time, the issue of better understanding the concept, potential drivers, as well as related resistances arose and was considered relevant by both scholars and practitioners involved. Hence, it was possible to gain trust-based access to a rich set of data relevant to the research objective of this dissertation. In doing so it could be compared how different factors as well as operational changes influenced productivity perceptions of the actors involved. Thus, engagement fostered nuanced understanding instrumental for the generation of constructive knowledge (Goldkuhl, 2012) in the form of explanations (Gregor, 2006). Replication of findings across both case settings should increase confidence in the emerging theoretical insights (Miles et al., 2013; Yin, 2014).

In the following both case settings are described in greater detail. In order to protect respondents' privacy, identifying information was anonymized.

2.2.1   Research setting

The first case setting of networked service delivery investigated was *eMobilizer*, a non-profit, digital service platform that aimed to enhance the public acceptance of e-mobility. Via the platform, the providers of eMobilizer collaboratively offered dedicated online courses as well as an online community to foster knowledge-transfer concerning the topic of e-mobility. The platform was operated from July 2015 until October 2017 as part of a research project funded by the German Ministry of Education and Research.

A university chair focusing on innovation research and a university chair focusing on data analytics were responsible for the overall project management and operation of eMobilizer. They can be considered as the focal providers in this case setting (i.e., focal providers A, B). For service delivery, they were supported by a set of interdisciplinary co-providers from science (i.e., co-providers A, B, C, D) and three co-providers from industry (i.e., co-providers E, F, G). Whereas industrial co-providers mainly supported public relations and the technical functioning of the service platform, scientific co-providers developed the learning content based on the latest scholarly insights. In doing so, it should be ensured that people informing themselves via eMobilizer (i.e., customers) can make an educated decision concerning the personal utilization of e-mobility. Besides learning about different aspects of e-mobility (e.g., history, technology, advantages and disadvantages, environmental impacts), customers could share any open questions concerning e-mobility, discuss their own experiences, and respond to calls for ideas initiated by the providers. Among others, the questions addressed requests for new learning content on the platform as well as ideas for and comments on new services in the context of e-mobility. In doing so, the goal was to identify knowledge gaps that should be addressed in future online courses as well as untapped potentials for improving e-mobility in the future. After analysis by the focal providers, this information was shared with co-providers to initiate the development of new learning content as well as concepts on how to improve the public acceptance of e-mobility in the future.

As mentioned above, realizing eMobilizer was a collaborative effort. The representatives of the different providers had to regularly interact with each other and coordinate activities. In this context, the author of this dissertation was as a member of focal provider A and his operational role was mainly concerned with project management, platform design and improvement, community interactions, and service development. In doing so, the author was part of the social system examined as he continuously worked together with representatives of the other stakeholders (Van de Ven, 2007). However, the main research activities for this case study (i.e., development of instruments for data collection, interviews, and data analysis) remained outside of daily operations. In this context, it is acknowledged that these activities were informed by the other participants involved similar to what Van de Ven (2007) calls collaborative basic research.

The second case setting, *OI-Lab*, is operated since May 2014 in the city center of a major German city. Via OI-Lab, a for-profit, R&D service is offered by an applied contract research organization (i.e., focal provider) supported by a university chair focusing on innovation management (i.e., co-provider A) that, among others, provided methodological expertise. Until the year 2019, OI-Lab is supported by the Bavarian State Ministry of Economic Affairs and Media, Energy, and Technology.

At the point of writing, the service of OI-Lab was carried out the following way: Organizations hired the focal provider of OI-Lab to conduct open prototyping and testing cycles for the period of three months. Throughout this time, customers received feedback on their innovation prototypes (i.e., new products or services) by potential users visiting OI-Lab and interacting with respective prototypes via purposefully designed testing booths. For this purpose, initially a formal project was initiated among the customers and the focal provider. Having discussed the customers' requirements, an appropriate research design was defined. Based on that, the physical environment was set up. This typically included components provided by the customers (e.g., prototypes of new products or services) as well as by the focal provider (e.g., furniture, means of data collection such as emotion tracking cameras, tablets for giving feedback). Once the physical surrounding for prototyping and testing was completed, the staff on site receives an in-depth briefing concerning the background of the customer, how to use the prototypes, and how to collect data from the visitors. Explicit and implicit feedback was either shared in direct interaction with the staff of the focal provider (e.g., in the form of short interviews or via observations) or indirectly via specific surrogates (e.g., sticky notes or self-service voting technology). In doing so, the visitors of OI-Lab took the role of a co-provider for service delivery (i.e., co-provider B) as they contribute to development activities of the customers. For attracting these visitors, a coffee shop (i.e., co-provider C) and a gadget shop (i.e., co-provider D) on site played an important role. At the end of a feedback cycle, users' feedback was analyzed by the focal provider and customers receive a detailed report supporting future development activities based on the insights derived.

In the context of OI-Lab, the operational role of the author was mainly concerned with active consultation of customers when planning their prototyping and testing cycles. For this purpose, the author received an unpaid access contract by the focal provider, collaborated with the staff on site, analyzed feedback generated, and presented it to the customer. However, he was not involved in actual interactions with visitors nor was he involved in any legal issues concerning contracting or payment. With respect to the research activities for this case study, like in the case of eMobilizer, it is acknowledged that the author was internally attached to the social system being studied. In doing so, he collaborated with both insiders and outsiders in order to generate in-depth insights (Van de Ven, 2007).

When comparing eMobilizer and OI-Lab, it becomes obvious that in both case settings service delivery was carried out by a network of providers and the main value proposition of the service was related to knowledge transfer. However, as presented in Table 8, they can be distinguished according to several aspects. As discussed above, OI-Lab was offered as a commercial service. For this purpose, there existed a formal service contract between the focal provider of OI-Lab and customers. As the service was strongly dependent on individual users interacting with existing prototypes, the service was realized in a physical environment. Moreover, customers could freely choose to include additional co-providers as well (e.g., external consultants), which have never been in contact with the focal provider before. eMobilizer, on the other hand, was a non-profit service targeting people interested in e-mobility. To reach as many interested people as possible, it was realized via a digital service platform. Thus, interactions mainly occurred in an online environment. Having been a part of an interdisciplinary research project, there existed a formal contract between the focal provider and the co-providers describing their individual roles and activities. Thus, individual users could not proactively influence the network of organizational co-providers. Having described the two case settings investigated in this study, next, the procedures of data collection and analysis are illustrated.

Table 9: Comparison of both case settings of networked service delivery.

eMobilizer	OI-Lab
Service type	
Education and research (non-profit)	Knowledge-intensive business service (for-profit)
Customer type	
Private users	Organizations
Focal provider	
Focal provider A: University chair for innovation research Focal provider B: University chair for data analytics	Applied contract research organization
Co-providers	
Co-provider A: University chair for sustainability management Co-provider B: University chair for learning management Co-provider C: University chair for marketing and communications Co-provider D: Applied contract research organization Co-provider E: Competence cluster for the energy industry Co-provider F, G: Industrial partners for service platform technology	Co-provider A: University chair for innovation research Co-provider B: Varying number of visitors Co-provider C: Coffee shop Co-provider D: Gadget shop Co-provider E: Varying number of third-party providers (e.g., external consultants)
Interaction environment	
Mainly online	Mainly offline
Formality among focal provider and co-providers	
Rather high	Rather low
Degree of customer freedom in selecting co-providers	
Rather low	Rather high

2.2.2   Data collection and analysis

In the context of OI-Lab, data collection started in April 2015 whereas in the context of eMobilizer, it commenced in July 2015. In both case settings, data collection continued until June 2017. Data collection resembled a systematic combining approach aiming at theory elaboration (Dubois & Gadde, 2002). In doing so, data collection represented a continuous process and overlapped with analysis. In line with this approach, interview and observational themes were adapted based on previous learnings (Dubois & Gadde, 2002). In both case settings, a variety of primary and secondary data sources were utilized. In this regard, the main impetus for multiple data sources was not to verify data but to reveal previously unknown aspects relevant to the research problem (Dubois & Gadde, 2002).

For qualitative case studies, interviews are typically seen as one of the most important sources of evidence (Eisenhardt & Graebner, 2007; Yin, 2014). For this study, both in-depth interviews (typically lasting around 60 minutes) as well as short interviews (lasting approximately ten minutes) were conducted. In this context, several short interviews were part of longer interviews focusing on another subject (i.e., only a few questions of the overall interview were related to the topic of service productivity). For interviews, a semi-structured interview guide was collaboratively developed with three other researchers (see Appendix D). It was adopted to the particular case setting and type of actor to elucidate individual actions, drivers, and related resistances affecting service productivity from the respective actor's point of view.

Interviews were conducted with experienced representatives of the different network actors. In the context of eMobilizer, interviewees included active community members who were willing to contribute to this study as well as the responsible project members of both focal and co-providers. In the context of OI-Lab, interviews were conducted with the responsible representatives of organizational customers who already finished their prototyping and testing projects. Depending on the company, this included either chief executive officers (CEOs) or responsible project managers. Concerning the focal provider, both strategic decision makers as well as operational staff on site were interviewed. For each organizational co-provider (i.e., co-provider A, C, D, E), the decision makers responsible for contributing to OI-Lab were considered.

Note that co-provider B refers to the individual visitors of OI-Lab providing feedback on the prototypes of the customer. Due to their heterogeneity, a greater number of visitors were interviewed in order to gain an in-depth understanding with respect to their productivity-related activities and perceptions.

Additionally, problem-centric group discussions (lasting between 240-480 minutes) were conducted focusing on opportunities for enhancing productivity for the different actors involved. Interviews and group discussions were conducted by a team of researchers in close coordination with the author. All interviews and parts of the group discussions were audio-recorded and subsequently transcribed. Moreover, observations on site were conducted leading to an extensive set of field notes. Besides that, available documentation such as reports, protocols of meetings involving the focal provider and co-providers as well as social media postings were collected. These documentations fostered a better understanding concerning operational changes as well as the effects of service delivery for the different actors under consideration. All in all, these different sources and types of data fostered a rich understanding of each case. A summary of the primary and secondary data collected for the exploratory case study is presented in Table 10.

For thematically organizing and analyzing the textual data generated, a template was utilized as suggested by King (2004). A template represents a list of codes, i.e., labels that are used to index text sections as relating to a particular issue or theme relevant to the research problem (King, 2004). Typically, the initial template is derived from literature, exploratory research, informal evidence, or personal experience. In the course of analysis, this initial template is revised as inadequacies reveal themselves. In doing so, new codes are inserted and/or existing ones are deleted. Other revisions may include changes to the scope or the higher-order classification of codes (King, 2004). This approach was selected due to the flexible and pragmatic use of coding, which can be adopted to the particular needs of the research. Moreover, it is argued that template analysis is particularly suitable for larger sets of qualitative data and for comparing heterogeneous perceptions of study participants (King, 2004).

Table 10: Primary and secondary data collected for the exploratory case study.

eMobilizer			OI-Lab		
Interviews					
Actors *(interviewees)*	**No.** *(type)*	**Date**	**Actors** *(interviewees)*	**No.** *(type)*	**Date**
Customers *(community members)*	7 *(in-depth)*	02/2016- 04/2016	Customers *(CEOs; project managers)*	10 *(in-depth)*	04/2015- 04/2017
Focal provider A *(Project co-lead)*	1 *(in-depth)*	10/2016	Focal provider *(deputy head; project lead; staff)*	6/4 *(in-depth /short)*	04/2015- 08/2016
Focal provider B *(project co-lead; project staff)*	2 *(in-depth)*	08/2016- 10/2016	Co-provider A *(chair, co-chair; staff)*	4 *(short)*	04/2015- 05/2015
Co-provider A *(project staff)*	1 *(in-depth)*	08/2016	Co-provider B *(visitors of OI-Lab)*	40 *(short)*	04/2015- 05/2015
Co-provider B *(project staff)*	1 *(in-depth)*	09/2016	Co-provider C *(CEO, sales manager)*	2 *(short)*	04/2015- 06/2015
Co-provider C *(project staff)*	1 *(in-depth)*	11/2016	Co-provider D *(CEO)*	1 *(short)*	07/2015
Co-provider D *(project staff)*	1 *(in-depth)*	08/2016	Co-provider E *(project manager)*	1 *(in-depth)*	04/2016
Co-provider E *(project staff)*	1 *(in-depth)*	11/2016			
Co-provider F *(project staff)*	1 *(in-depth)*	08/2016			
Group discussions					
Participants		**Date**	**Participants**		**Date**
Reps. of focal provider and co-providers A, B, C, D, G		03/17	3 reps. of customers, 4 reps of focal provider and co-provider A		02/2016
Observations, regular reports & social media					
Type		**Date**	**Type**		**Date**
Observations/documentations of tri-weekly jour fixes		07/2015- 06/2017	Daily reports		02/2016- 06/2017
Social media posts		07/2015- 06/2017	Observations/documentations of weekly jour fixes		01/2016- 06/2017
			Social media posts		04/2014- 06/2017

Due to the significant amount of data collected, for coding a computer-aided qualitative data analysis software was utilized (i.e., MAXQDA 12). The initial template was based on the theoretical foundations presented in Part II of this dissertation. In detail, it included the following higher-order codes: (1) *context for participation*, (2) *inputs*, (3) *network interactions*, (4) *outputs/outcomes*, (5) *perceived service productivity*, (6) *productivity learnings*, (7) *drivers and related resistances* of NSP for the different actors. Throughout the research process, the existing template was modified continuously based on the empirical observations and emergent need for theoretical explanations (Dubois & Gadde, 2002). Thus, it was modified "partly as a result of unanticipated empirical findings, but also of theoretical insights gained during the process" (Dubois & Gadde, 2002, p. 559). In doing so, following the hierarchical coding procedure, similar lower-order codes were clustered together to create more general higher-order codes (King, 2004). Coding was independently conducted by two researchers and repeatedly discussed with a third researcher. In doing so, justifications for revisions were presented and the definitions for the utilization of codes were generated (King, 2004). The results were compared until a satisfactory level of agreement was realized concerning the evolving template. This procedure was initially conducted for each case on its own leading to an in-depth understanding of the particular context. Afterward, patterns were investigated across both case settings of networked service delivery and the template was adopted accordingly. The highest-order codes and the two levels of lower-order codes of the resulting template are depicted in Figure 16. It is reflected in the conceptual productivity model and in the productivity drivers and related resistances detailed in the next chapter.

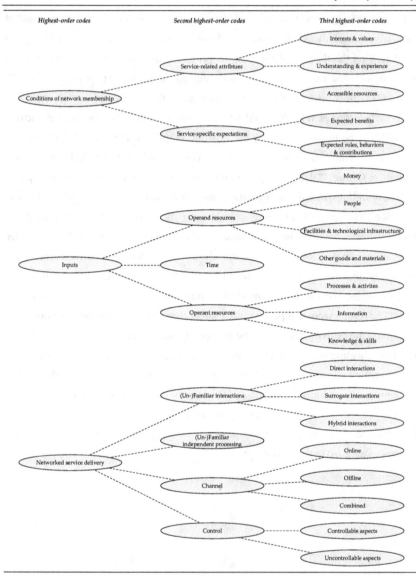

Figure 16: *Final template for data analysis. Own illustration.*

Figure 16 (cont.): *Final template for data analysis. Own illustration.*

3   Findings

 This chapter details the findings of the exploratory case study. As highlighted above, following an abductive research approach, the findings combine both empirical observations and established theoretical insights in order to elaborate theory (Dubois & Gadde, 2002). In the following section, the conceptual model of networked service productivity is introduced and its components are explained. Afterward, the identified drivers and related resistances are presented.

3.1   Conceptual model of networked service productivity

The findings suggest that productivity within a service delivery network can be conceptualized as a subjective, dynamic, and multi-level phenomenon comprising both effectiveness and efficiency dimensions. In order to explicitly distinguish it from monadic and dyadic service productivity models, in the following the phenomenon is coined networked service productivity (NSP). On the individual level, NSP can be described as an actor's satisfaction with the perceived effects of networked service delivery at a given time (i.e., effectiveness dimension) considering its resource contributions for reaching these effects (i.e., efficiency dimension). On the aggregated level, NSP comprises the collective satisfaction of two or more actors contributing resources to one or more instances of networked service delivery. Visually it is depicted in Figure 17. It focuses on a generic network actor (i.e., the customer or a particular provider of a service delivery network) and portrays patterns that could be discovered in both case settings. In the following subsections, its components are illustrated in more detail and exemplified with illustrative quotes from both case settings.

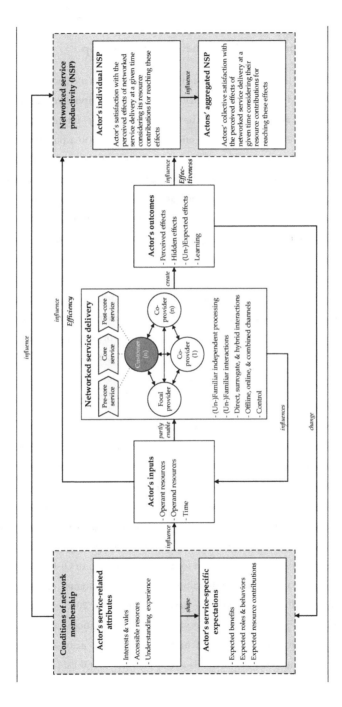

Figure 17: Conceptual model of networked service productivity. Own illustration.

3.1.1   Actor's conditions of network membership

The data suggest that for each actor, network membership is characterized by certain idiosyncratic conditions. First, each actor has particular service-related attributes. In this respect, each actor was found to have certain high-level interests and values that guide its decisions and behavior beyond the contribution to a particular instance of networked service delivery (Dobni, Ritchie, & Zerbe, 2000; Lessard, 2015). High-level interests and values affect an actor's preferences concerning service outcomes and how networked service delivery should be carried out. For participation in the service delivery network, each actor has preferential access to specific operand resources (e.g., money, OI-Lab facility, physical prototypes) as well as operant resources (e.g., technology for eMobilizer service platform, knowledge about e-mobility, skills for data collection and analysis) (Constantin & Lusch, 1994). For instance, in the context of eMobilizer, a very active community member stressed that the usage of the platform and similar service offerings is driven by his overall interest in the topic and the wish to share his personal experiences in this regard: *"[I participate] since I have great interest in electro mobility and try, wherever I can, to push the topic a bit further [i.e., service-related interest]. I think I already have a bit of experience [i.e., operant resource] and can also make a contribution. And then I thought, I am in"* (eMobilizer: Customer A).

Furthermore, at any given time, each actor has a particular service-related understanding and experience informing its general beliefs concerning the service offering under consideration. In both case settings, beliefs and experiences drew on previous communication with other network actors, potential contractual arrangements, as well as past network interactions in the context of the specific service or related offerings. It was found that these service-related attributes shape an actor's service-specific expectations. Each network actor intends to gain particular generic benefits (e.g., monetary compensation for the focal provider of OI-Lab) and/or specific benefits (e.g., learning and entertainment by the customer of eMobilizer) for participating in the service delivery network (Sampson, 2012). Moreover, service-related attributes shape an actor's service-specific expectations concerning the roles and resource contributions of itself and other network actors. For example, the respondent of a customer stressed: *"As a company I see . . . [OI-Lab] like this [i.e., service-*

related understanding], I have to assign some budget and time [i.e., expected resource contributions] and in the end, I want my revenues to increase [i.e., service-related interest]. . . . We decided to engage with . . . [OI-Lab] because we believe that we will develop and improve by doing so. How will we get better? We may have contacts to retailers, or we change something in our product, which will lead to increased sales of our product or we get more visibility [i.e., expected service-specific benefits]" (OI-Lab: CEO of customer E).

3.1.2   Actor's inputs, networked service delivery, and outcomes

Influenced by its individual conditions of network membership, each actor provides particular inputs to realize the pre-core, core, and/or post-core period of one or more customer journeys. These inputs comprise both operant and operand resources as well as temporal resources. They are utilized for independent processing (e.g., maintaining the OI-Lab or the eMobilizer website) as well as for interactions with one or more other network actors (Sampson, 2012; Tax et al., 2013). At any point in time, independent processing and interactions are either familiar or unfamiliar to the specific actor under consideration. Interactions are mediated by channels (Halvorsrud, Kvale, et al., 2016), which can be offline (e.g., the OI-Lab facility), online (e.g., the eMobilizer platform), or any combination of the two (e.g., testing an online device at the OI-Lab facility) (Halvorsrud, Kvale, et al., 2016; Neslin, Thomas, & Verhoef, 2006; Roth, Fritzsche, Jonas, Danzinger, & Möslein, 2014). Interactions are conducted directly (i.e., person to person) and/or via a surrogate (i.e., using a nonhuman resource of another actor) (Sampson, 2012). Moreover, in both case settings, interactions were identified that are a hybrid of direct and surrogate interactions. For example, when providing feedback in the context of OI-Lab, visitors (i.e. co-provider B) interacted with a surrogate (i.e., the prototype of the customer) while at the same time personally discussing their thoughts with the staff of the focal provider. These hybrid interactions were considered critical to foster effective knowledge-transfer: *"The guides [i.e., the staff of the focal provider] . . . make sure that the visitors understand everything [related to the customer's prototype]. . . . The interaction that is the core concept of . . . [OI-Lab] and I noticed that the more . . . [the guides] motivate visitors and can engage them, the more time they spend there and the more ideas are communicated, the more insights can be gained from that (OI-Lab: Project manager of customer F).*

As different actors provide inputs, no actor has full control over networked service delivery (Sampson, 2012, 2015). Thus, in both case settings, there existed extensive dependencies between the different actors leading to uncertainties concerning efficiency and effectiveness (Tax et al., 2013). For example, in the context of eMobilizer, representatives of the different co-providers repeatedly stressed that they experienced extensive delays due to dependencies on other co-providers: *"There was the infrastructure . . . which was also connected with delays because if one then said for example, 'here, we now have a usability problem', we call one of them, for example . . . [Co-provider F], who explain to you after they first checked it themselves, 'anyway that's not up to us, but. . . [co-provider G] is responsible' and so it just went back and forth"* (eMobilizer: Project staff of co-provider B).

Independent processing and interactions create outcomes that change an actor's service-related attributes for future instances of networked service delivery. From the perspective of a particular actor, outcomes include a broad range of effects for the actor itself as well as for other actors (Yalley & Sekhon, 2014). The data suggest that certain outcomes directly address an actor's expected benefits whereas others were unexpected. The latter include negative experiences such as stress due to unforeseen problems arising throughout networked service delivery. However, other unexpected effects are perceived as highly valuable as they address an actor's high-level interests (Lessard, 2015). For example, customers of OI-Lab experienced a wide range of benefits besides gaining insights regarding their prototypes. Among others, they connected to future customers, new business partners, gained inspiration concerning internal development processes, overall business logic, and corporate branding. For example, the respondent of a customer stressed: *"Without a traditional sales pitch we identified our first real customer . . . [we] would not have envisaged that . . . we roamed the country and tried to convince everyone of the advantages of this technology and then we figured out that it is enough to exhibit [the prototype] at . . . [OI-Lab] and then some people will get it and engage with us . . . like this I would not have expected it and for us it was the most pleasant side effect"* (OI-Lab: CEO of customer E). Besides these perceived effects, network interaction can lead to outcomes that remain hidden to the actor affected. For example, in the context of eMobilizer, it was found that the platform inspired a community member to initiate the development of a similar service platform in another country. As this actor initially did not inform the providers of eMobilizer about the initiative, this effect was only disclosed with a temporal delay.

Furthermore, in line with previous claims, the data suggest that, over time, productivity-related learning can take place (Grönroos & Ojasalo, 2004, 2015). Continuous interactions among actors throughout multiple instances of networked service delivery allow them to familiarize with each other and mutually improve efficiency and effectiveness of interactions based on previous experiences. For example, the interviewee of an OI-Lab customer stressed that whereas there were challenges in the beginning, interactions with the focal provider could be optimized by mutual adaptations: *"Let's put it like this, . . .we seemed to have a bit different demands than others. . . which led to stress on both sides [i.e., the customer and the focal provider]. But I believe we mutually adapted well. . . . I believe they [i.e., the interactions] are now already quite efficient, yes. . . . Now, I don't think they [i.e., the interactions] can be optimized even more"* (OI-Lab: *Project manager of customer D).*

Learning changes the conditions of network membership by affecting the service-related attributes of an actor. In doing so, it reshapes its service specific-expectations, which influences future inputs. For instance, in the context of eMobilizer, an employee of focal provider B highlighted, that the effort for building up a community was initially underestimated and triggered changes concerning the promotion of the platform and its content: *"One underestimated what kind of work it is to bring people to such a community . . . and I think that was massively underestimated by all . . . [co-providers] at the beginning . . . Especially since the real interest of the platform is to inspire and reach people who . . . are not [yet] interested in electro mobility. . . . Where it turned out that it makes sense to bring a certain offline context into the project . . . which perhaps should be emphasized a little bit more and to say, okay we also go out to events, to fairs, to congresses and try to push our content there, to activate the people, to question them, what I think was a very meaningful thing"* (eMobilizer: *Project staff of focal provider B).*

3.1.3   Networked service productivity

Based on the findings described above, on the individual level, NSP can be defined as an actor's satisfaction with the perceived effects of networked service delivery at a given time considering its resource contributions for reaching these effects. It is determined by the individuals deciding about network participation (e.g., individual customers or organizational decision makers) and comprises both effectiveness and efficiency dimensions. Whereas this satisfaction is subjective, it can be influenced by objective measurements. In both case settings, respondents highlighted that measuring quantitative service effects (e.g., number of platform users of eMobilizer, revenues per period for OI-Lab) is rather uncomplicated. For instance, in the context of eMobilizer, the project co-lead of focal provider B highlighted: *"Of course our main goal is to have this community in a size that it can achieve the related . . . project goals. Namely that it contributes to service innovation, that it contributes to the higher acceptance of electro mobility and for this we need a certain . . . quantity and quality in the community, and that can actually be measured well. So this is a relatively trivial connection, the more we have on the platform, and the more meaningful contributions are placed there . . . the more successful the project as such is"* (EM-PCL-FPB). In contrast to that, objectively measuring qualitative effects (e.g., innovation impact, knowledge creation, entertainment), was found more challenging. In this regard, several representatives of OI-Lab customers highlighted that for them, the application of financial measures would make little sense to inform their individual NSP: *"I think to try and financially measure the project at . . . [OI-Lab] is difficult. Yes, . . . [it] is expensive and the design [of the testing environment] costs a lot of money as well but if you compare what you can save because you gained insights that you didn't have before and maybe need to change directions, then it becomes priceless. It is also beneficial for the image. You are at . . . [OI-Lab], that raises awareness. . . . I think it is wrong for a company to try to measure it [financially]. . . . [It is] the positive image, this positive positioning. . . and also internally we gained so many insights that steered our work in a certain direction. I am really satisfied with the results"* (OI-Lab: Project manager of customer H).

NSP on the individual-level positively or negatively influences NSP on the aggregated level. The latter refers to two or more actors' collective satisfaction with the perceived effects of networked service delivery at a given time considering their resource contributions for reaching these effects. Taking into account the importance of collective performance for sustained operational success of networked service delivery (e.g., Gummesson, 2007; Hillebrand et al., 2015; Verleye et al., 2017) it is suggested that NSP should be considered for all actors relevant to repeatedly delivering the connected, overall service (Tax et al., 2013). Next, the drivers and related resistances of aggregated NSP identified in both case settings are depicted.

3.2   Drivers of aggregated NSP and related resistances

Following the data collection and analysis procedure described in Chapter 2, as presented in Figure 18, five interrelated drivers of aggregated NSP and twelve related resistances were identified. Just like the model of NSP, the drivers and resistances were derived by synthesizing the empirical observations with existing literature (Dubois & Gadde, 2002). Next, these factors are explicated in more detail. For this purpose, the following subsections are structured according to the five drivers identified. The identified resistances are explained in relation to these drivers.

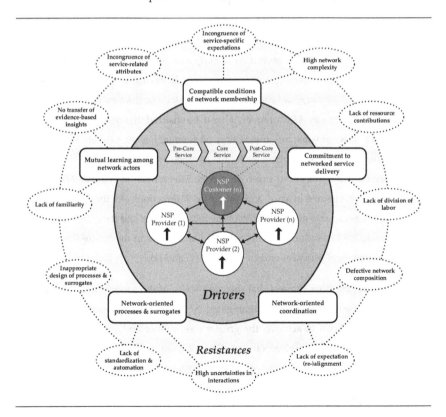

Figure 18: Identified drivers and related resistances of aggregated NSP. Own illustration.

3.2.1   Compatible conditions of network membership

In both case settings, it was found that aggregated NSP was contingent on network actors' compatibility regarding their idiosyncratic conditions of network membership. In this context, the (in-)congruence of network actors' service-related attributes (i.e., high-level interests, values, accessible resources, and understanding) plays an important role. Depending on that, mutually productive ties can or cannot be established as it is (im-)possible to set service-specific expectations concerning benefits, roles, behaviors, and resource contributions that can be commonly fulfilled (Hakanen & Jaakkola, 2012; Lehmann & Möslein, 2014). For instance, customers of OI-Lab had to be compatible with its particularities (e.g., qualitative feedback from self-selected visitors) and value expected outcomes given their particular research needs. In this context, the project manager of an OI-Lab customer highlighted: *"However, at the end of the day . . . the visitors themselves [i.e. co-provider B] do not fit to every company and . . . the results [are not suitable] either, because it doesn't help us so much if, for example, a 40-year-old lady has given feedback ten times . . .because our product is aimed at 16-17-year-old girls. And that's the point. We are faster and cheaper when we work on feedback on our own"* (OI-Lab: Project manager of customer A). Moreover, it has to be ensured that customers' prototypes and feedback mechanisms are interesting and engaging to OI-Lab visitors (i.e., ensuring effectiveness for co-provider B). In case the focal provider does not consider these dependencies throughout pre-core service interactions, it reduces NSP for the customer and/or visitors in core and post-core interactions. In the long-run, such incompatibilities can also decrease NSP for the focal provider and the coffee and gadget shop as it may lead to reduced numbers of OI-Lab visitors in the future (i.e., reduced effectiveness for focal provider and co-providers C and D).

Additionally, the data suggest that the complexity of the service delivery network influences compatibility and thus aggregated NSP. A high degree of compatibility becomes more difficult to achieve, the greater the number and variety of actors that contribute to networked service delivery (Choi & Krause, 2006; Tax et al., 2013). For instance, in the context of eMobilizer, respondents of the focal provider repeatedly stressed that it was a challenge to efficiently manage a large number of diverse co-providers: *"[The different providers have] simply completely different target constellations. That makes it always more difficult [to manage]. And the multitude of partners, the diversity of partners, small industrial enterprises, large [university] chair, small [university] chair. These are all things that play a role. . . . The coordination effort is simply always greater. And that's something that goes into the efficiency factor" (eMobilizer: Project co-lead of focal provider A).*

3.2.2   Commitment to networked service delivery

Second, the data suggest that aggregated NSP is contingent on network actors' commitment to networked service delivery. Whereas compatibility ensures that network actors' service-related attributes and service-specific expectations are congruent with each other, commitment affects the actual appointment of required resources in the context of networked service delivery (Sekhon, Yalley, Roy, & Shergill, 2016). Committed network actors are willing to provide resources as they value the potential benefits of networked service delivery and want to sustain the relationship with other network actors (Little & Dean, 2006). In both case settings, it was found that commitment influences the role-dependent and trustful division of labor. For example, the project manager of a particularly satisfied OI-Lab customer summarized a situation in the pre-core service period where different co-providers were dedicated to collaboratively setting up an appealing test environment: *"It was great. We all met at . . . [OI-Lab] one day and had a look around. The graphic designer and the printing agency that did the banners were there and took measurements and talked to [the staff]. . . .It was a really open communication that everyone was engaged in. A really brilliant creative collaboration. [OI-Lab] was really accommodating and [a staff member] said that they will ask if they . . . [can modify the environment] for us, that other . . . [customers] might benefit from [the modification] afterward as well. It was really great" (OI-Lab: Project manager of customer H).*

In case one or more relevant network actors do not commit themselves to service delivery, it can limit NSP for other actors. For example, in the context of eMobilizer, several providers aimed to modify the service-platform to attract more customers by improving its content and usability (i.e., improve effectiveness and efficiency for customers). A higher number of customers would in turn improve effectiveness for the focal providers as well as for most other co-providers. However, due to the lack of resource contributions by one co-provider, changes could not be implemented and aggregated NSP could not be enhanced. In this regard, the project co-lead of focal provider B reflected about her experiences: *"[It] has also been shown over the two years, or*

I think that is critical for success . . . that all the . . . partners [i.e., co-providers] commit themselves to their tasks, that they contribute time, that they bring in interest . . . especially if some . . . partners depend on the results or on the quality of the results of the other" (eMobilizer: Project co-lead of focal provider B).

3.2.3   Network-oriented coordination

Third, the data suggest that aggregated NSP is driven by pro-active and swift coordination among network actors in order to overcome defective network composition and prevent misaligned expectations. In this context, it was found that certain human and/or technological entities must have an appropriate understanding of customers' and potential co-providers' conditions of network membership. Based on that, these entities need to be able to determine which actors should provide resources to realize the different periods of the overall customer journey (Sampson et al., 2015) and (re-)align actors' expectations accordingly (Hakanen & Jaakkola, 2012). For this purpose, suitable operational and relational coordination mechanisms have to be in place. In both case settings, this included a particular combination of coordination institutions (e.g., contractual arrangements, regular meetings, managerial roles, constant contact persons) and governance mechanisms (e.g., activities for strengthening interpersonal relations). Moreover, supportive ICT (e.g., web-based collaboration software) was employed (Breidbach, Reefke, & Wood, 2015). For instance, the respondent of a co-provider of eMobilizer highlighted: *"At the beginning we only had a jour fixe, which included . . . [focal provider A, co-providers A, B]. In my opinion, the cooperation has become much more efficient . . . and effective since the introduction of a triweekly jour fixe, which included [all partners via ICT]" (eMobilizer: Project staff of co-provider A).* In this context, it was further stressed that the right frequency of meetings had to be found: *"You always have a bit of a trade-off in between, we now have a two-hour meeting every week, where we talk a lot and then there's not much . . . content, and we don't coordinate at all and everyone somehow marches to his own drummer. So you just have to strike the right balance, which is difficult with so many partners" (eMobilizer: Project staff of focal provider B).*

Building on these coordination mechanisms, resource allocation within a service delivery network can be improved, positively influencing NSP on the aggregated level.

For example, in the context of eMobilizer, respondents of the focal provider and co-providers repeatedly attributed gains in NSP to the establishment of personal contacts and trustful relationships among each other. This fostered a better understanding of each other's conditions of network membership, high-quality communication, and ultimately led to better outcomes and more efficient network interactions. Similarly, in the context of OI-Lab, the respondent of co-provider E stressed that a diverse set of coordination mechanisms is required for efficient and effective interactions: "*As soon as one has a contact person [i.e., coordination institution] for whichever group [i.e., network actor], as soon as everyone is aware of the processes and . . . even if the processes are not clear, dares and says . . . [that one] didn't understand it [result of relationship management], then something like this works*" (OI-Lab: Project manager of co-provider E).

3.2.4   Network-oriented processes and surrogates

Next, in line with previous claims, it was found that in both case settings of networked service delivery direct interactions were substituted with surrogate interactions to enhance their efficiency (Sampson, 2012; Sampson et al., 2015). Processes relying on direct interactions among network actors are typically characterized by high uncertainties due to a variation in humans' attitudes and behaviors (Chase, 1981). Surrogate interactions (e.g., via self-service technology) on the other hand can reduce uncertainties and related inefficiencies (Sampson, 2012). In doing so, surrogates can overcome a lack of standardization (Carlborg, Kindström, & Kowalkowski, 2013) and automation (Field et al., 2018) of network interactions. Thus, as long as it does not reduce effectiveness for relevant network actors, surrogate interactions can drive aggregated NSP. In this context, the data indicates that actors' expectations how respective processes and surrogates should be designed were shaped by their service-related attributes, i.e., their interests, values, resources, understanding, and experience. For instance, whereas representatives of most customers of OI-Lab were satisfied with the efficiency of interactions, the CEO of a customer from the IT-industry highlighted that, from his point of view, efficiency could be enhanced by integrating the different interaction tools into a coherent solution: "*I am probably more digitally progressive than many others. . . . There is phone, there is mail, . . . I have the documents shared, I think there can be more effective [meaning efficient] ways . . . just one piece where everything comes together for the service engagement with [OI-Lab]. . . . I need to think about where to put the document you were sending me, the report, and that is an extra effort I am putting in and when you provide a tool, where the whole structure and interaction is already built in, nobody has to create a folder" (OI-Lab: CEO of co-provider E).*

In case processes and surrogates are designed inappropriately, i.e., not in line with actors' conditions of network membership, aggregated NSP can reduce even in the context of surrogate interactions. For example, in the context of eMobilizer, for collaboratively creating online courses, the platform contained a content management system provided by co-provider E. However, other co-providers lacked the procedural as well as technological understanding and experience for effectively using the content management system having a negative influence on aggregated NSP. In this regard, a representative of co-provider E highlighted: *"You have to know in advance how this works and what you're doing. . . . [Using the content management system] I have to think about how I structure the content and which media I use beforehand, I have to file them all neatly, tag them, describe them so that I can find them again and use them again, otherwise I'm doing double and triple work. . . . Content was sometimes cobbled together [by the co-providers] . . . a lot of text, just a picture, no multimedia . . . So that in the end we have fundamentally reworked [the courses] . . . and the structure of the contents anyway. Which was an additional effort . . . that wasn't originally planned"* (eMobilizer: Project staff of co-provider E).

3.2.5 Mutual learning among network actors

Lastly, the data suggest that high levels of aggregated NSP are contingent on continuous and mutual learning among the different network actors involved. Extending the understanding of service productivity as a dyadic learning process (Grönroos & Ojasalo, 2004, 2015), the data suggest that with continuous duration of relationships, the focal provider, customers, and co-provider familiarize with each other on a personal and operational level and correspondingly adjust their service-related attributes. For example, concerning the former, the respondent of eMobilizer's co-provider E highlighted that aggregated NSP improved due to a better understanding concerning the preferences and competencies of individual representatives of the co-providers. This was considered particularly beneficial in situations when responsibilities were somewhat unclear: *"You just got to know each other better. . . . Of course, everyone has his duties . . ., but also . . . tasks that are not necessarily defined. . . . And of course at some point you get to know that, okay this person is particularly interested in these tasks or topics and [one] can then . . . involve the person more strongly in such things"* (eMobilizer: Project staff of co-provider E).

To foster mutual learning, in both case settings the data suggest that it is critical to gain evidence concerning outcomes of networked service delivery for the different network actors, reflect upon them, and share relevant insights with affected network actors. In this context, the representative of an OI-Lab customer highlighted: *"Of course . . . it is about how I can optimize the results with my given presence and time. From . . . [OI-Lab's] side documentation of best practice would be beneficial whether this is contents wise, links to other company projects, or tools that have been successful in other projects. The beauty is that you [i.e. the focal provider of OI-Lab] can create a knowledge base as time goes on. . . . If you then . . . make these things available and I can see oh great this company did something similar, I will get in touch with them directly, then I just received added value"* (OI-Lab: CEO of co-provider E). In order to share related evidence and foster mutual learning among network actors, in both case settings, operational and relational coordination mechanisms described above were utilized (e.g., daily mailings reporting about service inputs and outcomes, weekly jour fixes). In this respect, sharing evidence may also shed light on previously hidden effects. For example, in the context of OI-Lab, each testing cycle is typically followed by extensive media coverage. Respective information (e.g., outlet and reach) is continuously collected and analyzed by the focal provider and shared with the customers of OI-Lab. Customers are often keen on gaining publicity for their prototypes. Thus, they typically value this effect.

Having presented the identified drivers and related resistances for aggregated NSP, the next chapter discusses the findings of the exploratory case study.

4 Discussion

 This chapter discusses how the findings of the exploratory case study contribute to theory and inform organizational practitioners. Moreover, implications for the following parts of this dissertation are derived. Limitations of the study as well as possibilities for future research are presented in Part VI.

4.1 Theoretical contributions

The exploratory case study presented in this part answers the second research question of this dissertation: *how can networked service productivity be conceptualized and what are its drivers and related resistances?* In doing so, the study contributes to the largely unexplored topic of service productivity in the context of networked service delivery (Ostrom et al., 2015). Building on Gregor's (2006) taxonomy of theory types, both the model of NSP as well as the identified drivers can be considered theories for explaining. Such theories present what is and explain questions like how or why phenomena occur but do not aim to predict with any precision (Gregor, 2006).

The model of NSP contributes to the contemporary understanding of service productivity by taking into account the networked nature of many contemporary services (e.g., Alexander et al., 2016; Field et al., 2018; Tax et al., 2013) and overcoming a manufacturing-based understanding of service productivity (e.g., Aspara, Klein, Luo, & Tikkanen, 2017; Rust & Huang, 2012). According to the model, NSP can be subjectively considered for the different actors of a service delivery network. It is argued that NSP perceptions originate in an actor's conditions of network membership comprising its service-related attributes and service-specific expectations. These conditions, in turn, are dynamically changed by service outcomes such as perceived effects and operational learnings (Grönroos & Ojasalo, 2004, 2015). So far, the dynamic relationships of service-related attributes, service-specific expectations, and individual perceptions of different network actors have been neglected in contemporary service productivity models (cf. Grönroos & Ojasalo, 2004; Yalley & Sekhon, 2014).

The model of NSP implies that the idea of measuring service productivity merely as an objective ratio of total outputs to total inputs should be reconsidered. It overcomes a sole focus on financial indicators as "the only theoretically correct and practically relevant approach to measuring service productivity" (Grönroos & Ojasalo, 2004, p. 421). Similar to the claims of Yalley and Sekhon (2014), NSP addresses actors' satisfaction with effectiveness and efficiency as a more relevant consideration point. Depending on the particular context, this satisfaction may very well be influenced by objective measures (e.g., amount of revenue generated, amount of feedback received, amount of customers served). However, it is also dependent on subjective aspects such as personal believes about the perceived (un-)expected effects or feelings about the efficiency of network interactions. Additionally, the model sheds light on the role of hidden effects for the different network actors contributing resources to one or more instances of networked service delivery. So far, hidden effects have not received scholarly attention in the context of productivity management. However, the findings reveal that they may be used as a source for enhancing NSP when they are brought to light and shared with the network actor affected.

Distinguishing between individual and aggregated NSP, the model presents a new theoretical consideration point when striving to enhance productivity in the context of networked service delivery. As highlighted above, improving individual NSP for one network actor may negatively influence individual NSP for one or more other actors. Considering the dependencies of actors in the context of networked service delivery this is a vital issue for sustained network performance (Scerri & Agarwal, 2018; Tax et al., 2013; Verleye et al., 2017). Thus, instead of aiming to optimize NSP for one actor, it is proposed that NSP should be considered thoroughly for all relevant network actors when planning productivity-related interventions. In this regard, it should be noted that relevant actors may only comprise a subset of all actors actually contributing resources to a particular service delivery network. As highlighted above, for each customer, the service delivery network is potentially unique (Tax et al., 2013). Thus, from an operational point of view, considering NSP for all actors seems unfeasible. Rather, the goal should be to consider NSP for those actors that are relevant for repeatedly realizing networked service delivery for the anticipated customers of an overall, connected service.

All in all, reflecting on the empirically-based conceptualization and building on the conceptualization of Misterek, Dooley, and Anderson (1992), theoretically, there exist five relationships that can explain intervention-based enhancements of aggregated NSP. These relationships are depicted in Table 11. First, in the (1) *ideal scenario*, a productivity-related intervention may improve the collective satisfaction of relevant network actors with both effectiveness and efficiency of networked service delivery. This relationship may be realized by harnessing mutually accepted technological surrogates, which enhance resource utilization while at the same time better fulfill actors' expected benefits. Second, an intervention may lead to an improvement of network actors' collective satisfaction with effectiveness while efficiency remains unchanged. This may be the result of (2) *working smarter* throughout networked service delivery, for instance by uncovering previously hidden effects that are considered beneficial by one or more network actors. Third, an intervention can contribute to (3) *managed growth*, i.e., by improving actors' collective satisfaction with effectiveness overcompensating reduced satisfaction with efficiency. An example would be the replacement of surrogate interactions with direct interactions in case the latter better meet customers' demands. In doing so, the intervention may positively influence customers' willingness to re-engage with respective providers in the future.

Table 11: Theoretical relationships for improving aggregated NSP.

Theoretical relationship	Description
The ideal	Improvement of network actors' collective satisfaction with both effectiveness and efficiency
Working smarter	Improvement of network actors' collective satisfaction with effectiveness while efficiency remains unchanged
Managed growth	Improvement of network actors' collective satisfaction with effectiveness overcompensating reduced satisfaction with efficiency
Greater efficiency	Improvement of network actors' collective satisfaction with efficiency while effectiveness remains unchanged
No frills	Improvement of network actors' collective satisfaction with efficiency overcompensating reduced satisfaction with effectiveness

Next, (4) *greater efficiency* refers to improving the collective satisfaction with resource utilization while effectiveness remains unchanged, for instance by automating repetitive interactions throughout networked service delivery. Finally, a (5) *no frills* approach refers to improving actors' collective satisfaction with efficiency overcompensating reduced satisfaction with effectiveness, for example by collaboratively providing a new, low cost, connected service offering targeting price-sensitive customers.

Furthermore, the study contributes to theory by identifying five interrelated drivers and twelve related resistances of aggregated NSP. It is proposed that managing these drivers and, in doing so, mitigating related resistances can positively affect NSP for the focal provider, customers, as well as relevant co-providers. In this regard, it was found that respective actors need to have compatible conditions of network membership and commit to their expected role in the particular service delivery network. The importance of resource commitment is in line with the results of Sekhon et al. (2016) who found that resource commitment influences employee and customer readiness, which in turn has a positive influence on service productivity. Moreover, the findings substantiate that network coordination can be structured along the pre-core, core, and post core-service periods of the overall journey, providing a more fine-grained understanding for related research endeavors (e.g., Sampson et al., 2015). Lastly, the study provides empirical evidence for the role of network-oriented interaction surrogates (Sampson, 2012) as well as mutual learning (Grönroos & Ojasalo, 2004, 2015) among network actors for enhancing aggregated NSP.

4.2 Implications for practitioners

For practitioners, the model of NSP may provide a new lens for a more holistic productivity management. It reveals the importance of understanding and balancing subjective productivity perceptions of all relevant network actors for sustained operational success. Actors are only expected to continuously contribute resources to networked service delivery if effects are subjectively perceived beneficial and adequate taking into account their individual resource contributions. Hence, successfully managing service productivity requires considering the perceptions of all relevant network members (Gummesson, 2008; Quero & Ventrua, 2015; Scerri & Agarwal, 2018; Verleye et al., 2017). Thus, decisions concerning the improvement of individual-level

NSP should be rooted in an understanding concerning their effects for NSP on an aggregated level.

To identify the relevant network actors whose perceptions should be considered, first, a focal provider has to gain an in-depth understanding of the customer journey of the anticipated customers (Tax et al., 2013). Building on this understanding, a focal provider can reflect upon the appropriate co-providers to include and establish corresponding relationships. Afterward, the focal provider can strive to foster the improvement of aggregated NSP by mutually identifying and seizing productivity improvement opportunities. The managerial questions depicted in Table 12 may support this process. They are rooted in the drivers and related resistances of aggregated NSP presented in Chapter 3.2. Moreover, potential indicators that may support the focal provider to answer respective questions are illustrated.

Table 12: Managerial questions and indicators supporting the improvement of aggregated NSP.

Driver	Managerial questions	Indicators
Compatible conditions of network membership	- Are actors compatible regarding interests and values? - Do actors have a compatible service-related understanding and expectations? - Can we effectively and efficiently fulfill actors' expectations given the resources accessible via the service delivery network? - Do we need to involve additional actors or dismiss existing ones?	- Degree of congruence with customers' and co-providers' service-related attributes and service-specific expectations - Number of heterogeneous actors involved in service delivery network - Frequency of disputes with customers and/or co-providers about service-related interests and values - Frequency of disputes with customers and/or co-providers concerning service-specific expectations
Commitment to networked service delivery	- Are actors willing to contribute required resources to networked service delivery? - Do actors value the expected outcomes and are they interested in long-term relationships? - Is there a reliable division of labor with co-providers?	- Willingness of co-providers to respond to new demands of network members - Willingness of co-providers to participate in coordinative meetings - Frequency of complaints by customers and/or co-providers about lacking commitment of network members - Frequency of operational disputes with customers and co-providers

Table 12 (cont.): Managerial questions and indicators supporting the improvement of aggregated NSP.

Driver	Managerial questions	Indicators
Network-oriented coordination	- Are the right actors involved in pre-core, core, and post-core service interactions of the overall customer journey? - Do we regularly ensure that actors have aligned expectations concerning roles, behaviors, and resource contributions throughout the customer journey? - Do we harness the appropriate coordination institutions and governance mechanisms? - Do we have information and communication systems in place for effectively and efficiently sharing information across organizational boundaries?	- Availability of information concerning interests, values, expected roles, behaviors and resource contributions of customers and co-providers - Appropriateness of established coordination institutions (e.g., contracts, meetings, roles) - Appropriateness of established governance mechanisms (e.g., interpersonal activities) - Degree of automated coordination
Network-oriented processes and surrogates	- Are there any interactions repeatedly failing in daily operations? - Do we harness potentials of surrogate interactions? - Are interactions surrogates built on an in-depth understanding of actors' conditions of network membership	- Prevalence of uncertain interactions - Degree and appropriateness of standardized interactions - Degree and appropriateness of digitized/surrogate interactions - Ease of use of surrogates
Mutual learning among network actors	- Do we apply means and measures to gain evidence with respect to multisided outcomes of networked service delivery? - Do we share productivity-related insights with affected actors? - Do we continuously trial improvements and evaluate results?	- Availability of means and measures to gain evidence concerning multi-sided outcomes - Degree of familiarity among network actors - Regularity of sharing evidence-based insights among network actors - Frequency of productivity-improvement interventions

4.3   Implications for the remainder of this dissertation

All in all, as depicted in Table 13, the findings of the exploratory case study have the following implications for the remainder of this dissertation. The conceptual model of NSP informs the DSR study presented in Part V and the design principles developed in Part VI. Building on the arguments presented above, an objective of the technique developed is to mutually improve NSP for all actors required to realizing networked service delivery for the anticipated customers. For this purpose, the different network actors should be integrated into the systematic identification and analysis of opportunities to enhance aggregated NSP throughout the overall customer journey. In doing so it shall be ensured that their idiosyncratic conditions of network membership and heterogeneous perceptions are adequately considered. Moreover, as for each actor NSP is conceptualized as a dynamic phenomenon affected by a set of drivers, NSP should be improved iteratively. Concerning the design principles developed in Part VI, these objectives were transferred into considerations and boundary conditions to inform the creation of other artifacts supporting a focal provider to improve aggregated NSP. In Part VI, these principles are explicated in detail.

Table 13: Summary of implications for the remainder of this dissertation.

Insight	Implications for this dissertation
Aggregated NSP as a critical consideration point for productivity-related interventions	Part V: Objective to improve aggregated NSP for all relevant network actors of a connected, overall service Part VI: Importance to consider the effects of interventions on aggregated NSP; ability to recognize interrelations as boundary condition
Aggregated NSP as a phenomenon influenced by actors' idiosyncratic conditions of network membership, actors' inputs, and interactions throughout the pre-core, core, and post-core service periods of one or more customer journeys	Part V: Objective to integrate relevant network actors into the identification and analysis of NSP improvement opportunities throughout the overall customer journey Part VI: Importance to integrate network actors into the process of improving aggregated NSP and to consider the overall customer journey from the customers' and an operational point of view; access to appropriate qualitative and quantitative data as boundary condition
Aggregated NSP as a phenomenon dynamically changed by actors' past learning; affected by five interrelated drivers whose management may mitigate related resistances over time	Part V: Objective to foster an iterative improvement process of aggregated NSP Part VI: Importance to include activities and means to support iterative learning and improvements; actors' willingness to share related insights as boundary condition

Part V

Design science research study:

Proposing a technique for driving networked service

productivity

© Springer Fachmedien Wiesbaden GmbH, part of Springer Nature 2020
C. F. Daiberl, *Driving Networked Service Productivity*, Markt- und
Unternehmensentwicklung Markets and Organisations,
https://doi.org/10.1007/978-3-658-29580-6_5

1 Objectives and structure[11]

 This dissertation has the overall goal to explore *how a focal provider can drive productivity in the context of networked service delivery.* Part V supports this goal by designing and evaluating a corresponding technique. The research problem and the design objectives are derived from the findings of the systematic literature review presented in Part III and the exploratory case study presented in Part IV. The systematic literature review found that there is a lack of practical approaches that are in line with an integration strategy and aim to improve productivity for the different actors of a service delivery network. Afterward, the exploratory case study introduced the concept of NSP that serves as this study's theoretical foundation for productivity in the context of networked service delivery. It was established that NSP represents a subjective, dynamic, and multi-level phenomenon. On the individual level, NSP addresses an actor's satisfaction with the perceived effects of networked service delivery at a given time considering its resource contributions for reaching these effects. These perceptions influence NSP on the aggregated level, i.e., the collective perceptions of two or more actors of a particular service delivery network. In order to foster sustained operational success, it was argued that NSP should be considered for all network actors relevant to carry out networked service delivery for the anticipated customers. Building on these insights, Part V addresses the following research question:

RQ3: How can a focal provider systematically and iteratively discover and seize opportunities to enhance networked service productivity for itself, customers, and relevant co-providers?

For answering this research question, an organized set of design artifacts is iteratively developed and evaluated. The set of artifacts is called NSPIRET – an acronym for **n**etworked **s**ervice **p**roductivity **i**mp**r**ov**e**ment **t**echnique. The remainder of Part V is organized as follows: Chapter 2 depicts the theoretical background for the

---

[11] Part V of this dissertation builds upon and extends a conference contribution presented and discussed at the R&D Management Conference 2018 in Milan, Italy (Daiberl, Naik, & Roth, 2018). An adapted version is currently prepared to be submitted to a service management-oriented journal.

design of NSPIRET. For this purpose, approaches for modeling networked service delivery from the customers' and an operational point of view are introduced. Moreover, research on the usage of FMEA, i.e., the failure modes and effects analysis, as a systematic for enhancing service productivity is summarized. Next, Chapter 3 introduces the DSR approach and the process applied in this study. Subsequently, Chapter 4 presents the design and evaluation of the alpha and beta version of the designed technique. Finally, Chapter 5 discusses this study's contributions and implications.

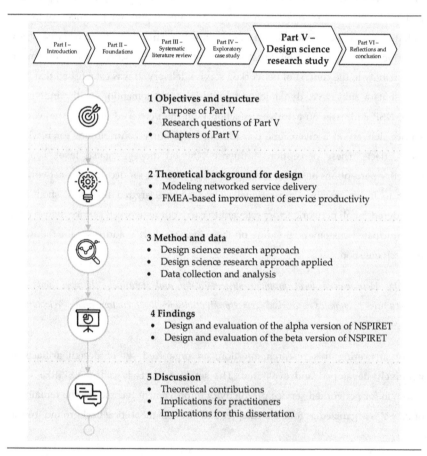

Figure 19: Structure of Part V. Own illustration.

2   Theoretical background for design

 This chapter reviews relevant literature for designing NSPIRET, a technique that aims to drive aggregated NSP for the different actors of a service delivery network. The necessary theoretical foundations are derived following the analysis-synthesis bridge model (Dubberly et al., 2008). According to this model, design processes should start with a model-based investigation of the current, problematic situation (i.e., analysis) before deriving a preferred future or solution (i.e., synthesis). In this context, models bridge the gap between analysis and synthesis (Dubberly et al., 2008). Against this backdrop, in the next section, approaches for modeling networked service delivery are introduced. Afterward, an FMEA-based technique for the model-based identification and evaluation of opportunities for driving service productivity is presented.

2.1   Modeling networked service delivery

In order to foster a holistic understanding of the current situation of networked service delivery, it is proposed to model it from both the customers' and from an operational point of view. The following subsections briefly introduce several approaches that can be applied for this purpose and demarcate the ones which are adopted for designing NSPIRET.

2.1.1   Modeling networked service delivery from the customers' point of view

For depicting service delivery from the customers' point of view, so-called customer journey models are often utilized to visually communicate related insights and foster empathy (Segelström, 2013; Stickdorn & Schneider, 2011). As highlighted in Part II, scholars argue that the customer journey represents a series of interactions between the customer and one or more service providers, which may span across an extended period of time (Tax et al., 2013; Voorhees et al., 2017; Zomerdijk & Voss, 2010). Customer journey models aim to depict these interactions placing the customer at the heart of the illustration (Halvorsrud, Kvale, et al., 2016; Zomerdijk & Voss, 2010). Over the past decades, a diverse set of customer journey models has been developed that often provide rich and creative illustrations (Følstad, Kvale, & Halvorsrud, 2013; Stickdorn & Schneider, 2011; Trischler & Zehrer, 2012). Nevertheless, most authors do not depict the elements of the customer journey on any formal grounds (Halvorsrud, Kvale, et al., 2016; Segelström, 2013).

In order to foster a more systematic approach, recently the customer journey modeling language (CJML) has been proposed (Halvorsrud, Haugstveit, & Pultier, 2016; Halvorsrud, Lee, Haugstveit, & Følstad, 2014). CJML is part of the customer journey analysis introduced in Part III (Halvorsrud, Kvale, et al., 2016). Being rooted in service design, it is customer-centric and reflects upon the role of co-providers. Thus, it can be applied to depict the customer journey in the context of networked service delivery. In CJML, touchpoints form the basic unit of analysis. They refer to discrete interactions between the customer and the different co-providers (Halvorsrud et al., 2014). In CJML, each touchpoint is presented as a circle and is labelled with an identifier (T_0, T_1, etc.) representing the temporal sequence. Each touchpoint has a certain initiator (i.e., the customer, a focal service provider, or a co-provider) depicted by the boundary color of a touchpoint circle. Within the area inside of each touchpoint circle the particular channel mediating the touchpoint is visualized. Channels are represented by the consistent use of suited symbols in order to foster an immediate association with the type of touchpoint represented (Halvorsrud, Haugstveit, et al., 2016).

CJML has been empirically evaluated and was found to be applicable to a wide range of service domains (Halvorsrud, Haugstveit, et al., 2016; Halvorsrud, Kvale, et al., 2016; Halvorsrud et al., 2014). All in all, CJML can provide a formal, high-level visual overview of the customer journey under consideration. As part of NSPIRET, it is adopted for modeling networked service delivery from the customers' point of view. However, CJML does not detail networked service delivery from an operational perspective as it lacks the description of resources required for realizing respective touchpoints. Next, modeling approaches relevant for this purpose are introduced.

2.1.2   Modeling networked service delivery from an operational point of view

There exist different approaches that can be applied to model operational processes such as the unified modeling language or the business process modeling notation (Recker et al., 2009). Whereas the former is primarily utilized for object-oriented modeling in the context of software development, the latter, as presented in Part III, is commonly used for business process documentation and improvement (Recker et al., 2009; Sampson, 2012). However, both approaches are highly formalized, complex, and rather unsuited for depicting largely unstructured processes common to service delivery (Alter & Recker, 2017; Recker et al., 2009).

In the field of services, a well-known tool for depicting service processes from an operational point of view is service blueprinting (Bitner et al., 2008; Fließ & Kleinaltenkamp, 2004). Service blueprinting differentiates between service process steps that are visible to the customer and the ones that are hidden from the customer (Milton & Johnson, 2012). Whereas traditional service blueprints focus on dyadic interactions between the customer and one provider, more recent adaptations, such as the information service blueprint presented in Part III, reflect upon the role of co-providers as well (Lim & Kim, 2014). However, in this context, the representation of co-providers remains on an abstract level and does not detail activities conducted by them. Another approach introduced in Part III and specifically tailored to networked service delivery is a PCN-diagram. These diagrams model networked service delivery as a series of direct and surrogate interactions between network entities to solve a certain need for the customer (Sampson, 2012; Sampson, Schmidt, Gardner, & Van Orden, 2015). It is particularly designed to model co-productive steps that simultaneously include various process entities (Sampson et al., 2015). However, this tool mainly focuses on the nature of interactions and lacks the representation of resources that are required for systematic productivity analysis and synthesis.

A relatively informal, textual approach applicable for modeling the operational perspective on networked service delivery is Alter's (2006) work system snapshot (WSS). WSS is a business-oriented system description that builds upon ideas of work system theory (Alter, 2013b). Being rooted in information systems research, work system theory is an integrated body of knowledge that has been developed to guide the analysis and design of sociotechnical systems within and across organizations (Alter, 2006, 2010b, 2013b, 2018; Truex, Alter, & Long, 2010). In work system theory, the central unit of analysis is the work system defined as "a system in which human participants and/or machines perform work (processes and activities) using information, technology, and other resources to produce specific products/services for specific internal and/or external customers" (Alter, 2013, p. 75). In this context, a work system that is exclusively applied to service delivery can be defined as a service system (Alter, 2012).[12] Work system theory acknowledges the role of both operand and operant resources but does not emphasize that distinction as, depending on the particular context, certain system elements can represent a resource of both types (Alter, 2013a). For instance, as indicated in the work system metamodel (Alter & Recker, 2017), participants (i.e., entities performing work) possess knowledge and skills (operant resources). However, the same participants may also serve as an operand resource such as a patient who receives treatment after he or she has specified the conditions (Alter, 2013a; Sampson, 2012). Thus, the explicit differentiation between both types of resources may unnecessarily complicate modeling.

In the context of services, WSS represents a one-page, text-based summary of six system elements: it highlights the (1) *customers*, labels the (2) *services* generated and summarizes the (3) *major processes and activities* that are carried for service delivery. Moreover, it details the (4) *participants*, (5) *technology*, and (6) *information* that are required for executing these processes and activities (Alter, 2010b, 2013b). Such snapshots have been applied in various research projects for system analysis and improvement (Alter, 2015; Daiberl, Oks, Roth, Möslein, & Alter, 2019; Johnson, Fruhling, & Fossum, 2016; Recker & Alter, 2012). WSS provides a generic structure for analyzing operational resources common to most settings of networked service delivery. In this study, WSS is applied for depicting the operational view on networked

---

[12] Note that in the context of work system theory, service is defined as "acts performed for others, including the provision of resources that others will use" (Alter, 2012, p. 220). Thus, it is different to the conceptualization of this dissertation presented in Part II but compatible regarding its consequences. Work system theory acknowledges that service should be considered from a process perspective, i.e., customers and one or more providers contribute both operand and operant resources (i.e., participants, technology, information, other resources) into a transformation process.

service delivery. Having introduced the modeling approaches applied for the design of NSPIRET (i.e., CJML and WSS), next, FMEA is presented. The latter represents a technique that fosters the model-based analysis to identify and evaluate opportunities for driving service productivity.

2.2   FMEA-based improvement of service productivity

This subsection introduces the usage of FMEA for improving service productivity. For this purpose, first, it provides some background related to the technique. Afterward, the FMEA-based portfolio approach to productivity improvement is introduced, which serves as a building block for designing NSPIRET.

2.2.1   Background related to FMEA

FMEA is an inductive technique for reliability analysis of systems (McDermott, Mikaulak, & Beauregard, 2008; Teng & Ho, 1996). FMEA requires the system under consideration to be broken down into subsystems and related components, for instance by using the modeling approaches depicted above. In doing so, it is possible to analyze these components for potential root failures, prioritize these failures and come up with solutions to prevent negative effects on the next higher system level (Sharma, Kumar, & Kumar, 2005). Originally being developed by NASA in the 1960s, FMEA has soon been adopted in industrial engineering (Puente, Pino, Priore, & de la Fuente, 2002; Sharma, Kumar, & Kumar, 2005). Recently, this technique has also been adopted for improving service design and productivity from a dyadic perspective (Chuang, 2007; Geum, Cho, & Park, 2011; Geum, Shin, et al., 2011).

In traditional FMEA, effects of so-called failure modes are evaluated based on their (1) *severity*, their (2) *probability of occurrence* and their (3) *ease of detection* typically using a five or ten point Likert scale (Chuang, 2007; H. Liu, Liu, & Liu, 2013). The individual scores are multiplied to derive a risk prioritization number (RPN). RPN serves as a quantitative score to highlight the most critical failures, which should be corrected by decision makers (Puente et al., 2002). The higher a particular RPN, the higher the need to intervene (Chuang, 2007).

Geum, Shin, et al. (2011) propose to use FMEA for enhancing productivity in the context of services. Unlike traditional FMEA, the authors apply a portfolio approach for the assessment of failure modes to foster a more multilateral assessment than RPNs provide. This approach is described in the next subsection.

2.2.2   FMEA-based portfolio approach to service productivity improvement

Portfolio management refers to dynamic decision processes through which a list of new projects is constantly evaluated and prioritized leading to resource allocations for implementing the most promising ones (Cooper, Edgett, & Kleinschmidt, 1999). A portfolio can be visualized in the form of a multi-dimensional matrix to visualize and swiftly compare opportunities for action (Day, 1990). Developing and analyzing failure portfolios is based on the idea that risk implications can be very different even if two RPNs are identical (Geum, Shin, et al., 2011).

Following the FMEA-based portfolio approach to service productivity improvement (Geum, Shin, et al., 2011), initially, the service process is delineated in the form of a flowchart to identify the different service steps. Based on this, sub-processes are analyzed to identify potential failure modes using a five-point Likert scale. Geum, Shin, et al. (2011) define failure modes as occurrences causing a failure in service delivery and thus reduce productivity for the provider or the customer. For their evaluation, the authors propose to retain the probability of occurrence and severity but exclude the ease of detection as a factor for consideration. The authors argue that the latter is relatively negligible in the service industry as the success of a service is based on the customer's perception about whether a service works well rather than actual service delivery (Geum, Shin, et al., 2011).

Besides merely focusing on failure modes as in traditional FMEA (see above), Geum, Shin, et al. (2011) highlight the necessity to develop a portfolio of innovation modes as well. In this context, failure modes are occurrences causing service failure and thus reducing productivity. Innovation modes, on the other hand, are opportunities to improve productivity for the customer or provider by harnessing driving forces such as new technologies, organizational change, market opportunities, or knowledge.

Thus, innovation modes are focusing on creating new value and improving productivity in the future. As priority measures for innovation modes, the authors propose to rate the expected (1) *impact* on productivity and its (2) *feasibility* of implementation given existing resource constraints of the service provider. Again, for evaluation, a five-point Likert scale is applied. A comparison of both modes is presented in Table 14.

Table 14: Comparison of failure and innovation modes. Based on Geum, Shin, et al. (2011, p. 1832).

Description	Failure mode	Innovation mode
Definition	Operational point that can cause a service failure	Operational point that can cause innovation in the service
Consequence	Reduce productivity	Potentially improve productivity
Priority measures	• Severity • Occurrence	• Impact • Feasibility

Given the different evaluation criteria for failure and innovation modes detailed above, portfolios of failure and innovation modes are developed each comprising four quadrants as depicted in Figure 20. Geum, Shin, et al. (2011) argue that failure modes falling under the (1) *highly dangerous* quadrant should be given the highest priority as they are characterized by a high expected severity and a high likelihood of occurrence. (2) *Big shots* on the other hand, are particularly critical. However, as their occurrence is low, it is difficult to anticipate them in daily operations. Thus, mechanisms should be enacted to prevent them from (re-)occurring. (3) *Casual failures* are often everyday occurrences that do not have severe effects but may be difficult to prevent. Thus, they should only be addressed if the costs do not outweigh the benefits of improvement. Lastly, (4) *insignificant failures* do not have a notable impact on overall productivity. Thus, in case resource constraints exist, they can be ignored (Geum, Shin, et al., 2011).

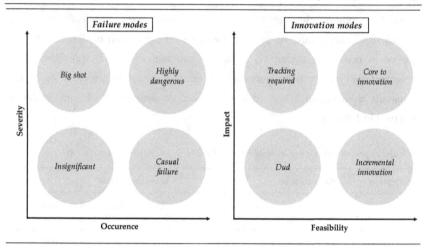

Figure 20: Portfolios of failure and innovation modes. Based on Geum, Shin, et al. (2011, pp. 1834-1835).

With respect to innovation modes, Geum, Shin, et al. (2011) argue that it is most important to focus on the (1) *core to innovation*. Innovation modes in this quadrant are expected to have a great impact on productivity and can be implemented given the accessible resources. The quadrant (2) *tracking required*, on the other hand, encompasses innovation modes that are expected to have a great impact but, considering the current resource constraints of the provider, are difficult to implement. However, due to changes to the resource base of the provider, these innovation modes may become feasible in the future. (3) *Incremental innovations* may have a limited impact on future productivity improvements. However, in case there are no potentials for radical improvements, for instance in the case of mature service delivery processes, incremental gains should be harnessed as well. Lastly, innovation modes subsumed under the (4) *dud* quadrant should be ignored as their impact on productivity improvement is low while also being resource intensive to implement (Geum, Shin, et al., 2011).

The authors have piloted this approach in the context of a hospital service together with a sample of patients in order to learn about failure and innovation modes from their perspective. The authors found that patients identified various failure and innovation modes and they claim that this approach can contribute to rational decision making for productivity improvements. All in all, Geum, Shin, et al. (2011) provide a way to operationalize the identification and evaluation of opportunities for improving service productivity. However, their approach still focuses on dyadic productivity perspective and thus does not consider the role of co-providers. Furthermore, they do not suggest how to systematically depict and analyze resources applied throughout the service delivery process. Finally, the authors do not provide practical recommendations for interventions based on the prioritized failure and innovation modes. Next, the research approach of this study is introduced and it is explicated how the theoretical background is synthesized and extended for developing NSPIRET.

3   Method and data

 This chapter presents the method and data used for developing and evaluating NSPIRET. In the next section, the DSR approach is introduced. Afterward, the phases of the specific DSR process applied are described in more detail.

3.1   Design science research approach

For developing NSPIRET, DSR was conducted (Hevner et al., 2004; March & Storey, 2008; Peffers et al., 2007). Rooted in engineering and the sciences of the artificial (Simon, 1996), DSR is an iterative research process to construct and evaluate sociotechnical artifacts that address an observed problem while contributing to scientific knowledge (Gregor & Hevner, 2013). In this context, artifacts are broadly defined and refer to any designed object that depicts an embedded solution to a defined research problem (Peffers et al., 2007). Thus, the output of DSR can address a broad range of contributions such as specific instantiations to more general methods, models, as well as abstract design theories (Gregor & Hevner, 2013; March & Smith, 1995). For this study, DSR was chosen as it suits the paradigm and objective of this research. Concerning the former, DSR is in line with the paradigm of pragmatism as it focuses on action, intervention, and constructive knowledge (Goldkuhl, 2012). Concerning the latter, DSR presents a rigorous approach for problem-solving in environmental contexts that are ill-defined and characterized by complex interactions (Gregor & Hevner, 2013). Moreover, DSR has been proclaimed as a valuable method for service research due to the ever-growing role of technology for service delivery (Ostrom et al., 2015).

As indicated above, the core activities of DSR are building and evaluating an artifact that addresses a relevant organizational need. For this purpose, researchers draw from the existing knowledge base comprising both the theoretical foundations for design as well as methods for its evaluation (Hevner et al. 2004). Moreover, the envisaged solution has to present a research opportunity. For that, the developed artifact has to better solve a known problem than existing contributions (i.e., improvement) or present a new solution to a new problem (i.e., invention). Moreover, new knowledge can be created by extending existing solutions to new problems (i.e., exaptation)

(Gregor and Hevner 2013). This study aims to synthesize and extend existing solutions (i.e., CJML, WSS, and the FMEA-based portfolio approach to service productivity improvement) to a previously unsolved problem (i.e., improving productivity in the context of networked service delivery). Hence, it presents a form of exaptation. Next, the research design is presented.

3.2   Research design

Scholars have proposed different DSR process models (Gregor & Hevner, 2013; Hevner et al., 2004; Peffers et al., 2007; Sein, Henfridsson, Rossi, & Lindgren, 2011). For this study, the DSR process of Peffers et al. (2007) was applied as shown in Figure 21.

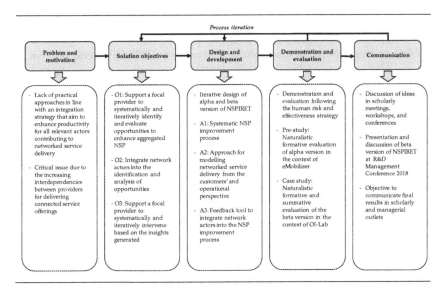

Figure 21: *DSR process applied. Adapted from Peffers et al. (2007).*

This process was selected as it is widely accepted in literature (Deng & Ji, 2018), stresses the iterative nature of DSR, and explicitly highlights the necessity for communicating DSR results to foster impact. In doing so it takes into consideration that the outputs of DSR studies are dynamically shaped by interaction and communication with other researchers and practitioners. Throughout the DSR process, all three forms of reasoning, i.e., deduction (theory-driven reasoning), induction (empirically-grounded reasoning), and abduction (creative imagination, reasoning by analogy) were applied (Fischer & Gregor, 2011). The phases of the DSR process are discussed in the following subsections in greater detail.

3.2.1 Problem and motivation

Following Peffers et al. (2007), initially, the problem has to be identified and the value of a solution has to be justified. In this regard, the systematic literature review found that there is a lack of practical approaches that are in line with an integration strategy and aim to enhance productivity for all relevant actors contributing resources to networked service delivery. Considering the increasing dependencies among specialized providers for delivering connected service offerings highlighted in Part I and Part II, this is a critical issue and should be addressed by new solutions. Thus, building on these theoretical considerations, the need for NSPIRET was established.

3.2.2 Objectives of the solution

Next, the objectives (O) of the solution need to be specified (Peffers et al., 2007). For this purpose, insights generated in Part III and IV were utilized: First, (O1) NSPIRET should support a focal provider to systematically and iteratively identify and analyze opportunities to enhance NSP for itself, customers, and relevant co-providers. In this context, given the conceptualization of NSP, improvement opportunities can address the pre-core, core, and post-core periods of a connected, overall service and encompass both efficiency and effectiveness dimensions. Second, (O2) NSPIRET should integrate the different network actors into the identification and analysis of opportunities. Thus, it shall be ensured that their individual conditions of network membership as well as their perceptions of NSP are adequately considered. Third, (O3) NSPIRET should support the focal provider to systematically and iteratively intervene based on the insights generated. All in all, fulfilling these goals should inform the overall service productivity life cycle acknowledging the dynamic nature of NSP as well as the demand for enhancing collective satisfaction of relevant network actors for operational success.

3.2.3   Design and development

The iterative design and development process has to be based on an appropriate theoretical underpinning and research methods (Peffers et al. 2007; Hevner et al. 2004). The necessary theoretical foundations for constructing NSPIRET were chosen in line with the analysis-synthesis bridge model, which has been applied for method development in service research before (e.g., Patrício et al. 2011). Following its ideas, for enhancing aggregated NSP, it is necessary to initially model the current situation before deriving suggestions for future improvements. For this purpose, NSPIRET adapts complementary contributions from service design (i.e., CJML) and information systems (i.e., WSS) to visualize the current and the preferred situation of networked service delivery. Additionally, a contribution rooted in the field of engineering (i.e., the FMEA-based portfolio approach) is adopted to foster the systematic identification and evaluation of opportunities to enhance aggregated NSP. Whereas these approaches serve as building blocks, they were further elaborated throughout the DSR process in order to meet the particularities of the problem domain, i.e., improving aggregated NSP.

NSPIRET was developed in an iterative manner comprising an alpha version, a beta version, and a revised beta version. All three versions of NSPRIET consist of an organized set of three artifacts: The first artifact, a (1) *systematic process of improving aggregated NSP* describes the activities that need to be performed. It guides the application of a (2) *dedicated modeling approach* to depict networked service delivery at a given time and a (3) *feedback tool* for the integration of actors into the process of improving aggregated NSP. The designs of the artifacts are detailed in Chapter 4.

3.2.4   Demonstration and evaluation

Demonstration and evaluation aim to establish how well the artifacts solve one or more instances of the problem identified (Peffers et al., 2007). For choosing the right evaluation strategy, the framework for evaluation in design science (FEDS) was applied (Venable et al., 2016). According to FEDS, each evaluation activity can be assessed according to its functional purpose and its guiding paradigm. Concerning the former, evaluation can either be more formative or summative. Whereas formative evaluation aims to improve the outcome generated by the evaluand, summative evaluation assesses if outcomes are in line with expectations of affected stakeholders (Venable et al., 2016). Concerning the paradigm of evaluation, FEDS distinguishes between artificial and naturalistic evaluation. Artificial evaluation is positivist and reductionist in nature (Venable et al., 2016). Throughout a purely artificial evaluation, artifacts are not applied to any reality (i.e., real users, real systems, real tasks) (Sonnenberg & vom Brocke, 2012). Typical evaluation methods include laboratory experiments, simulations or criteria-based analysis (Sonnenberg & vom Brocke, 2012; Venable et al., 2016). Naturalistic evaluation, on the other hand, is more interpretive in nature and explores the evaluand's performance in the real world (Venable et al., 2016). Thus, methods include case studies, ethnography, or hermeneutic approaches (Venable et al., 2016).

As indicated in Figure 22, the evaluation of NSPIRET was successively conducted in the context of the two empirical settings of networked service delivery introduced in Section 2.2 of Part IV. These settings were selected due to their operational differences as well as the possibility for trust-based access described before. Whereas the different settings fostered insights concerning the applicability of NSPIRET across diverse service domains, trust-based access helped to mitigate the risk associated with early development projects (Venable et al., 2016). For evaluation, the so-called "human risk and effectiveness strategy" was chosen, which focuses on naturalistic formative evaluations before moving into more summative evaluations (Venable et al., 2016). This strategy is particularly suited when, as in the case of NSPIRET, the major design risk is user-oriented (Venable et al., 2016). For this purpose, initially, a pre-study was conducted in the context of eMobilizer to assess the main ideas of the alpha version of NSPIRET. As the results of the pre-study seemed promising, secondly, a holistic case study was conducted to evaluate the refined beta version of NSPIRET in the context of OI-Lab. Having introduced the overall evaluation strategy, next, the evaluation designs are discussed in greater detail.

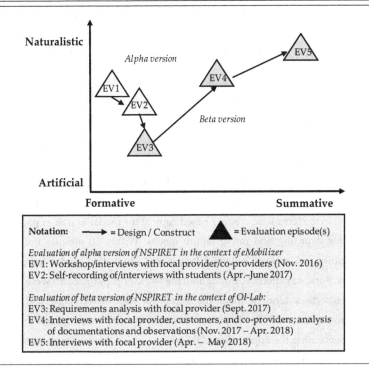

Naturalistic

Alpha version

EV1

EV2

EV4

EV5

Beta version

EV3

Artificial

Formative   Summative

Notation: ──▶ = Design / Construct   ▲ = Evaluation episode(s)

Evaluation of alpha version of NSPIRET in the context of eMobilizer
EV1: Workshop/interviews with focal provider/co-providers (Nov. 2016)
EV2: Self-recording of/interviews with students (Apr.–June 2017)

Evaluation of beta version of NSPIRET in the context of OI-Lab:
EV3: Requirements analysis with focal provider (Sept. 2017)
EV4: Interviews with focal provider, customers, and co-providers; analysis
      of documentations and observations (Nov. 2017 – Apr. 2018)
EV5: Interviews with focal provider (Apr. – May 2018)

Figure 22: *Evaluation episodes of the DSR study. Adapted from Venable et al. (2016).*

3.2.4.1   Evaluation design for the alpha version of NSPIRET

At the time of the evaluation, the service platform eMobilizer had been online for over one year and the co-providers wanted to identify opportunities to improve aggregated NSP for the different actors regularly involved. Thus, decision makers supported the pre-study of the alpha version of NSPIRET to evaluate its general effectiveness, utility, and understandability (Prat, Comyn-Wattiau, & Akoka, 2015). In this context, assessing effectiveness is related to how well NSPIRET fulfills the objectives specified above. Utility and understandability, on the other hand, provide additional nuanced insights concerning the practicability of NSPIRET (Prat et al., 2015). For evaluation, initially, an NSP improvement team was formed consisting of the author of this dissertation and one representative of focal provider A as well as one representative of focal provider B (see Table 9 presented in Chapter 2 of Part IV). Team members applied the alpha version of NSPIRET and modeled networked service delivery using insights derived by observations and available documentations (i.e., platform statistics, existing interview transcripts from the exploratory case study, protocols of meetings).

As depicted in Figure 22, for identification of failure and innovation modes from the focal and co-providers' perspective, a workshop was conducted, which lasted 120 minutes in total (EV1). Workshop participants were three employees of two industrial partners as well as seven researchers of four research organizations. Throughout the workshop, the model developed before served as the basis to identify failure and innovation modes for the different network actors involved. For this purpose, workshop participants were divided into two groups. Each group received an introduction to the technique, a paper-based copy of the model as well as paper-based templates for depicting and rating failure modes. Within 60 minutes both groups should identify and analyze potential failure and innovation modes for particular touchpoints. For data collection, throughout the workshop, participants were observed by two researchers (one of them the author of this dissertation) and relevant observations were noted. Furthermore, participants were asked to self-record any problems concerning the application of the alpha version. Moreover, semi-structured interviews with three workshop participants who provided particular insightful feedback were conducted to learn about their experiences with using the alpha version of NSPIRET. These interviews were audio recorded, lasted between 30 and 50 minutes, and were successively transcribed (see Appendix E for the interview guideline).

The integration of customers throughout the pre-study (EV2) was based on event-contingent self-recording (Wheeler & Reis, 1991). This method was selected as it is considered suitable to collect evidence over an extended period of time in a non-intrusive way and reduce recall bias (Halvorsrud, Kvale, et al., 2016; Wheeler & Reis, 1991). As participants for this study, 17 undergraduate students of a German university were recruited. The students' view represented the perspective of the customers as they actively used the service platform as part of a university course on new media, which lasted from April to June 2017. At the beginning of the course the students were instructed to self-record and rate any failure or innovation modes identified when using the platform with the help of a paper-based feedback tool. At the end of the course, students presented their findings and were interviewed in four groups in order to learn about their experiences with identifying and evaluating failure and innovation modes (see Appendix E for the interview guideline). Presentations and interviews lasted approximately 25 minutes per group. For data analysis, relevant information was transcribed and the different documents were consolidated. All documentations and interview transcripts were coded utilizing the qualitative data analysis software MAXQDA 12. For this purpose, the highest-order codes reflected the established DSR evaluation criteria indicated above, i.e., (1) *effectiveness*, (2) *utility*, and (3) *understandability*. For each highest-order code, (a) *positive perceptions*, (b) *negative perceptions*, and (c) *required design changes* for the artifacts of the beta version were analyzed. The findings of the evaluation of the alpha version and resulting design changes for the beta version are presented in Subsection 4.1.4.

3.2.4.2   Evaluation design for the beta version of NSPIRET

For evaluation of the beta version an encompassing case study was conducted in the context of OI-Lab lasting from mid-September 2017 until the end of May 2018. In the context of DSR, a case study is understood as the application of the designed artifacts to a real-world situation and assessing their effects on this situation (Peffers, Rothenberger, Tuunanen, & Vaezi, 2012). Again effectiveness, utility, and understandability were utilized as evaluation criteria. Additionally, as in the case study it was possible to evaluate the application of NSPIRET for several months, operational feasibility could be evaluated as well (Prat et al., 2015),

For the case study, in consultation with the decision makers of the focal provider of OI-Lab, an NSP improvement team was formed consisting of five employees of the focal provider who collaborated with the author of this dissertation. Building upon the extensive experiences of the team members, available documentation, and existing transcripts of in-depth interviews with three customers, networked service delivery was modeled and a web-based version of the feedback tool was set up. For programming the web-based tool, the author of this dissertation collaborated with another researcher. Afterward, the collection of failure and innovation was initiated and lasted until the end of April 2018. For this purpose, the NSP improvement team decided to focus on representatives of the focal provider, past customers, and individual visitors as co-providers in the context of OI-Lab.[13] In this context, representatives of six customers who recently finished their prototyping and testing projects and were willing to support this research were selected. The focus was on past customers in order to ensure that they had the necessary experience to provide feedback. Moreover, customers reflected different types of organizations (i.e., multinational enterprises, small and medium companies, public institutions) hiring the service of the OI-Lab. In doing so, it should be ensured that heterogeneous perspectives are revealed. Throughout the case study, representatives of the focal provider as well as customers could access the feedback tool via a link using their own computer. Representatives of co-providers could access the feedback tool via a stationary tablet positioned within the testing facility of OI-Lab (see Appendix F).

As indicated in Figure 22, initially, semi-structured interviews with five experienced representatives of the focal provider were conducted for requirements analysis prior to implementation on site (EV3, see Appendix E for the interview guideline). Afterward, formative interviews with seven employees of the focal provider utilizing NSPIRET were conducted at different development stages (EV4). Furthermore, interviews with representatives of six customers and with 20 individual co-providers who contributed to the case study were carried out (see Appendix E for the interview guideline). Whereas interviews with the focal provider and customers typically lasted around 60 to 90 minutes, interviews with co-providers were rather short and typically took around 10 minutes. Moreover, meetings, self-recordings of the NSP improvement team, and ad-hock feedback (e.g., e-mails highlighting problems) were utilized for data collection. Finally, after the test phase was over, summative interviews were conducted with four representatives of the focal provider to learn about how well NSPIRET met their expectations (EV5). Each of these interviews lasted around 60 minutes (see Appendix E for the interview guideline).

Data analysis was similar to the pre-study. Again, interview transcripts and relevant documentations were coded using MAXQDA 12. In doing so, the highest-order codes were pre-defined and encompassed the following criteria: (1) *effectiveness*, (2) *utility*, (3)

---

[13] These visitors were classified as representatives of co-provider B in the exploratory case study (see Chapter 4.2.2 of Part IV).

understandability, and (4) *operational feasibility*. For each highest-order code, the (a) *positive perceptions*, (b) *negative perceptions*, and (c) *required design changes* for future applications were investigated. The findings of the evaluation of the beta version and proposed design changes for future applications are presented in Subsection 4.2.4.

3.2.5   Communication

As the last phase of DSR, Peffers et al. (2007) stress the importance of communicating the results to both scholars and practitioners. Thus, preliminary ideas and different development stages of NSPIRET were regularly discussed with both scholars and practitioners in the context of meetings, workshops, and scientific conferences (i.e., Service Operations Management Forum 2015, Annual RESER Conference 2016, Doctoral Colloquium of 2017 European Academy of Management Conference). Moreover, the initial beta version of NSPIRET was presented at the 2018 R&D Management Conference. A future goal is to publish the final results of this study in scholarly well as managerial outlets to foster dissemination.

Having described the research design of the DSR study, in the next chapter, the findings are presented. In line with the DSR communication scheme of Gregor and Hevner (2013), first the artifacts of the respective version of NSPIRET are described before detailing the results of the evaluation.

4   Findings

This chapter introduces the developed artifacts and the results of their evaluation. All in all, NSPIRET represents an organized set of three artifacts as presented in Figure 23. The (1) *NSPIRET Navigator* (i.e., the process of improving aggregated NSP) guides the application of (2) *NSPIRET Snapshotting* (i.e., the modeling approach) as well as the utilization of the (3) *NSPIRET Shoutbox* (i.e., the feedback tool). Modeling, on the other hand, informs the set-up of the feedback tool by depicting the connected customer journey as well as operational resources. This information is utilized in the feedback tool to classify failure modes and innovation modes identified. Next, the design and evaluation of the alpha version of NSPIRET are presented in greater detail.

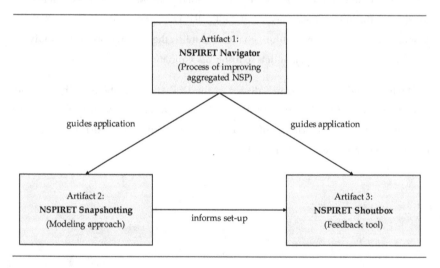

Figure 23: Interrelationships of NSPIRET's artifacts. Own illustration.

4.1   Alpha version of NSPIRET: Artifacts and evaluation results

This section presents the alpha version of NSPIRET. As mentioned above, it contains the initial ideas and was applied to motivate or discourage further development. At this stage, it did not contain all of the conceptual foundations presented in Chapter 2.

Next, the different artifacts of the alpha version are introduced successively. Afterward, the results of the naturalistic formative evaluation are presented.

4.1.1   Artifact 1: Alpha version of the NSPIRET Navigator

The conceptual structure of the alpha version of the NSPIRET Navigator is visualized in Figure 24. It depicts how the conceptual foundations of the initial process of improving aggregated NSP are synthesized. In the alpha version, process activities are realized throughout two sequential phases. First, in the (1) *preparation phase*, the following activities are conducted: An NSP improvement team is set up and responsibilities as well as internal procedures are clarified together with decision makers of the focal provider (P1). Next, team members collect data and apply NSPIRET Snapshotting to model the expected customer journey as a series of touchpoints (P2), depict the underlying service systems (P3), and actors' expected benefits (P4). Focusing on the customer journey is grounded in the concept of the service delivery network (SDN) (Tax et al., 2013). Whereas in the alpha version modeling of touchpoints does not follow any formal approach, the depiction of underlying service systems builds on WSS (Alter, 2013). Similar to established approaches from the field of service design, required data for modeling is collected qualitatively (e.g., interviews, observations, focus groups) in order to gain an in-depth customer understanding (Patrício et al., 2011). Afterward, a participatory workshop with representatives of the different providers as well as a self-recording initiative with customers are prepared (P5).

Having developed a snapshot for the current situation of networked service delivery, next, in the (2) *execution phase*, opportunities for improving aggregated NSP are identified and assessed together with representatives of the different network actors (E1, E2). These activities harness the NSPIRET Shoutbox that operationalizes ideas of the FMEA-based portfolio approach for enhancing service productivity (Geum, Shin, et al., 2011). It builds on the idea that each service system element underlying a particular touchpoint can be the source of one or more failure or innovation modes. Whereas the former represent service system elements that reduce NSP for one or more network actors, the latter are modified or new system elements that may enhance NSP for one or more network actors. Each failure mode is assessed according to its severity and likelihood of occurrence. Innovation modes, on the other hand, are rated according to their expected positive impact and feasibility for implementation (Geum, Shin, et al., 2011). Afterward, team members reflect upon failure and innovation modes and decide upon purposeful interventions considering their expected effects on aggregated NSP (E3). Finally, team members remodel networked service delivery (E4) before intervening according to specified responsibilities and procedures (E5). A summary of these activities is presented in Table 15.

Table 15: Activities of the alpha version of the NSPIRET Navigator.

Process phases	Activities
Preparation	P1: NSP improvement team is set up in accordance with decision makers of the focal provider and objectives, responsibilities, and procedures are clarified
	P2: Team members collect data/use existing insights and apply NSPIRET Snapshotting to model the customer journey as a series of touchpoints
	P3: Team members collect data/use existing insights and apply NSPIRET Snapshotting to model the service system for each touchpoint
	P4: Team members collect data/use existing insights and apply NSPIRET Snapshotting to depict expected benefits for each network actor
	P5: Team members prepare workshop with representatives of the different providers and self-recording of customers
Execution	E1: Team members conduct a workshop with representatives of the different providers to jointly identify and evaluate failure and innovation modes using the NSPIRET Shoutbox
	E2: Team members support customers to individually identify and evaluate failure and innovation modes for each touchpoint using event-contingent self-recording
	E3: Team members decide upon interventions after reflecting upon their effects on aggregated NSP
	E4: Team members apply NSPIRET Snapshotting to re-model networked service delivery
	E5: Team members intervene according to specified responsibilities and procedures

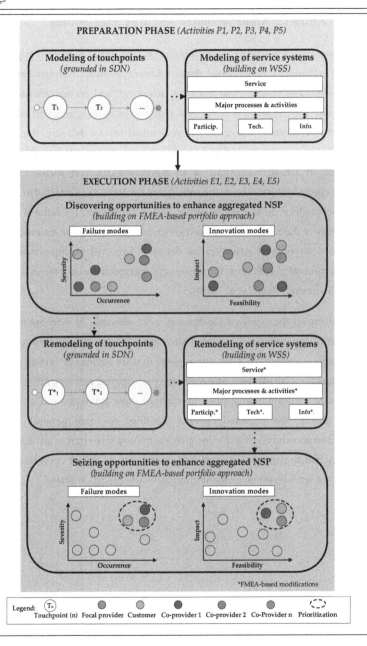

Figure 24: *Conceptual structure of the alpha version of the NSPIRET Navigator. Own illustration.*

4.1.2   Artifact 2: Alpha version of NSPIRET Snapshotting

The alpha version of NSPRIET Snapshotting, i.e., the initial modeling approach, is exemplified in Figure 25. As indicated above, it fosters productivity-related analysis by depicting networked service from both the customers' and an operational point of view. Following the suggestions of Tax et al. (2013) to focus on aggregated interactions for planning operations in the context of networked service delivery, the modeling approach of the alpha version depicts interactions with the anticipated customers. Thus, instead of actual touchpoints of an individual customer journey, modeling focuses on expected touchpoints of the anticipated clientele. As illustrated in Figure 25, an individual model is developed for each expected touchpoint. The latter is portrayed in the first row of the model and denoted generically to summarize different possible manifestations throughout actual service delivery. Expected touchpoints serve as a common denominator reflecting the customers' perspectives on networked service delivery (Halvorsrud, Kvale, et al., 2016).

Having depicted the expected touchpoints, next, elements of WSS are adapted to illustrate the operational point of view (Alter, 2013b). For each expected touchpoint, the major process and activities are summarized that are commonly carried out by the network actors for its realization. Moreover, the participating network actors as well as technologies and information applied throughout these processes and activities are delineated. Lastly, the expected benefits identified for each network actor are summarized on an extra sheet. Whereas such a summary is not part of an original WSS, it was developed to support the workshop participants to reflect upon the effects of changes to any service system element throughout the execution phase.

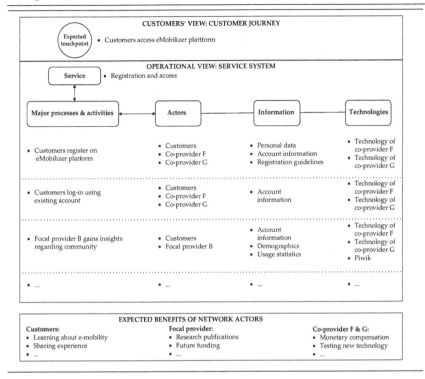

Figure 25: Exemplary snapshot developed in the context of eMobilizer (anonymized excerpt). Own illustration.

4.1.3   Artifact 3: Alpha version of the NSPIRET Shoutbox

For structuring the contributions from representatives of the different network actors, the alpha version of the NSPIRET Shoutbox is realized as a set of paper-based feedback sheets. The specific wording and categories of these sheets are adapted to fit the context of the workshop and self-recording respectively. The feedback sheets provide a standardized structure for actors' representatives to share any failure or innovation mode identified. Besides depicting the content of a particular failure or innovation mode, they should also reflect upon effects and sources of these modes. Moreover, they are expected to rate each failure and innovation mode on a five-point Likert scale as highlighted above. An anonymized excerpt of a feedback sheet filled out in the context of eMobilizer is depicted in Table 16.

Table 16: Feedback sheet applied in the context of eMobilizer (anonymized excerpt).

Failure modes for T₂	Effect on customer	Source of failure	Rating* Severity					Occurrence				
Registration benefits unclear	Less likelihood to register	Information	1	2	⊠	4	5	1	2	⊠	4	5
Password demands unclear	Repetitive data entry	Information	⊠	2	3	4	5	1	2	3	4	⊠
No possibility to remain logged-in	Additional effort for access	Technology	1	⊠	3	4	5	1	2	3	4	⊠
...	...	...	1	2	3	4	5	1	2	3	4	5

Innovation modes for T₂	Effect on customer	Source of innovation	Rating* Impact					Feasibility				
Explanatory pop-up	Simplifies usage	Information	1	⊠	3	4	5	1	2	⊠	4	5
Single sign-on	Less effort for registration	Technology	1	2	⊠	4	5	⊠	2	3	4	5
Gamification of courses	Higher likelihood use platform	Technology	1	2	3	4	⊠	1	⊠	3	4	5
...	...	...	1	2	3	4	5	1	2	3	4	5

*Note that 1= very low/unlikely; 5=very high/very likely

4.1.4   Evaluation results

The results of the evaluation episodes EV1 and EV2 (see Figure 22 in Subsection 3.2.4) served as a proof-of-concept and motivated further development of NSPIRET. Nevertheless, the findings also revealed several pitfalls regarding effectiveness, utility, and understandability for all three artifacts, which needed to be addressed in order to improve the outcomes of NSPIRET.

4.1.4.1   Effectiveness of the alpha version

Effectiveness refers to the degree to which NSPIRET achieves its objectives in a real situation (Prat et al., 2015). As illustrated in Table 17, the application of the alpha version fostered the systematic identification and analysis of 108 failure modes (FMs) and 100 innovation modes (IMs) in the context of eMobilizer. All in all, 25 failure modes (approximately 23% of the total number of failure modes), and 25 innovation modes

(25% of the total number of innovation modes) led to productivity-related interventions aiming to enhance aggregated NSP.

Table 17: Number of failure and innovation modes identified and interventions in the context of eMobilizer.

Actor	FMs identified	FMs interventions	IMs identified	IMs interventions
Focal providers & co-providers	25	7	19	9
Customers	83	18	81	16
∑	108	25	100	25

Tables 18 and 19 present how failure and innovation modes were distributed across the service system elements. It can be seen that failure modes primarily addressed the technologies applied, followed by information and human participants. Likewise, most innovation modes were rooted in technologies and information followed by the demand for new processes and activities throughout the connected customer journey.

Table 18: Distribution of failure modes across service system elements in the context of eMobilizer.

Actor	Source of failure modes					
	Services	Processes & Activities	Participants	Information	Technologies	Others
Focal provider & co-providers	1	2	9	5	7	2
Customers	2	2	3	21	58	0
∑	3	4	12	26	65	2

Table 19: Distribution of innovation modes across service system elements in the context of eMobilizer.

Actor	Source of innovation modes					
	Services	Processes & Activities	Participants	Information	Technologies	Others
Focal provider & co-providers	1	4	2	5	10	0
Customers	13	11	0	19	47	0
∑	14	15	2	24	57	0

The results provide an indication that, if iteratively applied, the main ideas of NSPIRET ingrained in the alpha version have the potential to meet the goals specified in Subsection 3.2.2. Nevertheless, several challenges for the effectiveness of the alpha version could be identified as well. Whereas self-recording of customers provided detailed insights how to improve NSP from their perspective, the workshop with representatives of the focal provider and the co-providers was less effective. It could be observed that some representatives seemed reluctant to openly discuss operational issues in front of representatives of other network actors. This led to a limited understanding of failure and innovation modes from the focal and co-providers' perspective. Thus, for improving effectiveness, the following design change (DC) was conducted: The workshop-setting was dismissed in favor of collecting individual feedback from self-selected representatives of all network actors (DC-A1.1). Additionally, several representatives stressed that they lacked the relevant knowledge to rate the likelihood of occurrence of failure modes identified and the feasibility of innovation modes proposed. Hence, in the beta version, these criteria should only be evaluated by the members of the NSP improvement team (DC-A1.2). Finally, throughout (re-)modeling the operational point of view on networked service delivery, the WSS-based categorization of service system elements was not yet considered exhaustive. Repeatedly, resources were identified that could not be assigned to any of the exiting elements (such as monthly prices for particular active community members). Thus, the WSS-based modeling was extended to include the element *other critical resources* (DC-A2.1)

4.1.4.2   Utility of the alpha version

Utility measures the worth of achieving NSPIRET's goals considering the costs for achieving it (Prat et al., 2015). In this regard, it was highlighted that, as the overall application of NSPIRET is a rather time-consuming undertaking, the results should lead to a holistic picture of failure and innovation modes perceived by the different network actors: *"Considering what we invested, and it was also simply about testing it, [results were] absolutely okay, but I think, that the main advantage . . . has to be, that you . . . [gain] a holistic picture, because if you do not have this, then . . .we can also simply do a brainstorming" (EV1: Member of NSP improvement team).* However, gaining a holistic picture concerning network actors' individual perceptions of NSP was limited by the design of the NSPIRET Navigator as feedback was only given by a limited number of respondents at pre-determined events. Moreover, it was criticized that the failure and innovation modes collaboratively identified throughout the workshop often remained on a generic level, reducing the value of these contributions. In contrast to that, it could be observed that self-recording by customers fostered more detailed feedback. Possibly being captured in the moment of interaction, failure and innovation modes were more specific and thus fostered understanding of the NSP improvement team.

For improving the utility of the beta version concerning the first and second objective, the following modifications were conducted. In order to gain a more holistic picture of network actors' NSP perceptions, the sequential process of the NSP Navigator was dismissed in favor of continuous process phases. Failure and innovation modes should not only be provided at particular events but continuously by individual representatives (DC-A1.3) via a web-based version of the NSPIRET Shoutbox (DC-A3.1). In doing so, the goal was to overcome any temporal and spatial restrictions in order to reach as many network actors as possible who can provide relevant insights on how to improve NSP from their particular perspective. In line with the third objective of NSPIRET, realizing this digital medium should support a steady influx of failure and innovation modes and thus foster an iterative improvement process. Moreover, in order to reduce the effort for analyzing feedback and planning interventions, the modified NSPIRET Shoutbox should support and, if possible, automate respective activities (DC-A3.2).

4.1.4.3   Understandability of the alpha version

According to Prat et al. (2015), understandability addresses how the different artifacts making up NSPIRET can be understood at a global level and at a detailed level considering the different elements and relationships inside the artifact. In this regard, interviewees could mostly understand the functions and content of respective artifacts and their interrelations on a global level. The NSPIRET Navigator was considered logical and the purpose of the different process phases and related activities could be understood. However, the developed NSPIRET Snapshots and the NSPIRET Shoutbox were not fully understood on a detailed level. Concerning the former, representatives were partly confused by the technical terms presented and found it challenging to process all of the information provided in the context of a workshop. Concerning the latter, it was found important to improve the visual representation to foster understandability: *"I believe that the most important step is . . . making it vivid, both concerning the user [i.e., customer] journey as well as concerning the partners, because then you can work with something, being a picture or pictogram or something . . . just because of this visualization you become aware of, ah okay, I now have to deal with the partner [for instance]"* (EV1: Member of NSP improvement team). Moreover, the utilization of numeric rating scales within the NSPIRET Shoutbox was criticized as it may not be easily processed and thus lead to misunderstandings by individual raters.

For improving understandability of the beta version, the NSPIRET Navigator, Snapshotting and the Shoutbox were modified. In the beta version, only members of the NSP improvement team should interact with the models developed whereas network actors' representatives solely interact with the feedback tool (DC-A1.4). Snapshotting should follow a more formalized approach including more visual elements for depicting the customer journey. For this purpose, CJML was adopted to extend the WSS-based description of the different stages of networked service delivery (DC-A2.2). Finally, with respect to the new digital version of the feedback tool, any unnecessary technical terms should be prevented and the numeric rating scales should be exchanged with a descriptive graphic rating scale (DC-A3.3).

4.1.5   Summary of design changes

The design changes derived by the findings of the pre-study are summarized in Table 20. In the next section, the revised artifacts of the beta version are presented.

Table 20: Design changes to the alpha version of NSPIRET.

Artifact	Design changes
	DC-A1.1: Dismissal of workshop in favor of collecting individual feedback from self-selected representatives of the network actors to enhance *effectiveness*
	DC-A1.2: Members of NSP improvement team rate occurrence of failure modes and feasibility of innovation modes to enhance *effectiveness*
NSPIRET Navigator	
	DC-A1.3: Adoption of a continuous, iterative improvement process to enhance *utility*
	DC-A1.4: Self-selected representatives of the network actors only interact with feedback tool to enhance *understandability*

Table 20 (cont.): Design changes to the alpha version of NSPIRET.

Artifact	Design changes
NSPIRET Snapshotting	DC-A2.1: Inclusion of new service system element "other critical resources" to enhance *effectiveness*
	DC-A2.2: Inclusion of CJML to enhance visualization of the customer journey to improve *understandability* for NSPIRET team
NSPIRET Shoutbox	DC-A3.1: Web-based feedback tool supporting the collection, evaluation, and implementation of feedback from network actors to enhance *utility*
	DC-A3.2: Removal of technical terms to improve *understandability*.
	DC-A3.3: Adoption of descriptive graphic rating scale to improve *understandability*.

4.2   Beta version of NSPIRET: Artifacts and evaluation results

Harnessing the evaluation results of the alpha version as well as insights derived throughout requirements analysis with representatives of the focal provider of OI-Lab, the initial design of the beta version of NSPIRET was developed. In the next subsection, its artifacts are described in greater detail. Afterward, the evaluation results are presented and the implemented design changes are delineated.

4.2.1   Artifact 1: Beta version of the NSPIRET Navigator

The NSPIRET Navigator of the beta version also follows the analysis-synthesis bridge model. However, building on the evaluation results of the pre-study, the sequential phases of planning and execution of the alpha version are replaced by an iterative and continuous process of modeling, discovery, and intervention supported by a facilitation phase. The conceptual structure of the beta version is depicted in Figure 26. The activities conducted throughout the four phases are described next.

Throughout the (1) *facilitation phase*, the necessary support activities are carried out. In this context, in accordance with decision makers of the focal provider, an NSP improvement team is set up and objectives, responsibilities, and procedures related to the initiative are clarified (F1). Afterward, team members operate and distribute the beta version of the Shoutbox, which is instantiated as a web-based tool (F2). Moreover, team members regularly motivate representatives of the different network actors to share their feedback (F3).

Next, throughout the (2) *(re-)modeling phase*, team members collect the required data and develop a snapshot depicting the customer's view on networked service delivery (M1). For this purpose, the graphical approach of CJML is adopted and the customer journey is depicted as a series of expected touchpoints throughout the pre-core, core, and the post-core service periods (Halvorsrud, Kvale, et al., 2016; Voorhees et al., 2017). Afterward, for each touchpoint, the respective service system is modeled using a modified version of WSS (M2) (Alter, 2013). Furthermore, network actors' expected benefits are depicted to support decision making with respect to productivity-related interventions (M3).

Once the current situation is modeled from the customer's and an operational perspective, opportunities to enhance aggregated NSP are identified and evaluated throughout the (3) *discovery phase*. Self-selected representatives of the different network actors utilize the NSPIRET Shoutbox to share failure and innovation modes identified and assess their individually perceived severity and impact respectively (D1). Team members use the NSPIRET Shoutbox to review, edit, and assess responses to decide upon interventions in order to improve aggregated NSP (D2). In this context, team members evaluate each failure mode according to its likelihood of occurrence and each innovation mode according to its feasibility of implementation.

Lastly, the (4) *intervention phase* takes place. Building on the results of the discovery phase, team members propose interventions after contemplating on their effects on aggregated NSP (I1). Next, team members initiate re-modeling and intervene according to the responsibilities and procedures detailed before (I2). In doing so, they record relevant intervention-related activities within the NSPIRET Shoutbox to ensure transparency of decisions and traceability of results (I3). Finally, team members communicate the results of interventions to ensure that network actors are aware of the impact of their contributions (I4). A summary of the process activities is presented in Table 21.

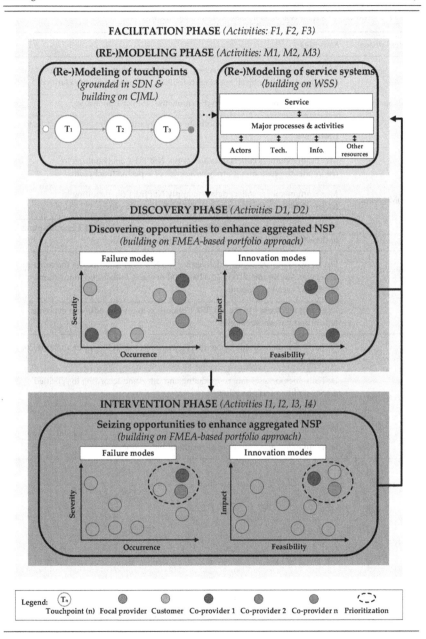

Figure 26: *Conceptual structure of the beta version of the NSPIRET Navigator. Own illustration.*

Table 21: Process activities of the beta version of the NSPIRET Navigator.

Process phase	Activities
Facilitation	F1: NSP improvement team is set-up in accordance with decision makers of the focal provider and objectives, responsibilities, and procedures are clarified
	F2: Team members operate and distribute the NSPIRET Shoutbox
	F3: Team members regularly motivate representatives of the network actors to contribute
(Re-)Modeling	M1: Team members collect data and apply NSPIRET Snapshotting to (re-)model the customer journey as a series of expected touchpoints
	M2: Team members collect data and apply NSPIRET Snapshotting to (re-)model the service system underlying each touchpoint
	M3: Team members collect data/use insights and apply NSPIRET Snapshotting to depict expected benefits for each network actor
Discovery	D1: Network actors' representatives use the NSPIRET Shoutbox in the context of regular service interactions to share and evaluate failure and innovation modes for each touchpoint
	D2: Team members use the NSPIRET Shoutbox to review, edit, and evaluate failure and innovation modes
Intervention	I1: Team members decide upon interventions after reflecting upon their effects on aggregated NSP
	I2: Team members initiate re-modeling and intervene according to specified responsibilities and procedures
	I3: Team members record intervention-related activities within the NSPIRET Shoutbox
	I4: Team members communicate results of interventions

4.2.2   Artifact 2: Beta version of NSPIRET Snapshotting

NSPIRET Snapshotting of the beta version extends the modeling approach of the alpha version by integrating CJML for depicting the customer journey in a systematic and visually enriched way. The first row of the snapshot highlights the considered period of the customer journey (i.e., pre-core, core, and post-core service). The second row visualizes the series of expected touchpoints following the notation of CJML. Each expected touchpoint is presented as a circle and is labeled with an identifier (T_0, T_1, etc.) representing the temporal sequence. Each touchpoint has a certain initiator (i.e., the customer, the focal service provider, or a co-provider) depicted by the boundary color of a touchpoint circle. Following the suggestions of Halvorsrud et al. (2014), for NSPIRET snapshotting, it is proposed to utilize different colors for each network actor in order to clearly distinguish among them. Within the area inside of each touchpoint circle the particular channel mediating the touchpoint is visualized. Channels are represented by the consistent use of suited symbols in order to foster an immediate association with the type of touchpoint represented. Unlike the notation of CJML, for developing an NSPIRET Snapshot, multiple possible channels for each touchpoint can be presented using a dotted frame. This was found necessary as certain interactions between the anticipated customers and the co-providers involved can be carried out via a range of channels. The possibility to denote optional channels shall enhance the flexibility of modeling in comparison to strictly sequential flowcharting.

From row three onwards, the different elements of the respective service system realizing each touchpoint are summarized. As described in Subsection 4.1.5, the service system element *other critical resources* is included to depict any resources relevant for realizing the respective touchpoint, which are not covered by the original WSS elements. Examples include physical components necessary for an offline service channel or monetary resources that need to be transferred in order to finish a payment process. A summary of the visual notation is presented in Figure 27. An anonymized excerpt of an NSPIRET Snapshot for two touchpoints of the pre-core service stage of OI-Lab is presented in Figure 28.

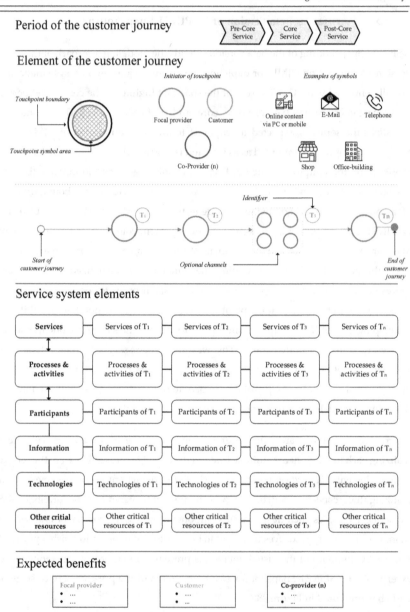

Figure 27: *Visual notation for modeling networked service delivery. Adapted and extended from Halvorsrud, Haugstveit, et al. (2016) and Alter (2013).*

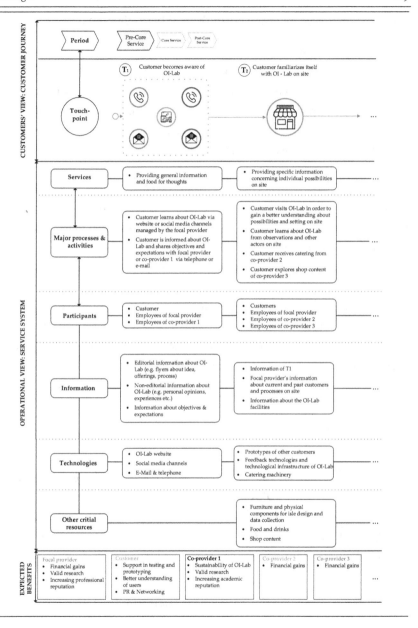

Figure 28: *Exemplary snapshot for two touchpoints in the context of OI-Lab (anonymized excerpt). Own illustration.*

4.2.3   Artifact 3: Beta version of the NSPIRET Shoutbox

The web-based tool enables representatives of the different network actors to share failure and innovation modes with the NSP improvement team. It is prototypically instantiated as a web-application to be accessible via mobile devices (e.g., laptop, smartphone) and stationary devices (e.g., feedback terminal in the physical service environment). Next, the architecture is briefly summarized before the interactions with the NSPIRET Shoutbox are presented.

4.2.3.1   Technical architecture of the beta version of the NSPIRET Shoutbox

The technical architecture of the NSPIRET Shoutbox is illustrated in Figure 29. When a user enters data into the client-side application, it gets transferred to the web server, which handles the incoming data. The server uses Node.js, which is a runtime environment for the server-side execution of JavaScript mainly used to develop web applications that can be extended easily through modules via the package manager npm. One of these is Express.js, a web framework for Node.js which contains features for building web applications and application programming interfaces. The data is written to the database with the help of mongoose.js, an object modeling tool for Node.js, with built-in features such as data validation and a range of extensions, e.g., for user management. MongoDB, a document-oriented NoSQL database, is used for data storage.

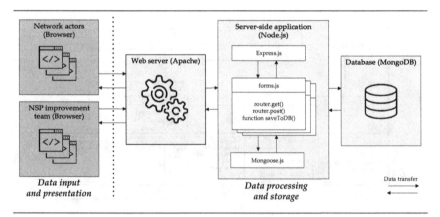

Figure 29: *Technical architecture of the beta version of the NSPIRET Shoutbox. Own illustration.*

4.2.3.2   Main interactions with the beta version of the NSPIRET Shoutbox

Representatives of the different network actors access the NSPIRET Shoutbox via an internet browser. On the landing page they select if they wish to report a problem (i.e., failure mode) or an opportunity for improving NSP (i.e., innovation mode). In order to foster understandability and ease of use, the interface was kept as simple as possible and any unnecessary technical terms were prevented. Next, representatives share and evaluate failure and innovation modes from their perspective. For this purpose, they can select one or more categories best addressing the source of the failure or innovation mode. These categories are derived from the service system elements specified in the modeling phase. After that, as depicted in Figure 30 and 31, they detail their qualitative feedback using the keyboard or voice entry function of the respective mobile or stationary feedback device. For rating, representatives select the smiley best addressing the perceived severity in the case of failure modes and impact in the case of innovation modes. After submission, gratitude is expressed and representatives are invited to share further feedback.

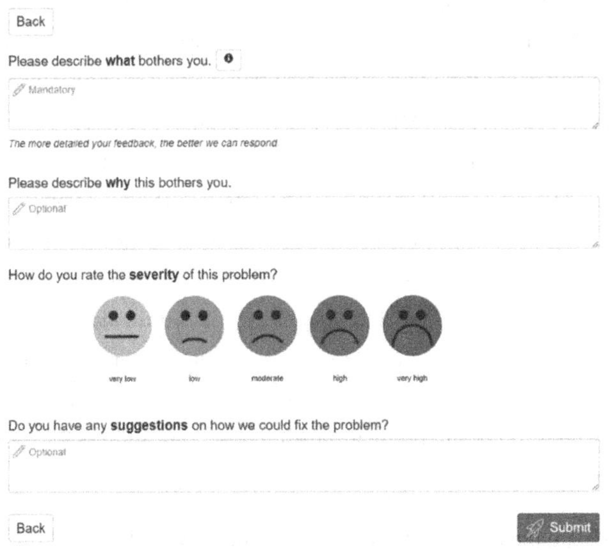

Figure 30: *Sharing of failure modes in the context of OI-Lab. Screenshot.*

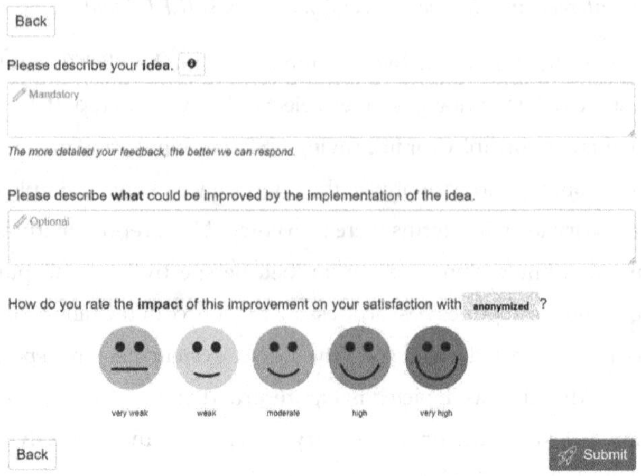

Figure 31: Sharing of innovation modes in the context of OI-Lab. Screenshot.

The NSP improvement team accesses the tool via a web-browser using an individual log-in. In the admin panel, the responsible team member reviews and edits the innovation and failure modes shared by the representatives of the different network actors. For this purpose, the admin panel includes a digital worksheet (see Figure 34). Building on best practices for FMEA-based software, this worksheet presents a unique ID for each failure and innovation mode as well as its creation date and time (Cândea, Kifor, & Constantinescu, 2014). Moreover, the type of network actors sharing failure and innovation modes is indicated as well as the selected categories and individual ratings. Editing includes the dismissal of obviously unserious contributions and the correction of the qualitative description (e.g., typos). Additionally, wrongly or non-categorized failure and innovation modes are adapted. Moreover, the appropriate touchpoints addressed by the respective failure and innovation modes are selected. Finally, individual contributions are grouped in case they address the same failure or innovation mode.

Next, based on the number of similar contributions as well as past experiences, the responsible team member rates the likelihood of occurrence for failure modes as well as the feasibility for implementing innovation modes. In case of grouped failure and innovation modes, the average of the individual ratings is automatically calculated.

Based on these ratings, portfolios of failure and innovations modes are automatically visualized as indicated in Figure 32 and 33. These portfolios inform the NSP improvement team concerning the priority to intervene using the generic intervention strategies described in Section 2.3. Each failure and innovation mode is depicted as a color-coded dot to indicate the actor under consideration. Moreover, in case several failure or innovation modes are grouped together, the diameter expands. In case the priority for intervention is considered high, responsible team members plan an intervention in the digital worksheet presented in Figure 34.

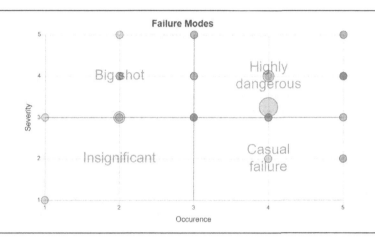

Figure 32: Exemplary portfolio of failure modes in the context of OI-Lab. Screenshot.

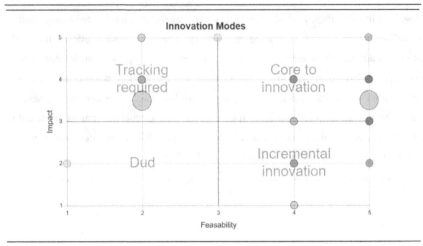

Figure 33: *Exemplary portfolio of innovation modes in the context of OI-Lab. Screenshot.*

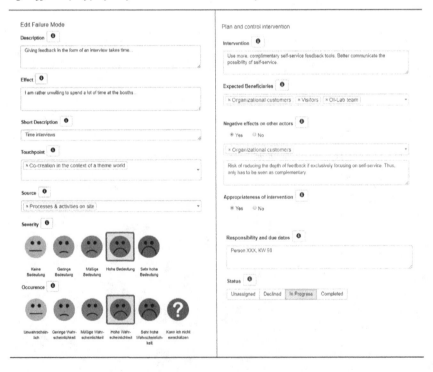

Figure 34: *Exemplary editing of failure mode and planning of intervention in the context of OI-Lab. Screenshot.*

4.2.4   Evaluation results

Harnessing the evaluation episodes EV3, EV4, and EV5 (see Figure 22 in Subsection 3.2.4) the beta version of NSPIRET was iteratively assessed and improved regarding its effectiveness, utility, understandability, and operational feasibility. Next, respective results are presented in detail.

4.2.4.1   Effectiveness of the beta version

As presented in Table 22, until the end of May 2018, the application of the beta version supported the NSP improvement team to identify and analyze 101 failure modes and 124 innovation modes. Whereas the former led to 61 interventions (approximately 60% of the total number of failure modes), the latter inspired 62 interventions (50% of the total number of innovation modes). In this context, it should be noted that the lower number of failure modes and innovation modes identified by customers may be because, as described in Subsection 3.2.4.2, only six organizational customers were invited to actively contribute to the evaluation of the beta version.

Table 22: Number of failure and innovation modes identified and interventions in the context of OI-Lab.

Actor	FMs identified	FMs interventions	IMs identified	IMs interventions
Focal provider	19	14	34	15
Customers	7	6	9	6
Co-providers	75	41	81	41
Σ	101	61	124	62

Table 23 illustrates how the failure and innovation modes as well as related interventions were distributed over time. It becomes clear that, using NSPIRET, team members could iteratively discover and seize opportunities to enhance aggregated NSP throughout the evaluation period. However, over time, the number of failure and innovation modes shared reduced. The drop of innovation modes starting in February 2018 may be partially due to changes to the wording in the NSPIRET Shoutbox as described in Subsection 4.2.4.3 (i.e., respondents seemed to have greater difficulties coming up with creative ideas for further development of OI-Lab than identifying opportunities for improvement of NSP).

Table 23: Distribution of failure and innovation modes over the evaluation period in the context of OI-Lab.

Type	Oct. - Nov. 17	Dec. 17- Jan. 18	Feb- Mar. 18	Apr. – May 18	Σ
FMs identified	34	27	24	16	101
FMs interventions	22	22	5	12	61
IMs identified	59	47	10	8	124
FMs interventions	25	28	3	6	62

Tables 24 and 25 present how failure and innovation modes were distributed across the service system elements. It can be seen that the NSP improvement team classified most failure and innovation modes to originate in a lack of information followed by defective technologies as well as problematic processes and activities. Similarly, most innovation modes were classified to originate in new or enhanced information, processes and activities as well as technologies. Several failure and innovation mode identified were considered to have more than merely one source. Thus, the numbers presented in Tables 24 and 25 do not reflect the numbers of Tables 22 and 23.

Table 24: Distribution of failure modes across service system elements in the context of OI-Lab.

Actor	Source of failure modes					
	Services	Processes & activities	Participants	Information	Technologies	Others
Focal provider	4	6	4	2	3	4
Customers	0	3	1	5	0	0
Co-providers	7	8	5	24	17	21
Σ	11	17	10	31	20	25

Table 25: Distribution of innovation modes across service system elements in the context of OI-Lab.

Actor	Source of innovation modes					
	Services	Processes & activities	Participants	Information	Technologies	Others
Focal provider	2	11	0	10	4	11
Customers	1	1	0	8	0	0
Co-providers	4	9	3	35	13	23
Σ	7	21	3	53	17	34

The data suggest that applying the beta version in the context of OI-Lab supported the systematic and iterative identification and analysis of opportunities to enhance aggregated NSP. Still, some members of the NSP improvement team highlighted that the systematics of the discovery phase could be further improved by implementing the possibility to clarify any ambiguous feedback shared by other network actors: *"You can't ask people. . . . I have had it a few times, where I would have liked to ask, because it was not quite clear to me what was meant by it [i.e., the failure or innovation mode shared via the Shoutbox], because I could not implement it then also for lack of information"* (EV5: Member of NSP improvement team). In order to address this issue, a function enabling actors' representatives to share contact information for respective inquiries was added to the NSPIRET Shoutbox (DC-A3.4) and a corresponding activity was added to the NSP Navigator (DC-A1.5). However, due to data privacy regulations in the context of OI-Lab, this feature could not be tested during the evaluation period.

Moreover, members of the NSP improvement team repeatedly stressed that the intervention phase suffered from organizational deficiencies. Repeatedly, interventions addressing the prioritized failure and innovation modes were prevented by limited resources and decision-making powers of the NSP improvement team: *"You can definitely recognize potentials [for improving aggregated NSP] very well. . . . [However] the person who works on it must have the resources and the authority to make any decision. . . . [I got much feedback] that I just can't solve. That's why this intervention step is a little bit frustrating for me"* (EV5: Member of NSP improvement team). In this regard, it was highlighted that there was a lack of regular intervention-related coordination among the team members and other responsible decision makers of the focal provider. This led to temporal delays and not following up on prioritized failure and innovation modes throughout the intervention phase. In order to address this issue, the NSPIRET Navigator was modified for future applications. To ensure a timely exchange of information and rapid decision-making about resource investments, it is proposed to establish intervention-related coordination institutions (e.g., regular coordinative meetings, roles) during the intervention phase (DC-A1.6).

From a summative perspective, the findings demonstrate that throughout the eight months studied, the first objective of NSPIRET could be largely achieved. Team members stressed that the different artifacts of NSPIRET supported the systematic identification and analysis of various opportunities to enhance aggregated NSP. The second objective of NSPIRET, i.e., integrating different network actors to consider their individual perspectives on NSP, can also be regarded as mostly fulfilled. Applying the NSPRIET Shoutbox helped to overcome restrictions in time and place and integrate representatives of all network actors to share their individual perspective on how to enhance NSP. In this regard, team members were satisfied with the number of contributions by the different network actors and the respective insights generated. However, as indicated above, objective three, i.e., supporting systematic and iterative interventions to enhance aggregated NSP, was not yet fulfilled satisfactorily.

4.2.4.2 Utility of the beta version

Almost all interviewees considered pursuing the objectives of NSPIRET as valuable. Nevertheless, it was repeatedly stressed that, with respect to the first and second objective of NSPIRET, utility can be further enhanced by collecting positive feedback as well. In doing so, the NSP improvement team can not only learn about failure and innovation modes, but also gain evidence about which specific service system elements already have a positive influence on aggregated NSP. Based on this feedback, respective elements should be maintained or elaborated in the future. In this regard, a representative of the focal provider highlighted: *"It's also important for us to keep track of what's going especially well, so that we can just record it somewhere, and so that we know . . . this and that . . . how we did it was super good"* (EV4: Representative of the focal provider). Thus, the NSPIRET Navigator (DC-A1.7) as well as the NSPIRET Shoutbox (DC-A3.5) were adopted accordingly by mid-February 2018 and positive feedback was shared almost daily until the end of May 2018.

Furthermore, it was found that the feedback did not only address interactions where the focal provider was involved. Actors' representatives also shared failure and innovation modes as well as positive feedback addressing interactions with other co-providers, which were not controlled by the focal provider. In this context, it was found that utility can be enhanced by sharing this feedback with the affected co-providers to foster interventions on their behalf. In doing so, in line with the third objective of NSPIRET, interventions by the co-providers may be systematically and iteratively supported. In this regard, a team member stated: *"You can really get a lot out of it [i.e., the application of NSPIRET]. . . . There are also such things in there as 'The salmon is not well done'. . . . And a bad experience in the café [i.e., co-provider] is also transferred to us and vice versa. And these are things that become clear again and I don't think we have them in our heads. And then you just have to take something like that . . . into conversations [with the affected co-provider] (EV4: Member of NSP improvement team).* Thus, a corresponding activity was added to the intervention phase of NSPIRET in November 2017 (DC-A1.8) and respective information was shared with affected co-providers throughout the rest of the evaluation period.

Additionally, concerning the third objective of NSPIRET, it was highlighted that the beta version lacks a formal mechanism to assess the impact of interventions. In this context, it was stressed that the NSP improvement team should regularly control if intended improvements of interventions are actually realized. In this regard, the utility can be enhanced by providing evidence for the actual outcomes of an intervention as highlighted by a team member: *"You implement a lot of things now and it could be that everything is worthless and has no impact [on aggregated NSP]. . . . there should be a control mode. . . . I think if we are doing the work . . . [we should assess the impact] (EV5: Member of NSP improvement team).* Consequently, for future applications, the specification and assessment of metrics to evaluate the impact of changes on aggregated NSP were added to the intervention phase of the NSPIRET Navigator (DC-A1.9) and a corresponding functionality was implemented in the Shoutbox (DC-A3.6).

NSPIRET Snapshotting was considered valuable as it can foster a better understanding of touchpoints in the context of networked service delivery at a given time. Particularly in the context of OI-Lab this was beneficial as, so far, a structured representation of processes was missing: *"I don't think I've ever seen [OI-Lab] processes so beautifully portrayed. Because we do everything rather in an agile flow . . . without portraying it in such a structured manner . . . thus, I think it is very good" (EV5: Member of NSP improvement team).* In this context, it was discussed that utility could be further improved by digitizing NSPIRET Snapshotting and integrating it within the admin panel of the NSPIRET Shoutbox. In doing so, re-modeling could be partly automated reducing the effort for continuous application. However, as the implementation of a digitized modeling tool represents a very time-intensive undertaking, it could not be implemented in the context of this study.

Moreover, members of the NSP improvement team repeatedly highlighted that for enhancing the utility of NSPIRET, the admin panel of the NSPIRET Shoutbox should be modified. In this context, particularly the visualization of the failure and innovation modes in a rigid worksheet was criticized as it led to information overload. Thus, the screening, editing, and evaluating of failure and innovation modes was unnecessarily time-consuming. To address this issue, additional possibilities for filtering and customized display of failure and innovation modes were iteratively added until the end of April 2018 (DC-A3.7). These changes enabled team members to filter feedback according to the user type, mode, touchpoint, underlying service system element, priority, and status. All in all, these revisions were considered valuable by team members as they significantly reduced their administrative effort.

Altogether, the application of NSPIRET was considered valuable in the context of OI-Lab. The focal provider has not strived to systematically and iteratively enhance aggregated NSP. Thus, after having been applied for over three months, a member of the NSP improvement team summarized: *"I think it [i.e., applying NSPIRET] is very, very important [for us], I really have to say that I think it is a pity that we only have applied it so late, as you can use it for very, very much to become better, and I also think that it is something that has to be . . . [utilized] in the future"* (EV4: Member of NSP improvement team).

4.2.4.3   Understandability of the beta version

Members of the NSP improvement team could comprehend the function, content, and interrelations of the NSPIRET Navigator, NSPIRET Snapshotting, and NSPIRET Shoutbox after receiving a personal briefing. However, in this regard, team members highlighted that they had to get used to the terms embedded in the different artifacts and the procedures prescribed. Related information was provided throughout the briefing and an accompanying manual. However, it was stressed that the latter was not always used when working with respective artifacts. For instance, with respect to using NSPIRET Shoutbox in daily operations, a member of the NSP improvement team indicated: *"Honestly, I have read it [i.e., the manual] but the problem is, I am someone who when I do it [i.e., using the admin panel] then I do not look into it again. When you have read it four weeks ago, you do not know it anymore"* (EV4: Member of NSP improvement team). Thus, related information was added directly within the admin panel of the NSPIRET

Shoutbox to foster understanding and decision making (DC-A3.8). Whereas this design change was considered positive, for future applications, team members also stressed that they would prefer a more interactive knowledge transfer, e.g., via dedicated workshops or videos. Additionally, with respect to NSPIRET Snapshotting, it could be observed that understandability for team members can be further enhanced when using a coherent color coding for the different service system elements applied. Thus, for future applications, the description of each service system element applied is complemented by colored rectangles signaling the different network actors contributing respective resources (DC-A2.3).

For providing feedback, representatives of the different network actors only interacted with the NSPIRET Shoutbox and most stressed that the content of the NPIRET Shoutbox was largely self-explanatory. However, team members and representatives stressed that user guidance could be further enhanced by using more symbols within the tool. Moreover, several representatives faced difficulties in distinguishing between failure and innovation modes based on the respective dialogue within the NSPIRET Shoutbox and thus the wording was reconsidered. *"Why do you differentiate between problem [i.e., failure mode] and suggestion for improvement [i.e., innovation mode]? . . . For me, it was a little bit tricky . . . a suggestion for improvement obviously is based on a problem. I thought problem – I do not have a solution, suggestion for improvement – I do have a solution. However, this is a little confusing"* (EV4: Representative of a customer). Similarly, it could be observed that actors' representatives repeatedly were confused by the option to select categories for describing the source of the respective failure or innovation mode identified. In order to address the identified pitfall and improve understandability, more symbols were implemented into the NSPIRET Shoutbox and instead of asking for a "suggestion for improvement", it is asked for a creative "idea for further development of OI-Lab". Moreover, the option to select categories was removed (DC-A3.9). Both team members and representatives stressed that these changes foster a better understanding of the NSPIRET Shoutbox.

All in all, the data suggest that the function and content of the different artifacts of NSPRIET were generally understandable. However, for the members of the NSP improvement team, receiving a proper briefing was considered vital to get acquainted with the different technical terms and concepts adopted by NSPIRET.

4.2.4.4   Operational feasibility of the beta version

As highlighted above, operational feasibility has not been evaluated for the alpha version. It presents the degree to which team members and representatives of the different network actors support the artifacts of NSPIRET, operate them, and integrate them into their daily practice (Prat et al., 2015). The data suggest that operational feasibility depends on how much value is attributed to NSPIRET by individual team members and representatives in comparison to other activities. In this regard, several members of the NSP improvement team highlighted that activities conducted in the context of NSPIRET were considered extra work that was not as highly prioritized as their regular tasks. Against this backdrop, it was stressed that operational feasibility could be enhanced if the initiative is supported continuously and visibly by management. In this regard, it was also highlighted that management should appoint a team member to drive the initiative, i.e., somebody who takes accountability for deliverables and regularly motivates other team members: *"I think this really needs someone who is really pushy and says 'hey guys, look, we have already achieved this and that is why we need you to take it further" (EV5: Member of NSP improvement team).* Thus, for future applications, a corresponding activity was added to the facilitation phase of the NSPIRET Navigator (DC-A1.10).

Representatives of the different network actors indicated their willingness to also share identified failure and innovation modes in the future as the temporal and cognitive effort for utilizing the NSPIRET Shoutbox was considered reasonable. However, in this regard, representatives repeatedly highlighted that they would wish to be informed about the impact of their contributions as for them, long-term support depends on knowing that their feedback is actually considered by the NSP improvement team: *"[I think] one would also have to make it transparent that somebody is looking at it [i.e., the feedback] and what is happening with it. . . . I don't write that in there just to have written it in, but that I also know, yes okay something is done with it" (EV4: Representative of the focal provider).* Thus, for future applications, during the intervention phase, team members should regularly communicate the effects of the feedback provided (DC-A1.11).

Moreover, a few of the representatives stressed that for them, operational feasibility is strongly dependent on the possibility to provide feedback anonymously, particularly when it addresses sensitive topics or personal criticism. Whereas for representatives using the stationary feedback tablet at OI-Lab it was possible to anonymously share failure and innovation modes right from the beginning, representatives of customers initially had to use a dedicated log-in. Against this backdrop, a respondent stressed that to foster utilization and honest feedback, the NSPIRET Shoutbox should be modified: *"It really would have to be anonymized. . . . I normally really would not do it when I am logged-in. Of course, it could be anonymized as well, but one is maybe not so sure about that . . . and if you want to receive direct, honest feedback, I think, it somehow has to work without any log-in at all"* (E5: Representative of customers). Thus, the DNSP Shoutbox was modified to enable all representatives to give feedback without having to be logged-in (DC-A3.10).

From a summative perspective, it was found that for network actors' representatives, operational feasibility was strongly influenced by perceptions concerning the possibility, relevance, and impact of providing feedback. In this regard, most representatives highlighted that they would continue to share failure and innovation modes in case they perceived them as relevant and had the perception that their feedback is actually used to improve networked service delivery. From the point of view of the team members, NSPIRET was not fully established in the eight months of demonstration. Whereas some members regularly conducted the respective activities expected of them, others only engaged after receiving a reminder. In this context, a team member pointed out: *"And for me, for the implementation, . . . a fixed date [is important] which I have to set myself. This is in fact also self-regulation and self-discipline"* (EV5: Member of the NSP improvement team).

4.2.5   Summary of design changes and revised beta version of NSPRIET

Table 26 summarizes the design changes to the artifacts of the beta version. The revised activities of the NSPIRET Navigator are depicted in Table 27. An excerpt of a color-coded Snapshot is presented in Figure 35. Modifications to the NSPIRET Shoutbox are illustrated by exemplary screenshots depicted in Figures 36, 37, and 38. Subsequently, Chapter 5 discusses the findings of the DSR study.

Table 26: Design changes to the beta version of NSPIRET.

Artifact	Design changes
	DC-A1.5: Network actors' representatives can share contact during discovery phase to answer questions about their feedback to enhance *effectiveness*
	DC-A1.6: Establishment of intervention-related coordination institutions to enhance *effectiveness*
	DC-A1.7: Representatives can share positive feedback during discovery phase to enhance *utility*
NSPIRET Navigator	DC-A1.8: Team members share feedback with affected co-providers during intervention phase to enhance *utility*
	DC-A1.9: Team members specify and assess metrics to control effects of changes during intervention phase to enhance *utility*
	DC-A1.10: Appointment of team member during the facilitation phase to drive the NSPIRET initiative to enhance *operational feasibility*
	DC-A1.11: Communication of effects of feedback during the intervention phase to enhance *operational feasibility*
NSPIRET Snapshotting	DC-A2.3: Coherent color coding of service system elements to enhance *understandability*
	DC-A3.4: Functionality to share contact address to the NSPIRET Shoutbox to enhance *effectiveness*
	DC-A3.5: Functionality to share positive feedback to enhance *utility*
	DC-A3.6: Functionality to add metrics for assessing effect of interventions to enhance *utility*
NSPIRET Shoutbox	DC-A3.7: Functionality to sort/filter feedback according to date, priority, mode, user type, status, touchpoint, and service system element to enhance *utility*
	DC-A3.8: Functionality to display relevant procedures in admin panel to enhance *understandability*
	DC-A3.9: Adaptations in design and wording to enhance *understandability*
	DC-A3.10: Functionality to share failure modes, innovation modes, and positive feedback anonymously to enhance *operational feasibility*

Table 27: Activities of the revised beta version of the NSPIRET Navigator.

Process phase	Activities
Facilitation	F1: NSP improvement team is set-up in accordance with decision makers of the focal provider and objectives, responsibilities, and procedures are clarified
	F2: Team members regularly motivate network actors to contribute
	F3: Team members operate and distribute the NSPIRET Shoutbox
	F4*: Decision makers continuously support the initiative and ensure that team members possess adequate resources and decision-making powers
(Re-)Modeling	M1: Team members collect data/use insights and apply NSPIRET Snapshotting to (re-)model the customer journey as a series of touchpoints
	M2: Team members collect data/use insights and apply NSPIRET Snapshotting to (re-)model the service system for each touchpoint
	M3: Team members collect data/use insights and apply NSPIRET Snapshotting to depict expected benefits for each network actor
Discovery	D1*: Network actors' representatives use the NSPIRET Shoutbox to share failure and innovation modes as well as positive feedback for each touchpoint
	D2*: Network actors' representatives share contact data if they are willing to provide further information and want to learn about interventions
	D3*: Team members use the NSPIRET Shoutbox to share failure modes, innovation modes and positive feedback verbally expressed
	D4: Team members use the NSPIRET Shoutbox to review, clarify, edit, and prioritize contributions
Intervention	I1*: Team members collaboratively plan and coordinate interventions considering expected effects on aggregated NSP together with decision makers
	I2: Team members initiate re-modeling and intervene according to specified responsibilities and procedures
	I3*: Team members share relevant feedback requiring external interventions with affected co-providers
	I4: Team members record intervention-related activities within the NSPIRET Shoutbox
	I5*: Team members specify and assess metrics to control effects of changes
	I6*: Team members communicate effects of feedback with network actors' representatives

*New/modified activities based on the evaluation of the beta version

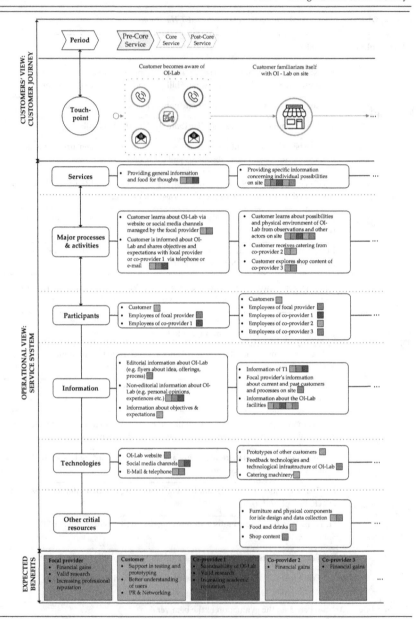

Figure 35: *Excerpt of color-coded NSIPRET Snapshot in the context of OI-Lab. Own illustration.*

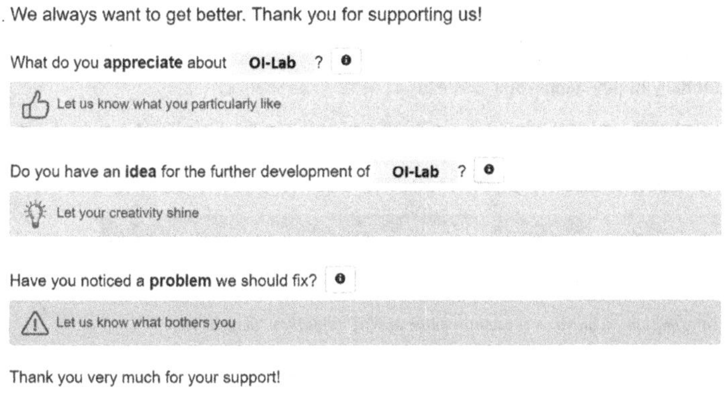

. We always want to get better. Thank you for supporting us!

What do you **appreciate** about   **OI-Lab**   ?   ❶

👍 Let us know what you particularly like

Do you have an **idea** for the further development of   **OI-Lab**   ?   ❶

💡 Let your creativity shine

Have you noticed a **problem** we should fix?   ❶

⚠ Let us know what bothers you

Thank you very much for your support!

Figure 36: Revised design of landing page for actors' representatives. Screenshot (anonymized).

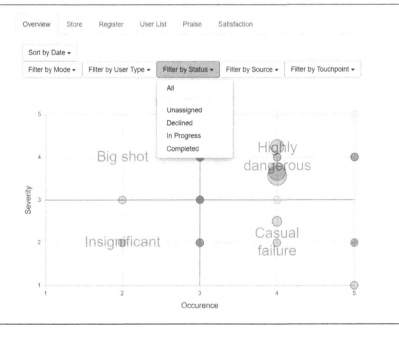

Figure 37: Sorting and filtering mechanisms in the admin panel of the NSPIRET Shoutbox. Screenshot.

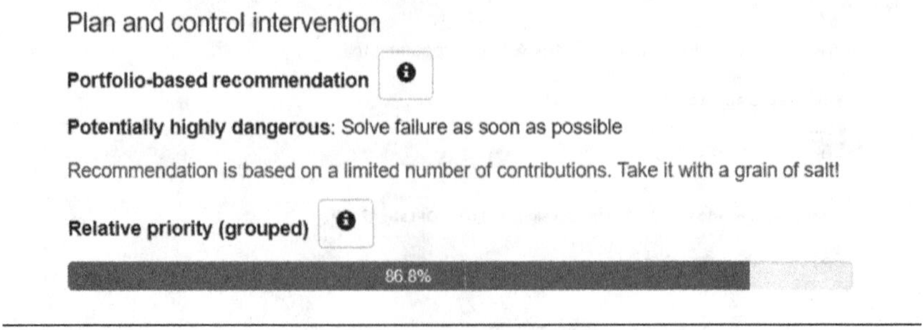

Plan and control intervention

Portfolio-based recommendation   ❸

Potentially highly dangerous: Solve failure as soon as possible

Recommendation is based on a limited number of contributions. Take it with a grain of salt!

Relative priority (grouped)   ❸

86.8%

Figure 38: *Information included in the admin panel of NSP Shoutbox. Screenshot.*

5   Discussion

 This chapter discusses the theoretical contributions and practical implications of the DSR study before highlighting the implications for the dissertation. Limitations and avenues for future research are presented in Part VI.

5.1   Theoretical contributions

Building on the findings of Part III and Part IV, the DSR study answers the third research question of this dissertation: *how can a focal provider systematically and iteratively discover and seize opportunities to enhance networked service productivity for itself, customers, and relevant co-providers?* This research question is answered by iteratively developing and evaluating an alpha and beta version of a new interdisciplinary productivity improvement technique called NSPIRET. According to the DSR contribution framework of Gregor & Hevner (2013), NSPIRET provides a theoretical contribution in the form of an exaptation. The technique synthesizes existing solutions to solve a new problem, i.e., exploring and seizing opportunities to enhance NSP for all relevant actors contributing resources to networked service delivery. Taking into account the increasing relevance of connected service offerings that require collective performance of different actors for sustained operational success (Gummesson, 2007; Hillebrand et al., 2015; Verleye et al., 2017), addressing this problem is considered critical.

NSPIRET contributes to literature by addressing the lack of practical approaches following an integration strategy and aiming to enhance productivity for the focal provider, customers, and co-providers throughout the overall service productivity life cycle. For this purpose, NSPRIET builds upon and extends CJML (Halvorsrud, Kvale, et al., 2016), WSS (Alter, 2006), and the FMEA-based portfolio approach for service productivity improvement (Geum, Shin, et al., 2011). Being rooted in the disciplines of service design, information systems, and engineering, so far, despite their complementary characteristics, respective approaches have been used in isolation. NSPIRET demonstrates that these approaches can be conceptually and operationally integrated and applied for real world improvements of aggregated NSP. Harnessing the classification scheme for productivity improvement approaches (see Chapter 2 of

Part III), on a high-level, NSPIRET can be positioned in comparison to the other integration approaches identified in the literature review as presented in Figure 39.

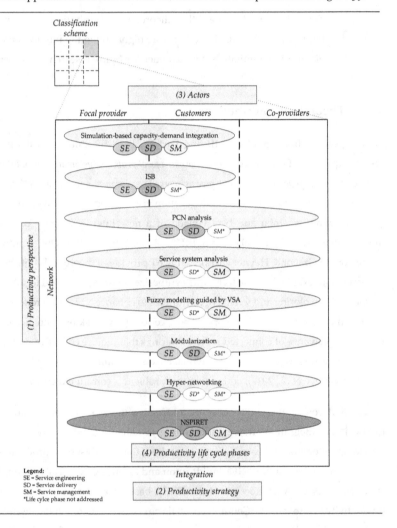

Figure 39: *Positioning of NSPIRET in comparison to other integration approaches presented in Part III of this dissertation. Own illustration.*

NSPIRET fosters the enhancement of aggregated NSP by systematically and iteratively (re)modeling networked service delivery, identifying and analyzing failure and innovation modes from the perspective of the different network actors, and intervening accordingly. In doing so, it informs all phases of the overall service productivity life cycle. NSPIRET provides a conceptual structure and contains operational means to analyze and (re-)engineer touchpoints and underlying service systems harnessing productivity-related indicators. In this context, a new web-based tool, the NSPIRET Shoutbox, was instantiated in order to facilitate the integration of the different network actors into the process of improving aggregated NSP. In doing so, the NSPIRET Shoutbox fosters the identification and analysis of opportunities for driving NSP throughout actual service delivery from their individual perspectives. Besides that, the tool structures the planning and control of interventions based on the evidence derived informing the service management phase of the service productivity life cycle. Overall, this study adds to the diversity of design science in the field of service research (e.g., Beloglazov, Banerjee, Hartman, & Buyya, 2015; Teixeira et al., 2017). As summarized in Table 28, each artifact presents constructive knowledge and thus contributes to nascent theory for design and action (Gregor, 2006).

Table 28: Theoretical contributions for design and action.

Artifact	Theoretical contributions
NSPIRET Navigator	The conceptual structure and process present a guideline on how to systematically harness interdisciplinary concepts and tools for identifying and analyzing opportunities to enhance aggregated NSP and intervene accordingly
NSPIRET Snapshotting	The modeling approach provides a systematic way of how to depict networked service delivery from the focal providers', customers' and co-providers' perspective
NSPIRET Shoutbox	The web-based feedback tool presents an instantiation enabling the integration of different network actors into the identification and analysis of opportunities for improving service productivity from their perspective

For the service research discipline, the paper addresses the call for using DSR in order to evolve system engineering approaches (Ostrom et al., 2015; Teixeira et al., 2017). The proposed technique presents a novel way how to systematically model, analyze, and intervene in networked service delivery with the goal to enhance NSP for the focal provider, customers, and relevant co-providers. In doing so, NSPIRET is in tune with the contemporary understanding of service productivity as it focuses on actors' subjective perceptions in terms of both efficiency and effectiveness dimensions (Yalley & Sekhon, 2014). It contributes to a formalized improvement process that takes into consideration the complexity of networked service delivery. Thus, it can be considered superior to ad-hoc changes based on a limited operational view often found in service practice (Halvorsrud, Kvale, et al., 2016; Shostack, 1984).

Furthermore, this study contributes to the field of service design by proposing a modeling approach that can help to visualize expected interactions in the context of any dyadic or networked service delivery process from both the customer's as well as the (co-)providers' point of view. In doing so, customer journey analysis (Halvorsrud, Kvale, et al., 2016) as well as related mobile ethnographic studies (e.g. Stickdorn, Frischhut, & Schmid, 2014) can be complemented by integrating an operational perspective. This can support the comparison of expected service interactions with actual interactions to identify deviation patterns concerning touchpoints and required service systems. Integrating both perspectives may foster a more detailed understanding of the status quo and thus support the systematic analysis and planning of changes to service delivery over time.

5.2   Implications for practitioners

The findings of this study are relevant to service engineers, designers, as well as managers of a focal service provider. For them, the revised beta version of NSPIRET provides a first step towards systematically and iteratively improving NSP for their own organization, customers and relevant co-providers. It provides an operationalized systematic that is theoretically anchored and was developed harnessing insights derived in two empirical settings. Based on the evaluation results, it can be assumed that the application of the revised beta version of NSPIRET has the potential to portray effectiveness, utility, understandability, and operational feasibility in other practical settings. It proposes to iteratively improve aggregated NSP by modeling the current situation of networked service delivery, collaboratively identifying and analyzing failure and innovation modes, remodeling the situation, and intervening accordingly. In doing so it addresses all phases of the service productivity life cycle in real-world situations of networked service delivery as illustrated in Table 29.

Table 29: Practical implications of the artifacts throughout the service productivity life cycle.

Artifact	Service engineering	Service delivery	Service management
NSPIRET Navigator	Proposes activities guiding the (re-)modeling of networked service delivery and interventions	Proposes activities guiding the discovery of opportunities to enhance aggregated NSP throughout networked service delivery	Proposes activities guiding the managerial facilitation of improving aggregated NSP
NSPIRET Snapshotting	Provides a representation of networked service delivery as a series of touchpoints and underlying service systems	Provides a blueprint of networked service at a given time	Provides elements to locate and quantify sources of failure and innovation modes
NSPIRET Shoutbox	Fosters insights concerning network actors' individual perceptions of NSP and opportunities for improvements; structures and documents intervention	Can be applied to integrate network actors throughout actual service delivery independent from temporal and spatial restrictions	Depicts indicators and portfolios supporting managerial decision making

The NSPIRET Navigator supports practitioners throughout the service engineering and service delivery phase by proposing activities guiding the (re-)modeling of networked service delivery, the discovery of opportunities to enhance aggregated NSP, and implementing change. Moreover, it supports the service management phase by comprising activities ensuring managerial support of the initiative. NSPIRET Snapshotting supports service engineering by enabling a structured representation of networked service delivery. These models can be used as a blueprint for realizing interactions throughout the service delivery phase and provide elements to locate and quantify sources of failure and innovation modes. Finally, the NSPIRET Shoutbox informs the service engineering phase by fostering insights concerning opportunities for improving aggregated NSP. Moreover, it structures and documents interventions. Furthermore, it can be applied for the time and location independent integration of network actors throughout the service delivery phase and informs service management by depicting indicators and portfolios fostering rational decision making.

Continuously applying NSPIRET may not only assist a focal provider in improving aggregated NSP, but may also support the building of strong ties with both customers and co-providers. Collaborating in the context of NSPIRET may support actors to familiarize with each other and learn about their individual conditions of network membership. Harnessing these insights, the focal provider may be able to take over a central role for the mutual evolution of network members and foster competitive advantages in the future (Tax et al, 2013).

5.3   Implications for the remainder of this dissertation

All in all, the DSR study contributes to the overall objective of this dissertation by iteratively developing the revised beta version of NSPIRET. The development and design build on the conceptual foundations presented in Part II and harness the results of the systematic literature review of Part III as well as the findings of the exploratory case study of Part IV. The findings of the evaluation of NSPIRET inform the development of design principles as summarized in Table 30. In Part VI, the resulting principles are explicated in detail.

Table 30: Summary of implications for the remainder of this dissertation.

Insights	Implications for this dissertation
Network actors have to be willing to contribute, require experience with networked service delivery and have to understand activities and supporting tools to share relevant failure and innovation modes	Part VI: Importance of activities and means to demonstrate value of contributions and foster understanding and anonymity; experience, perceived value and understandability as boundary conditions
Some network actors provide unclear descriptions of failure and innovation modes	Part VI: Importance to include activities and means to clarify productivity-related feedback; willingness to share contact information as boundary condition
NSP improvement team requires coordination, resources, and authority for interventions; application of NSPIRET presents extra work for team members in daily operations	Part VI: Importance to establish coordination institutions and IT-support of analysis activities; continuous managerial support and resource provision as boundary conditions
Beta version of NSPIRET lacked formal control of impact of interventions	Part VI: Importance to consider activities and means to control actual impact of interventions; access to appropriate qualitative and quantitative data as boundary condition

Part VI

Reflections and conclusion:

Driving networked service productivity

© Springer Fachmedien Wiesbaden GmbH, part of Springer Nature 2020
C. F. Daiberl, *Driving Networked Service Productivity*, Markt- und
Unternehmensentwicklung Markets and Organisations,
https://doi.org/10.1007/978-3-658-29580-6_6

1 Objectives and structure

 This dissertation explores *how a focal provider can drive productivity in the context of networked service delivery*. Part VI of this dissertation support this goal by summarizing what has been established so far, reflecting on these findings, and developing design principles. Moreover, it depicts limitations and directions for future research and concludes the dissertation.

As illustrated in Figure 39, the remainder of Part VI is organized as follows: Chapter 2 briefly summarizes the previous parts of this dissertation. Afterward, Chapter 3 reflects on the findings of this dissertation in order to develop design principles for the creation of new approaches supporting the systematic enhancement of aggregated NSP in other contexts. Chapter 4 delineates limitations of the scientific investigations presented and derives directions for future research. Finally, Chapter 5 concludes this dissertation by presenting final notes about driving NSP.

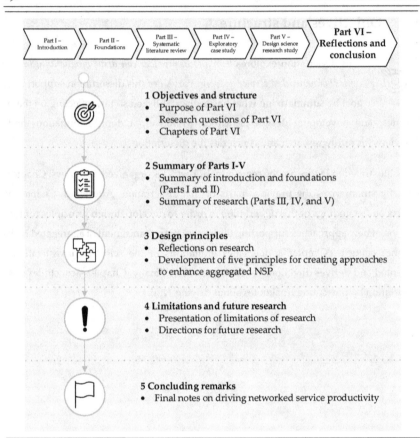

Part I – Introduction   Part II – Foundations   Part III – Systematic literature review   Part IV – Exploratory case study   Part V – Design science research study   **Part VI – Reflections and conclusion**

1 Objectives and structure
- Purpose of Part VI
- Research questions of Part VI
- Chapters of Part VI

2 Summary of Parts I-V
- Summary of introduction and foundations (Parts I and II)
- Summary of research (Parts III, IV, and V)

3 Design principles
- Reflections on research
- Development of five principles for creating approaches to enhance aggregated NSP

4 Limitations and future research
- Presentation of limitations of research
- Directions for future research

5 Concluding remarks
- Final notes on driving networked service productivity

Figure 40: Structure of Part VI. Own illustration.

2   Summary of Parts I-V

 This chapter briefly summarizes Parts I-V. Thus, it serves as a reminder of what has been established so far. In doing so, it can also be considered as an executive summary of the overall research project.

2.1   Summary of Part I

Initially, Chapter 1 highlighted the scholarly and managerial importance of driving service productivity. It was stressed that, from an economic perspective, improving productivity is critical for future growth and prosperity. From an organizational perspective, it was established that managing service productivity is vital for operational success and perceived as increasingly relevant by decision makers from both service and industrial organizations (Klingner et al., 2015). However, due to conceptual difficulties as well as the influence of customers and co-providers on service interactions, it was established that driving service productivity is a complex challenge. Moreover, it was depicted that due to technological progress and increasing specialization, contemporary services are often delivered by a network of providers (Tax et al., 2013). In this realm, it was highlighted that actors depend on each other for delivering efficient and effective services. Thus, it was stressed that a key challenge for scholars and practitioners is to understand *how a focal service provider can drive productivity in the context of networked service delivery*. Addressing this overall objective, Chapter 2 depicted the following research questions:

RQ1: Which systematic approaches are discussed in service research for the improvement of service productivity from a network perspective and what are their application-oriented qualities?

RQ2: How can networked service productivity be conceptualized and what are its drivers and related resistances?

RQ3: How can a focal provider systematically and iteratively discover and seize opportunities to enhance networked service productivity for itself, customers, and relevant co-providers?

Next, Chapter 3 introduced the overall research design and Chapter 4 summarized the structure of this dissertation.

2.2   Summary of Part II

Part II presented relevant theoretical foundations of this dissertation. Chapter 1 summarized the objectives and structure of Part II. Afterward, Chapter 2 introduced the concept of service by presenting different scholarly understandings. It was established that this dissertation follows the unified services theory that considers services as a process of productive activities relying on customer inputs (Sampson, 2010; Sampson & Froehle, 2006). Next, Chapter 3, scrutinized the concept of service productivity and presented considerations for its improvement. Concerning the former, it was stressed that the concept has evolved from a mere focus on operational efficiency to integrate both efficiency and effectiveness considerations (Grönroos & Ojasalo, 2004; Yalley & Sekhon, 2014). Moreover, different conceptual models of service productivity were compared reflecting the evolution of the theoretical understanding. In doing so, it was stressed that existing models neglect the networked nature of contemporary service interactions. Next, different types of service productivity improvement approaches were introduced. In this regard, it was stressed that tools are the least complex approaches followed by techniques, systems, and strategic approaches (van der Wiele et al., 2006). Afterward, it was established that each approach is in line with a particular service productivity strategy (Djellal & Gallouj, 2013) and can be applied throughout one or more phases of the service productivity life cycle (Janeschek et al., 2013).

Chapter 4 presented this dissertation's understanding of networked service delivery. For this purpose, first, network-related concepts in service research were introduced. It was highlighted that according to network theory, a network represents a set of nodes (e.g., actors) that are linked by ties (e.g., interactions) enabling or preventing some kind of flow (e.g., information, money, goods) (Borgatti & Foster, 2003; Borgatti & Halgin, 2011). Building on that understanding, the concept of the service delivery network was presented that informs the theoretical understanding of this dissertation. It was established that the service delivery network is defined as two or more actors that, from the perspective of the customer, are responsible for delivering a connected, overall service (Tax et al., 2013). The concept builds on the customer experience approach, focusing on the customer journey (Zomerdijk & Voss, 2010) that can be separated into pre-core service, core service, and post-core service periods (Voorhees et al., 2017). It was argued that applying such a network perspective sheds light on various operational and relational issues that otherwise would remain unconsidered. For instance, it stresses the importance of planning processes relying on external inputs from the focal provider, customers, and co-providers and coordinating among these actors throughout service delivery. Finally, Chapter 5 summarized and synthesized the key concepts introduced to establish a coherent understanding applied throughout the following parts.

2.3   Summary of Part III

Part III presented a systematic literature review focusing on approaches for enhancing service productivity from a network perspective. Chapter 1 introduced the objectives and structure of the review. It was highlighted that the review addresses the lack of an integrated understanding of how to improve productivity in the context of networked service delivery. In doing so, it answers the first research question of this dissertation depicted above.

Building on the theoretical foundations presented in Part II, Chapter 2 developed a theory-based classification scheme in order to guide analysis and structure the findings of the systematic literature review. The scheme distinguishes approaches for improving service productivity according to the productivity perspective, productivity strategy as well as the actors and the service productivity life cycle phases affected.

Chapter 3 presented the review procedure applied. It followed the process of Tranfield et al. (2003) and harnessed the advice of Webster and Watson (2002) as well as Wickham and Woods (2005). The review focused on leading service journals as well as general management and operations oriented journals. Moreover, the productivity toolbox of the funding priority "productivity of services" of the German Ministry of Education and Research was investigated. In doing so, all in all, 18 approaches presented in 19 core contributions as well as 62 related contributions were identified. The analysis of identified approaches was conducted using the software tool MAXQDA 12.

Chapter 4 presented the findings of the descriptive and thematic analysis. It was found that scholars from different disciplines such as engineering, marketing, information systems as well as operations research have proposed relevant approaches that can inspire productivity improvements in the context of networked service delivery. It was established that there exist several efficiency- and effectiveness-focused approaches that provide operational guidelines and demonstrate promising empirical evaluation results. However, it was found that that there is a lack of practical approaches that focus on enhancing efficiency and effectiveness for all relevant actors contributing resources to a connected, overall service. Moreover, it substantiated the need for a coherent conceptual understanding of productivity in the context of networked service delivery. Finally, Chapter 5 discussed the findings of the review. It depicts theoretical contributions, practical implications, and implications for the remainder of this dissertation. A summary of the main aspects of the systematic literature review is presented in Table 31.

Table 31: Summary of the systematic literature review.

Aspect	Description
Research need	Lack of an integrated understanding of approaches for systematically improving service productivity in the context of networked service delivery
Research questions	Which systematic approaches are discussed in service research for the improvement of service productivity from a network perspective and what are their application-oriented qualities?
Theoretical underpinning	Literature on service productivity, improving service productivity, and networked service delivery as presented in Part II
Research method	Systematic literature review
Data collection and analysis	Review in 12 leading service journals; 8 operations and general management-oriented journals; service productivity toolbox of the funding priority "productivity of services" Descriptive and thematic analysis using MAXQDA 12
Findings	Multi-criteria classification scheme Identification of 19 core contributions and 62 related contributions proposing 18 approaches for enhancing service productivity from a network perspective Description of 19 core contributions Classification of 18 approaches and overview of application-oriented qualities
Theoretical contributions	Novel classification scheme fosters high-level analysis of existing and new approaches for improving service productivity Discovery that there is a lack of practical approaches that are in line with an integration strategy and aim to enhance service productivity for the focal provider, customers, and relevant co-providers Substantiates the need for a coherent conceptual model of productivity in the context of networked service delivery
Implications for practitioners	Findings can support practitioners to reflect on their own initiatives for driving service productivity The identified approaches can serve as an evidence-informed and actionable knowledge base potentially relevant for different contexts of networked service delivery
Implications for this dissertation	Substantiates the need for establishing a coherent conceptual understanding of service productivity in the context of networked service delivery (Part IV) Depicts the need for practical approaches that integrate efficiency and effectiveness considerations for all relevant network actors (Part V) Informs the development of design principles (Part VI)

2.4   Summary of Part IV

Part IV presented an exploratory case study focusing on the content, drivers, and related resistances of productivity in the context of networked service delivery. Chapter 1 introduced the objective and structure of the study. It was argued that existing conceptual models do not account for situations when multiple providers contribute to overall service delivery. To address this research gap, the case study builds on the theoretical foundations presented in Part II and answers the second research question.

Chapter 2 described the research method as well as the procedure of data collection and analysis. The exploratory case study investigated productivity-related perceptions of network actors in two operationally different, but particularly revelatory settings of networked service delivery. Thus, it can be considered a multiple, embedded case design (Yin, 2014). In both case settings, themes and patterns were identified using abductive reasoning (Ketokivi & Choi, 2014). Replication of results across both case settings should improve the confidence in the emerging theoretical insights (Miles et al., 2013; Yin, 2014). Next, the two empirical settings were introduced: eMobilizer, a non-profit digital service and OI-Lab, a for-profit, professional research and development service. Data collection resembled a systematic combining approach (Dubois & Gadde, 2002) and included semi-structured interviews, group discussions, observations as well as a compilation of reports and social media postings. Analysis followed a template (King, 2004) using the software tool MAXQDA 12.

Chapter 3 presented the results. It was established that NSP represents a subjective, dynamic, and multi-level phenomenon. On the individual level, NSP addresses an actor's satisfaction with the perceived effects of networked service delivery at a given time considering its resource contributions for reaching these effects. These perceptions influence aggregated NSP, i.e., the collective perceptions of two or more network actors. Perceptions originate in actors' conditions of network membership comprising their service-related attributes and service-specific expectations. Moreover, five interrelated drivers for enhancing aggregated NSP were identified: (1) *Compatible conditions of network membership,* (2) *commitment to networked service delivery,* (3) *network-oriented coordination,* (4) *network-oriented processes & surrogates,* and (5) *mutual learning among network actors*. It is proposed that managing these drivers may help to overcome twelve related resistances. Chapter 4 discussed the findings of the case study. Relevant aspects of the case study are summarized in Table 32.

Table 32: Summary of the exploratory case study.

Aspect	Description
Presented in	Part IV
Research need	Lack of conceptual understanding regarding service productivity in the context of networked service delivery
Research question	How can networked service productivity be conceptualized and what are its drivers and related resistances?
Theoretical background	Literature on service productivity, improving service productivity, and networked service delivery as presented in Part II
Method	Exploratory case study following a multiple, embedded case design
Data collection and analysis	Data collected in two empirical settings (eMobilizer and OI-Lab) by means of interviews, group discussions, observations and compilation of regular reports and social media postings
	Template analysis using MAXQDA 12
Findings	Conceptual model of NSP depicting factors and relationships of productivity in the context of networked service delivery
	Highlights that for sustained operational success of networked service delivery, NSP should be considered for all relevant network actors
	Identifies five interrelated drivers of aggregated NSP and twelve related resistances
Theoretical contributions	Novel conceptual model is argued to better capture the particularities of contemporary service delivery than monadic or dyadic models
	Widens the concept of service productivity and proposes theoretical relationships for enhancing aggregated NSP
Implications for practitioners	New lens for a more holistic productivity management
	Managerial questions and related indicators may support the enhancement of aggregated NSP in organizational practice
Implications for this dissertation	Informs objectives of the DSR study (Part V)
	Informs the development of design principles (Part VI)

2.5   Summary of Part V

Part V presented a DSR study proposing NSPIRET – the networked service productivity improvement technique. Chapter 1 introduced the objectives as well as the structure of this study. It was highlighted that the development of NSPIRET addresses the lack of practical approaches for enhancing service productivity for the relevant actors contributing resources to networked service delivery. In doing so, it answered the third research question of this dissertation.

Chapter 2 presented the theoretical background for design. It was highlighted that the theoretical foundations were selected in line with the analysis-synthesis bridge model (Dubberly et al., 2008). According to this model, first, the current situation should be investigated before a preferred future is depicted. For this purpose, different approaches for (re-)modeling networked service delivery were introduced. In this regard, CJML was portrayed as a formal approach to depict service delivery as a series of touchpoints between the customer and one or more co-providers (Halvorsrud, Kvale, et al., 2016). Moreover, WSS was presented as a complementary tool to depict the operational resources required for realizing respective touchpoints (Alter, 2013b). Finally, FMEA-based portfolio approach to productivity improvement was presented (Geum, Shin, et al., 2011). It was argued that this technique might foster the model-based analysis of opportunities for improving aggregated NSP.

Chapter 3 introduced the research method and data. First, relevant background about DSR was shared (Hevner et al., 2004; Peffers et al., 2007). Afterward, the different phases of the particular DSR process applied were elucidated. In this context, it was highlighted that the current design of NSPIRET is the result of two iterations of development and evaluation in the empirical settings introduced in Part IV of this dissertation. Evaluation followed a human risk and effectiveness strategy (Venable et al., 2016). The alpha version of NSPIRET was evaluated in a pre-study in the context of eMobilizer to assess the initial ideas. For this purpose, observations and interviews with representatives of co-providers were conducted followed by event-contingent self-recoding of customers (Wheeler & Reis, 1991). The evaluation findings of the alpha version were applied to develop the beta version, which was assessed by carrying out a case study in the context of OI-Lab. It included a series of interviews with representatives of the focal provider, customers, and co-providers as well as analysis of documentations and observations on site. The collected data was analyzed using the software tool MAXQDA 12.

Chapter 4 presented the design of the alpha and beta version of NSPIRET as well as the respective evaluation results leading to the revised beta version. The alpha version consisted of an aggregated NSP improvement process integrating network actors by means of a workshop, a WSS-based modeling approach, and a paper-based feedback tool for depicting failure and innovation modes. The evaluation results indicated the necessity of significant design changes to enhance effectiveness, utility, and understandability. Building on these results, the beta version included an iterative improvement process harnessing feedback from individual representatives of the different network actors, a modeling approach integrating CJML and WSS, and a web-based feedback tool. The evaluation findings highlighted that the beta version was partly effective and its utility and understandability was mostly perceived as high. However, throughout the evaluation period, operational feasibility could only partly be established in daily operations of OI-Lab. To address the issues identified, a revised beta version was proposed, which is subject to future evaluation activities. Chapter 5 discussed the theoretical contributions as well as the implications for practitioners and the remainder of this dissertation. Table 33 summarizes key insights in this respect. Having presented a brief summary of the previous parts of this dissertation, the following chapter reflects on the findings and derives a set of design principles.

Table 33: Summary of the DSR study.

Aspect	Description
Presented in	Part V
Research need	Lack of practical approaches that are in line with an integration strategy and aim to enhance service productivity for the different actors contributing resources to networked service delivery
Research question	How can a focal provider systematically and iteratively discover and seize opportunities to enhance networked service productivity for itself, customers, and relevant co-providers?
Theoretical background	Fundamental concepts presented in Part II Contributions from service design (i.e., CJML), information systems (i.e., WSS), and engineering (i.e., FMEA-based portfolio approach for productivity improvement
Method	Design science research
Data collection and analysis	Data collected in two cases: eMobilizer (non-profit, digital service) and OI-Lab (for-profit R&D service) by means of interviews, observations, and event-contingent self-recording Template analysis using MAXQDA 12
Findings	Design and evaluation of alpha and beta version of NSPIRET Design of revised beta version of NSPIRET
Theoretical contributions	Knowledge contribution in the form of exaptation: Showcases how interdisciplinary approaches can be combined to address a new problem, i.e., productivity in the context of networked service delivery Constructive knowledge for discovering and seizing opportunities to enhance aggregated NSP
Implications for practitioners	Application of NSPIRET's artifacts may support practitioners to enhance aggregated NSP throughout the overall service productivity life cycle
Implications for this dissertation	Informs the development of design principles (Part VI)

3 Design principles

 This chapter reflects on the overall findings of this dissertation in order to detail design principles for improving aggregated NSP. Design principles present explicit prescriptions about constructing instances of a particular class of artifacts (Gregor, 2006; Gregor & Hevner, 2013; Sein et al., 2011). Thus, they can be considered as constructive knowledge (Goldkuhl, 2012) contributing to nascent theory for design and action (Gregor, 2006). For this purpose, design principles are purposefully described in an abstract manner in order to foster application in different use contexts (Gregor & Jones, 2007). In this respect Chandra, Seidel, and Gregor (2015) argue that descriptions should be both action and materiality oriented. Thus, design principles should not only prescribe "*what* an artifact should enable users to do" but also "*how* it should be built in order to do so" (Chandra et al., 2015, p. 4043). Furthermore, relevant boundary conditions, i.e., the relevant use contexts or intended user group, need to be considered (Chandra et al., 2015).

In line with the overall objective of this dissertation, the following design principles capture knowledge about the development of systematic approaches (i.e., artifacts) supporting a particular focal provider to enhance NSP for itself, its customers, and relevant co-providers. To a varying degree, all of these design principles are ingrained in the revised beta version of NSPIRET. Next, five principles are introduced building on the findings of the research presented in Part III, IV, and V as indicated in the respective discussion sections (see Figure 41). In doing so, both theory-driven and empirically-grounded reasoning was applied (Fischer & Gregor, 2011). For each principle actions, material properties, and boundary conditions that should be considered for developing new tools, techniques, systems, or strategic approaches to drive aggregated NSP are described (Chandra et al., 2015). Moreover, the way these principles were integrated into the design of NSPIRET is indicated.

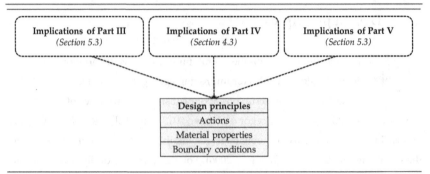

Figure 41: Derivation of design principles. Own illustration.

The first design principle stresses the importance to (1) *consider contextual complementarity* when developing new or improved approaches for enhancing aggregated NSP. As presented in Part III, several approaches were identified that can be applied to enhance service productivity from a network perspective. However, these approaches address different productivity-related criteria and are characterized by particular application-oriented qualities. Thus, new approaches should be based on an in-depth understanding of the contextual requirements and strive to complement already established productivity improvement initiatives to generate novel insights for improving aggregated NSP. In doing so, the focal provider should be able to harness individual experiences to successfully integrate new approaches into the particular application context and foster synergies with existing initiatives. For this purpose, new approaches require activity-related flexibility and adaptability of supporting tools. Against this backdrop, in-depth understanding of contextual requirements and established initiatives can be considered as relevant boundary conditions. Concerning the revised beta version of NSPIRET, this principle was taken into account as throughout the facilitation phase of the NSPIRET Navigator decision makers collaborate with members of the NSP improvement team to plan the initiative. In doing so, they can ensure that it is in line with contextual requirements such as available resources, established roles, and procedures concerning the service engineering, service delivery, and service management phase of the overall service productivity life cycle. Moreover, being implemented as a web-based tool, the NSPIRET Shoutbox can easily be integrated into existing communication infrastructures to foster operational feasibility.

The second principle is coined (2) *consider the connected, overall service*. In Part IV it was established that aggregated NSP is influenced by interactions throughout the pre-core service, core service, and post-core service periods of the customer journey. Throughout each period, the customer and one or more providers contribute resources that are transformed into particular outcomes. In order to identify previously untapped opportunities for improving aggregated NSP, the focal provider should consider all relevant network interactions throughout the connected, overall service. Therefore, new approaches should include means to systematically identify, depict, and analyze relevant actors and interactions from both the customers' and from an operational point of view. This shall foster an encompassing understanding of the status quo and reveal operational resources that can be modified to drive NSP for the actors considered. Moreover, it shall provide a structure to implement envisaged changes. An obvious boundary condition in this respect is to ensure adequate access to required qualitative and/or quantitative data in order uncover relevant actors, respective interactions, and related resources. This principle is ingrained in the revised beta version of NSPIRET by synthesizing and extending CJML, WSS, and the FMEA-based analysis of opportunities to enhance aggregated NSP based on understanding both touchpoints and underlying service systems throughout the connected, overall service.

The third principle is to (3) *consider actors' conditions of network membership*. Building on the findings of Part IV, for improving aggregated NSP, the focal provider has to learn about the heterogeneous service-related attributes as well as service-specific expectations of all actors required to realize networked service delivery. As highlighted in the conceptual model of NSP (see Figure 17), actors' individual conditions of network membership influence both inputs to networked service delivery and productivity related perceptions. Consequently, new approaches should support the integration of representatives of the focal provider, customers, and relevant co-providers into the process of improving aggregated NSP. In doing so, their individual conditions of network membership shall be considered in an adequate manner. For this purpose, as revealed in Part V, activities and means have to be adopted that demonstrate the value of contributions, foster understanding, and enable anonymous feedback for sensitive topics. Moreover, measures should be included in order to clarify any ambiguous feedback. Against this backdrop, boundary conditions include actors' experience with networked service delivery, willingness to contribute and share contact information, as well as an understanding of activities and tools for contributing to the process of improving aggregated NSP. This principle is considered comprehensively in the design of the revised beta version of NSPRET. The NSPIRET Navigator prescribes to integrate network actors throughout the (re-)modeling, discovery, and intervention phase. Moreover, the NSPIRET Shoutbox presents an instantiated software tool fostering their contributions independent of any spatial and temporal restrictions.

Next, it is proposed to (4) *consider the network-related effects of interventions*. In Part IV it was established that aggregated NSP addresses network actors' collective satisfaction with the perceived effects of networked service delivery at a given time considering their resource contributions for reaching these effects. Any particular intervention striving to improve individual NSP for a particular network actor can have a positive or negative impact on aggregated NSP as it may improve or reduce individual NSP for another actor. Hence, it was highlighted that the focal provider should, to the best of its ability, consider these effects in order to rationally decide about whether to carry out a particular intervention or not. Thus, new approaches should include means to foster reflection on network-related effects prior to intervention and, as substantiated by the findings of Part V, control actual effects after intervention. Relevant boundary conditions in this respect include the ability to recognize interrelations and evidence actual effects, which is dependent on the access to related qualitative and/or quantitative insights. This principle is acknowledged in the revised design of the beta version of the NSPIRET Navigator. It stresses the necessity to reflect on an intervention's effects on aggregated NSP based on the findings of NSPIRET Snapshotting, specify them in the NSPIRET Shoutbox, and define control measures throughout the intervention phase.

The last design principle stresses the necessity to (5) *consider the dynamics of aggregated NSP*. As presented in Part IV, for each actor NSP is a dynamic phenomenon that may change over time based on the perceived effects of network interactions and operational learning. In this regard, a high level of aggregated NSP is contingent of managing its drivers to mitigate related resistances. Thus, for sustainable enhancement of aggregated NSP, it is considered critical that the focal provider considers these dynamics and engages in an iterative improvement process. For this purpose, new designs should include activities and means that foster continuous learning about the compatibility of actors' conditions of network membership, actors' commitment to networked service delivery, as well as the appropriateness of network-oriented coordination activities, processes, and surrogates. In this respect, evidencing results and, as revealed in Part V, the establishment of intervention-related coordination institutions and supportive IT for carrying out improvement related activities is considered vital. Against this backdrop, boundary conditions include continuous managerial support and resource provisions. This design principle is ingrained in the revised beta version of NSPIRET by ingraining activities and means to continuously discover opportunities to enhance aggregated NSP and intervene accordingly. A summary of the design principles derived is presented in Table 34. Next, limitations of the scientific investigations presented and directions for future research are discussed.

Table 34: Summary of design principles.

Principle	Description		Building on
Consider contextual complement-arity	Action	Focal provider should gain complementary information and harness synergies throughout the service productivity life cycle	Part III
	Material property	Approaches require contextual flexibility and adaptability in terms of activities and supporting tools	Part III
	Boundary conditions	In-depth understanding of contextual requirements and established initiatives	Part III
Consider the connected, overall service	Action	Focal provider should consider all relevant actors and interactions to discover opportunities to enhance aggregated NSP	Part IV
	Material property	Approaches should include appropriate means to systematically identify, depict, and analyze actors and interactions throughout the pre-core, core, and post-core service stage from the customers' and operational point of view	Part IV
	Boundary conditions	Access to qualitative/quantitative data	Part IV
Consider conditions of network membership	Action	Focal provider should consider service-related attributes and service-specific expectations of network actors	Part IV
	Material property	Approaches should include appropriate activities and means for the integration of network actors into the process of enhancing aggregated NSP (e.g., demonstrate value, foster understanding and anonymity)	Part IV, V
	Boundary conditions	Experience with network service delivery; willingness to contribute; understanding of activities and supporting tools.	Part V
Consider network-related-effects of interventions	Action	Focal provider should consider the effects of interventions on aggregated NSP	Part IV
	Material property	Approaches should include appropriate activities and means to reflect on possible effects prior to intervention and control for effects after intervention	Part IV, V
	Boundary conditions	Ability to recognize interrelations; access to qualitative/quantitative data	Part IV, V
Consider dynamics of aggregated NSP	Action	Focal provider should consider the dynamic nature of aggregated NSP	Part IV, V
	Material property	Approaches should include appropriate activities and means to support iterative learning and improvements (e.g., evidencing, establishment of coordination institutions and supportive IT)	Part IV, V
	Boundary condition	Continuous managerial support and resource provisions	Part V

4 Limitations and directions for future research

 The findings of this dissertation have to be considered in light of its limitations. This chapter highlights several shortcomings of the research presented in chronological order and derives avenues for future research.

Concerning the systematic literature review presented in Part III, it is acknowledged that the classification of the identified approaches was conducted on a subjective basis. Thus, depending on the particular interpretation, several of the approaches may be repositioned within the classification scheme. Another limitation is the sample of outlets selected for the review. The review focused on leading service journals, pre-selected general and operations management-oriented journals, as well as the German funding priority "productivity of services". Consequently, the review does not provide a comprehensive collection of all published approaches possibly relevant for enhancing service productivity from a network perspective.

Future research could gain additional insights by focusing on scholarly and practitioner-oriented outlets from other relevant disciplines such as engineering or operations research. These insights would be useful to gain a more holistic understanding concerning the state of the art and provide a richer compilation of approaches for enhancing service productivity in the context of networked service delivery. Moreover, an extended review may also provide the possibility to evaluate further if the classification scheme is exhaustive and does not contain unnecessary criteria. Whereas all of the 18 approaches identified could be mapped within the scheme, future research may reveal the need to refine or extend existing criteria. Moreover, DSR studies should address the identified knowledge gaps and elaborate and empirically evaluate new, operationalized integration approaches for systematic and holistic service productivity improvements addressing all phases of the service productivity life cycle. In doing so, iterative productivity improvements may be fostered that is in line with the contemporary understanding of service productivity as a concept integrating both efficiency and effectiveness considerations.

A limitation of the findings of the exploratory case study presented in Part III is that they are derived from investigating productivity in merely two settings of networked service delivery. Whereas both case settings differ in important aspects such as the type of service, the customers, and the interaction environment, they reflect knowledge-intensive service offerings. Thus, it is acknowledged that generalization of findings is limited and further research should be conducted to (dis-)confirm, refine and extend initial insights. In this regard, an important direction would be to explore further context-specific factors and conceptual relationships influencing individual and aggregated NSP in different domains. Among others, relevant settings for future research include IT-related service delivery networks (e.g., Huang & Rust, 2013) potentially realized by the internet of things (e.g., Larivière et al., 2016) or people-focused service delivery networks as in the context of elderly care (e.g., Čaić et al., 2018). In this regard, other aspects such as power structures among actors or professionalism and corresponding organizational structures (e.g., Lewis & Brown, 2012) may be investigated concerning their influence on individual and aggregated NSP as well as related drivers and related resistances. Furthermore, future research could apply the model of NSP as well as the drivers proposed in Part IV to develop theoretical propositions and test emerging theory.

Next, a fertile ground for future research would be to explore microfoundations of individual and aggregated NSP. Research on microfoundations focuses on explanations on a low analytical level that underpin the macro constructs under consideration (Storbacka, Brodie, Böhmann, Maglio, & Nenonen, 2016). In line with the conceptualization of micofoundations in the context of dynamic capabilities (Teece, 2007), future research could shed light on distinct skills, processes, procedures, organizational structures, and decision rules required to ensure mutually effective and efficient interactions in service delivery networks. Emerging insights in this respect can inform systematic capability building initiatives (Agarwal & Selen, 2009) as well as the development of supportive indicators and measurement systems (Sahay, 2006).

With respect to the DSR study presented in Part V, it is acknowledged that the revised beta version of NSPIRET is still at an early stage and several design boundaries need to be considered for its application. Whereas it was iteratively developed building on the insights derived in two empirical settings, so far, it has not been entirely applied to a real-world scenario of networked service delivery. Thus, it is unclear if the implemented design changes will actually improve identified gaps in terms of effectiveness and further improve utility, understandability, and operational feasibility. It is likely that future evaluation activities will point out the need for further modifications.

Second, NSPIRET, focuses on improving NSP for the focal provider, customers, and relevant co-providers by depicting, analyzing, and modifying interactions throughout networked service delivery taking the customer journey as the common overriding process (Halvorsrud, Kvale, et al., 2016; Tax et al., 2013). The focus is on the expected touchpoints of the anticipated customers and underlying service system elements required for their realization. NSPIRET is not concerned with modeling individual customer journeys and therefore does not detail all possible instances of interaction within a particular service delivery network. Moreover, it does not prescribe on which level of detail service system elements should be depicted. This decision needs to be taken in light of the available resources as well as the context and complexity of networked service delivery. Additionally, for each (co-)provider, there exist several internal and supplier-oriented processes required for networked service delivery that may also portray potentials for gains in terms of effectiveness and efficiency (Liker & Morgan, 2006; Sampson, 2012; Staats et al., 2011). Hence NSPIRET should be considered complementary to other tools and techniques for improving service productivity. In this regard, future research could reveal possibilities and barriers for integration and adaptions with more established productivity improvement approaches.

Moreover, the revised beta version of NSPIRET lacks any formal solutions for balancing heterogeneous needs. In case conflicting demands of the different network actors are identified, responsible members of the NSP improvement team still have to contemplate on the trade-offs between the different subjective perspectives of NSP. Thus, NSPIRET does not address the enhancement of aggregated NSP as a formal optimization problem (cf. Rust & Huang, 2012) but requires thoughtful and creative decision making reflecting upon the possible multisided effects of envisaged changes. In this context, future research could focus on creating heuristics (Reijers & Mansa, 2005; Venable et al., 2016) as well as formal approaches (Ostrom et al., 2015) how to balance trade-offs among the different individual perceptions of NSP.

Furthermore, so far, NSPIRET is dependent on active contributions and explicit feedback from network actors. An obvious limitation in this context is the dependency on external actors whose contribution can only partly be controlled by the focal provider. Potential respondents need to be enabled and motivated to contribute. In this context, it is critical to ensure understandability (Prat et al., 2015) and ease of use of the feedback channel (Davis, 1989). Moreover, the potential material, immaterial and intrinsic motives for the contribution of the potential respondents need to be considered (Janzik, 2010). These drivers of motivation have to be adequately addressed throughout the discovery of failure and innovation modes. Furthermore, there is the risk that respondents overemphasize certain failures due to limited service experiences (Geum, Shin, et al., 2011) or are cogitatively biased (Liedtka, 2015). Moreover, due to the dependency on explicit feedback, NSPIRET is unsuited to uncover latent needs that are not addressed sufficiently and thus may provide opportunities to radically improve service productivity (Witell, Kristensson, Gustafsson, & Löfgren, 2011).

In order to address some of these challenges and to improve the effectiveness and utility of NSPIRET a fruitful direction for future research is to harness smart devices (Atzori, Iera, & Morabito, 2014; Marinova, Ruyter, & Huang, 2017; Zanella et al., 2014), artificial intelligence (Huang & Rust, 2018; Morris, Schlenoff, & Srinivasan, 2017) and related automation possibilities. In this regard, sensors of service devices employed in the context of network interactions may support the real-time identification of failure and innovation modes. Harnessing algorithm-based machine learning (Jordan & Mitchell, 2015) may foster the automated prioritization of failure and innovation modes and thus reduce the effort for applying NSPIRET. Similarly, it would be worthwhile to engage in atomization of (re-)modeling networked service delivery based on interventions conducted. Developing and evaluating an IT-based artifact for NSPIRET Snapshotting could not only enhance the utility of NSPRIET, but may also be applied in other service research projects focusing on understanding the overall customer journey. In this regard, an IT-based modeling tool could enhance the efficiency of analysis, particularly in longitudinal studies (e.g., Halvorsrud, Kvale, et al., 2016).

Regarding the design principles for improving aggregated NSP presented in the previous chapter it needs to be pointed out that they have not been evaluated naturalistically. Thus, whereas they are grounded in the findings of this research, assessing their effectiveness remains subject to future work. Therefore, future design-oriented research in different organizational settings is required to assess and further elaborate on the proposed design principles. In doing so, engaged scholars and practitioners may further specify new or improved required actions, material properties, and boundary conditions of new or improved artifacts for driving aggregated NSP in particular settings of networked service delivery. Having discussed the limitations of the scientific investigations of this dissertation and having highlighted potential avenues for future research, next, some concluding remarks are presented.

5   Concluding remarks

This dissertation presents pioneering work on the largely unexplored, yet highly relevant topic of productivity in the context of networked service delivery. Harnessing the results of a systematic literature review, an exploratory case study, and a design science research study, it develops constructive knowledge informing a focal service provider *how to drive productivity in the context of networked service delivery.*

Key findings include that, so far, there has been a lack of practical approaches that are in line with an integration strategy and aim to enhance service productivity for all relevant actors contributing resources to networked service delivery. Moreover, the need for a better coherent conceptual foundation of productivity in the context of networked service delivery was revealed. Against this backdrop, the concept of NSP was established. NSP is conceptualized as a subjective, dynamic, and multi-level phenomenon. On the aggregated level, it is influenced by actors' idiosyncratic conditions of network membership, their inputs, and interactions throughout the pre-core, core, and post-core service periods of one or more customer journeys. Building on these insights the current design of NSPIRET was iteratively developed and assessed. NSPIRET presents a technique aiming to support a focal provider to systematically discover and seize opportunities to improve NSP for itself, customers and relevant co-providers. It was found that the beta version of NSPIRET demonstrated promising levels of effectiveness, utility, understandability, and operational feasibility.

In line with the pragmatist paradigm guiding this research, the author hopes that the results of this dissertation are found useful by service researchers and practitioners alike. As highlighted before, future research is strongly encouraged to elaborate on and (dis-)confirm the initial insights. Let's strive towards new approaches for service engineering, delivery, and management overcoming a narrow, efficiency-focused understanding of productivity. Let's consider the interdependencies and effects of contemporary service delivery and collaborate in order to foster truly productive service interactions in a networked world. This dissertation is just a first step in this direction – hopefully many more will follow.

References

© Springer Fachmedien Wiesbaden GmbH, part of Springer Nature 2020
C. F. Daiberl, *Driving Networked Service Productivity*, Markt- und
Unternehmensentwicklung Markets and Organisations,
https://doi.org/10.1007/978-3-658-29580-6

References

acatech. (2015). *Smart Service Welt – Umsetzungsempfehlungen für das Zukunftsprojekt Internet-basierte Dienste für die Wirtschaft*. Berlin.

Agarwal, R., & Selen, W. (2009). Dynamic capability building in service value networks for achieving service innovation. *Decision Sciences, 40*(3), 431–475.

Alexander, A., Teller, C., & Roggeveen, A. L. (2016). The boundary spanning of managers within service networks. *Journal of Business Research, 69*(12), 6031–6039.

Allee, V. (2008). Value network analysis and value conversion of tangible and intangible assets. *Journal of Intellectual Capital, 9*(1), 5–24.

Alter, S. (2006). *The work system method: Connecting people, processes, and IT for business results*. Larkspur: Work System Press.

Alter, S. (2010a). Service systems and service-dominant logic: Partners or distant cousins? *Journal of Relationship Marketing, 9*(2), 98–115.

Alter, S. (2010b). Viewing systems as services: A fresh approach in the IS field. *Communications of the Association for Information Systems, 26*(11), 195–224.

Alter, S. (2012). Metamodel for service analysis and design based on an operational view of service and service systems. *Service Science, 4*(3), 183–294.

Alter, S. (2013a). From resources and activities to value for customers within systems of service systems. In *Proceedings of SIG-SVC 2013 Workshop* (pp. 1–17). Milan.

Alter, S. (2013b). Work system theory: Overview of core concepts, extensions, and challenges for the future. *Journal of the Association for Information Systems, 14*(2), 72–121.

Alter, S. (2015). Work system theory as a platform: Response to a research perspective article by Niederman and March. *Journal of the Association for Information Systems, 16*(6), 485–514.

Alter, S. (2018). System interaction theory: Describing interactions between work systems. *Communications of the Association for Information Systems, 42*(1), 233–267.

Alter, S., & Recker, J. C. (2017). Using a work system perspective to expand BPM use cases for research. *Journal of Information Technology Theory and Application, 18*(1), 47–71.

Anitsal, I., & Schumann, D. (2007). Toward a conceptualization of customer productivity: The customer's perspective on transforming customer labor into customer outcomes using technology-based self-service options. *The Journal of Marketing Theory and Practice, 15*(4), 349–363.

Aspara, J., Klein, J. F., Luo, X., & Tikkanen, H. (2018). The dilemma of service productivity and service innovation. *Journal of Service Research, 21*(2), 249–262.

Atzori, L., Iera, A., & Morabito, G. (2014). From "smart objects" to "social objects": The next evolutionary step of the internet of things. *IEEE Communications Magazine,* (January), 97–105.

Badinelli, R. D. (2012). Fuzzy modeling of service system engagements. *Service Science, 4*(2), 135–146.

Badinelli, R. D., Barile, S., Ng, I., Polese, F., Saviano, M., & Nauta, P. (2012). Viable service systems and decision making in service management. *Journal of Service Management, 23*(4), 498–526.

Baines, T., Bigdeli, A. Z., Bustinza, O. F., Shi, V. G., Baldwin, J., & Ridgway, K. (2017). Servitization: Revisiting the state-of-the-art and research priorities. *International Journal of Operations & Production Management, 37*(2), 256–278.

Baines, T., Lightfoot, H. W., Benedettini, O., & Kay, J. M. (2009). The servitization of manufacturing: A review of literature and reflection on future challenges. *Journal of Manufacturing Technology Management, 20*(5), 547–567.

Baines, T., & Shi, V. (2014). Servitization transformation: Drivers, benefit and barriers. In T. Baines, B. Clegg, & D. Harrison (Eds.), *Growth through servitization* (pp. 34–39). Birmingham: Aston University.

Baldwin, C. Y., & Clark, K. B. (1997). Managing in an age of modularity. *Harvard Business Review, 75*(5), 84–93.

Banker, R. D., & Chang, H. (2006). The super-efficiency procedure for outlier identification, not for ranking efficient units. *European Journal of Operations Research, 175*(2), 1311–1320.

Barile, S., Lusch, R., Reynoso, J., Saviano, M., & Spohrer, J. (2016). Systems, networks, and ecosystems in service research. *Journal of Service Management, 27*(4), 652–674.

Bartsch, S., Demmelmair, M. F., & Meyer, A. (2011). Dienstleistungsproduktivität: Stand der Forschung und Zusammenhang zu zentralen vorökonomischen Größen im Dienstleistungsmarketing. In M. Bruhn & K. Hadwich (Eds.), *Dienstleistungsproduktivität: Management, Prozessgestaltung, Kundenperspektive, Band 1* (pp. 35–59). Wiesbaden: Gabler Verlag.

Bateman, N., Hines, P., & Davidson, P. (2014). Wider applications for Lean: An examination of the fundamental principles within public sector organisations. *International Journal of Productivity and Performance Management, 63*(5), 550–568.

Bateson, J. E. G. (1979). Why we need service marketing. In O. C. Ferrell, S. W. Brown, & C. W. Lamb (Eds.), *Conceptual and theoretical developments in marketing* (pp. 38–40). Chicago: Amercian Marketing Association.

Beer, S. (1972). *Brain of the firm*. London: Penguin Press.

Beloglazov, A., Banerjee, D., Hartman, A., & Buyya, R. (2015). Improving productivity in design and development of information technology (IT) service delivery simulation models. *Journal of Service Research, 18*(1), 75–89.

Ben-Akiva, M., & Lerman, S. R. (1991). *Discrete choice analysis*. Cambridge, MA: MIT Press.

Berrone, P., Surroca, J., & Tribó, J. A. (2007). Corporate ethical identity as a determinant of firm performance: A test of the mediating role of stakeholder satisfaction. *Journal of Business Ethics, 76*(1), 35–53.

Bessant, J., Lehmann, C., & Möslein, K. M. (2014). Service productivity and innovation. In J. Bessant, C. Lehmann, & K. M. Möslein (Eds.), *Driving Service Productivity: Value creation through innovation* (pp. 3–15). Cham: Springer.

Bettencourt, L., & Ulwick, A. W. (2008). The customer-centered innovation map. *Harvard Business Review, 86*(5), 109–114.

Beyer, H., & Holtzblatt, K. (1997). *Contextual design: Defining customer-centered systems*. San Francisco, CA: Morgan Kaufmann.

Bicheno, J. (2008). *The lean toolbox for service systems*. Buckingham: PICSIE Books.

Biege, S., Lay, G., Zanker, C., & Schmall, T. (2013). Challenges of measuring service productivity in innovative, knowledge-intensive business services. *The Service Industries Journal, 33*(3–4), 378–391.

Bitner, M. J., Ostrom, A. L., & Morgan, F. N. (2008). Service blueprinting: A practical technique for service innovation. *California Management Review, 50*(3), 66–94.

Borchert, M., Hamburger, J., Brockhaus, N., Strina, G., Klinkhammer, S., & Heinen, E. (2011). Produktivitätsmanagement für Dienstleistungen aus der KMU-Perspektive. In M. . Bruhn & K. Hadwich (Eds.), *Dienstleistungsproduktivität: Management, prozessgestaltung, Kundenperspektive, Band 1* (pp. 89–120). Wiesbaden: Gabler Verlag.

Borgatti, S. P., & Foster, P. C. (2003). The network paradigm in organizational research: A review and typology. *Journal of Management, 29*(6), 991–1013.

Borgatti, S. P., & Halgin, D. S. (2011). On network theory. *Organization Science, 22*(5),

1168–1181.

Böttcher, M., & Klingner, S. (2011). Providing a method for composing modular B2B services. *Journal of Business & Industrial Marketing, 26*(5), 320–331.

Box, G., Jenkins, G. M., & Reinsel, G. C. (1994). *Time series analysis.* New Jersey: Prentice Hall.

Brax, S. A., Bax, A., Hsuan, J., & Voss, C. (2017). Service modularity and architecture: An overview and research agenda. *International Journal of Operations & Production Management, 37*(6), 686–702.

Breidbach, C. F., Reefke, H., & Wood, L. C. (2015). Investigating the formation of service supply chains. *Service Industries Journal, 35*(1–2), 5–23.

Bullinger, H. J., Fähnrich, K. P., & Meiren, T. (2003). Service engineering: Methodical development of new service products. *International Journal of Production Economics, 85*(3), 275–287.

Buxton, B. (2007). *Sketching user experiences: Getting the design right and the right design.* San Francisco, CA: Morgan Kaufmann.

Čaić, M., Odekerken-Schröder, G., & Mahr, D. (2018). Service robots: value co-creation and co-destruction in elderly care networks. *Journal of Service Management, 29*(2), 178–205.

Calabrese, A. (2012). Service productivity and service quality: A necessary trade-off? *International Journal of Production Economics, 135*(2), 800–812.

Cândea, G., Kifor, S., & Constantinescu, C. (2014). Usage of case-based reasoning in FMEA-driven software. *Procedia CIRP, 25*, 93–99.

Carlborg, P., & Kindström, D. (2014). Service process modularization and modular strategies. *Journal of Business & Industrial Marketing, 29*(4), 313–323.

Carlborg, P., Kindström, D., & Kowalkowski, C. (2013). A lean approach for service productivity improvements: synergy or oxymoron? *Managing Service Quality, 23*(4), 291–304.

Carroll, J. M. (2000). Five reasons for scenario-based design. *Interacting with Computers, 13*(1), 43–60.

Chan, W. K. V., & Hsu, C. (2009). Service scaling on hyper-networks. *Service Science, 1*(1), 17–31.

Chandler, J. D., & Vargo, S. L. (2011). Contextualization and value-in-context: How context frames exchange. *Marketing Theory, 11*(1), 35–49.

Chandra, L., Seidel, S., & Gregor, S. (2015). Prescriptive knowledge in IS research: Conceptualizing design principles in terms of materiality, action, and boundary conditions. In *Proceedings of the Annual Hawaii International Conference on System Sciences* (Vol. 2015–March, pp. 4039–4048).

Charmaz. (2006). *Constructing grounded theory: A practical guide*. Thousand Oaks, CA: Sage.

Charnes, A., Cooper, W. W., & Rhodes, E. (1978). Measuring the efficiency of decision making units. *European Journal of Operational Research, 2*(6), 429–444.

Chase, R. B. (1981). The customer contact approach to services: Theoretical bases and practical extensions. *Operations Research, 29*(4), 698–706.

Chase, R. B., & Haynes, R. M. (2000). Service operations managemnt: A field guide. In T. Schwartz & D. Iacobucci (Eds.), *Handbook of Service Marketing and Management* (pp. 455–471). Thousand Oaks: Sage Publications.

Chew, W. (1988). No-nonsense guide to measuring productivity. *Harvard Business Review, 66*(1), 110–118.

Chinosi, M., & Trombetta, A. (2012). BPMN: An introduction to the standard. *Computer Standards and Interfaces, 34*(1), 124–134.

Chintagunta, P. K., & Desiraju, R. (2005). Strategic pricing and detailing behavior in international markets. *Marketing Science, 24*(1), 67–80.

Choi, T. Y., & Krause, D. R. (2006). The supply base and its complexity: Implications for transaction costs, risks, responsiveness, and innovation. *Journal of Operations Management, 24*(5), 637–652.

Chuang, P.-T. (2007). Combining service blueprint and FMEA for service design. *Service Industries Journal, 27*(2), 91–104.

CIA World Factbook. (n.d.). GDP - Composition, by sector of origin. Retrieved March 19, 2018, from https://www.cia.gov/llibrary/publications/the-world-factbook/fields/2012.html

Constantin, J. A., & Lusch, R. F. (1994). *Understanding resource management*. Oxford, OH: The Planning Forum.

Constantine, L. L. (2009). Human activity modeling: Toward a pragmatic integration of activity theory and usage centered design. In A. Seffah, J. Vanderdonckt, & M. Desmarais (Eds.), *Human-Centered Software Engineering* (pp. 27–51). London:

Springer.

Cooper, H. M. (1988). Organizing knowledge synthesis: A taxonomy of literature reviews. *Knowledge in Society, 1*(1), 104–126.

Cooper, R. G., Edgett, S. J., & Kleinschmidt, E. J. (1999). New product portfolio management: Practices and performance. *Journal of Product Innovation Management, 16*(4), 333–351.

Corbing, J., & Strauss, A. (2008). *Basics of qualitative research: Grounded theory procedures and techniques*. Thousand Oaks: Sage.

Corsten, H. (1994). Überlegungen zum Produktivitätsmanagement für Dienstleistungsunternehmen - dargestellt am Beispiel bilateraler personenbezogener Dienstleistungen. In H. Corsten & W. Hilke (Eds.), *Schriften zur Unternehmensführung - Dienstleistungsproduktion* (pp. 43–77). Wiesbaden.

Corsten, H. (1997). *Dienstleistungsmanagement* (3rd ed.). München: Oldenbourg Wissenschaftsverlag.

Costa, E., Lucas Soares, A., & Pinho de Sousa, J. (2017). Institutional networks for supporting the internationalisation of SMEs: the case of industrial business associations. *Journal of Business & Industrial Marketing, 32*(8), 1182–1202.

Daiberl, C. F., Naik, H., & Roth, A. (2018). Proposing the NSPIRE technique: Improving productivity of networked service delivery. Paper presented and discussed at the *R&D Management Conference 2018*. Milan.

Daiberl, C. F., Oks, S. J., Roth, A., Möslein, K. M., & Alter, S. (2019). Design principles for establishing a multi-sided open innovation platform: Lessons learned from an action research study in the medical technology industry. *Electronic Markets. In Press.*

Daiberl, C. F., Roth, A., & Möslein, K. M. (2016a). Approaches for enhancing productivity of networked service delivery: A review and assessment. Paper presented and discussed at the *26th Annual RESER Conference*. Naples.

Daiberl, C. F., Roth, A., & Möslein, K. M. (2016b). Conceptualizing productivity within a service network: The case of JOSEPHS®. Paper presented and discussed at the *23rd EuROMA Conference*. Trondheim.

Daiberl, C. F., Roth, A., & Möslein, K. M. (2016c). Towards perceived service interaction productivity: A proposed conceptual model. In *Proceedings of the KSS Workshop 2016*. Karlsruhe.

Dale, B. G. (2003). *Managing Quality*. Oxford: Blackwell Publishers.

Davis, F. D. (1989). Perceived usefulness, perceived ease of use, and user acceptance of information technology. *MIS Quarterly, 13*(3), 319–340.

Day, G. S. (1990). *Market driven strategy: Processes for creating value.* New York: The Free Press.

De Blok, C., Meijboom, B., Luijkx, K., Schols, J., & Schroeder, R. (2014). Interfaces in service modularity: A typology developed in modular health care provision. *Journal of Operations Management, 32*(4), 175–189.

Deng, Q., & Ji, S. (2018). A review of design science research in information systems: Concept, process, outcome, and evaluation. *Pacific Asia Journal of the Association for Information Systems, 10*(1), 1–36.

Djellal, F., & Gallouj, F. (2008). *Measuring and improving productivity in services: Issues, strategies and challenges.* Cheltenham: Edward Elgar Publishing.

Djellal, F., & Gallouj, F. (2013). The productivity challenge in services: measurement and strategic perspectives. *The Service Industries Journal, 33*(3–4), 282–299.

Dobni, D., Ritchie, J. R. B., & Zerbe, W. (2000). Organizational values: The inside view of service productivity. *Journal of Business Research, 47*(2), 91–107.

Drucker, P. F. (1974). *Management: Tasks, responsibilities, practices.* New York: Harper & Row.

Drucker, P. F. (1991). The new productivity challenge. *Harvard Business Review, 69*(6), 69–79.

Dubberly, H., Evenson, S., & Robinson, R. (2008). The analysis-synthesis bridge model. *Interactions, 15*(2), 57–61.

Dubois, A., & Gadde, L. (2002). Systematic combining: An abductive approach to case research. *Journal of Business Research, 55*(7), 553–560.

Dyson, R. G., Allen, R., Camanho, A. S., Podinovski, V. V., Sarrico, C. S., & Shale, E. A. (2001). Pitfalls and protocols in DEA. *European Journal of Operational Research, 132*(2), 245–259.

Edgett, S., & Parkinson, S. (1993). Marketing for service industries - A review. *The Services Industry Journal, 13*(3), 19–39.

Edvardsson, B., Gustafsson, A., & Roos, I. (2005). Service portraits in service research: A critical review. *International Journal of Service Industry Management, 16*(1), 107–121.

Edvardsson, B., Kristensson, P., Magnusson, P., & Sundström, E. (2012). Customer integration within service development - A review of methods and an analysis of insitu and exsitu contributions. *Technovation, 32*(7–8), 419–429.

Eisenhardt, K. M. (1989). Building theories from case study research. *Academy of Management Review, 14*(4), 532–550.

Eisenhardt, K. M., & Graebner, M. E. (2007). Theory building from cases: Opportunities and challenges. *Academy of Management Journal, 50*(1), 25–32.

Ekman, P., Raggio, R. D., & Thompson, S. M. (2016). Service network value co-creation: Defining the roles of the generic actor. *Industrial Marketing Management, 56*(July), 51–62.

Fetke, P. (2008). Business process modeling notation. *Wirtschaftsinformatik, 50*(6), 504–507.

Field, J. M., Victorino, L., Buell, R. W., Dixon, M. J., Goldstein, S. M., Menor, L. J., … Enrico Secchi, J. J. Z. (2018). Service operations: What's next? *Journal of Service Management, 29*(1), 55–97.

Fischer, C., & Gregor, S. (2011). Forms of reasoning in the design science research process. In H. Jain, A. P. Sinha, & P. Vitharana (Eds.), *Service-oriented perspectives in design science research. DESRIST 2011* (pp. 17–31). Milwaukee, WI, USA: Springer.

Fitzsimmons, J. A. (1985). Consumer participation and productivity in service operations. *Interfaces, 15*(3), 60–67.

Fließ, S., & Kleinaltenkamp, M. (2004). Blueprinting the service company: Managing service processes efficiently. *Journal of Business Research, 57*(4), 392–404.

Følstad, A., Kvale, K., & Halvorsrud, R. (2013). *Customer journey measures: State of the art research and best practices.* Oslo. Retrieved from https://brage.bibsys.no/xmlui/handle/11250/2390670

Garrett, J. J. (2011). *Elements of user experience: User-centered design for the web and beyond.* Berkeley: New Riders.

Geum, Y., Cho, Y., & Park, Y. (2011). A systematic approach for diagnosing service failure: Service-specific FMEA and grey relational analysis approach. *Mathematical and Computer Modelling, 54*(11–12), 3126–3142.

Geum, Y., Shin, J., & Park, Y. (2011). FMEA-based portfolio approach to service productivity improvement. *The Service Industries Journal, 31*(11), 1825–1847.

Glaser, B., & Strauss, A. (1967). *The discovery of grounded theory: Strategies for qualitative research*. Chicago: Aldine.

Goldkuhl, G. (2012). Pragmatism vs interpretivism in qualitative information systems research. *European Journal of Information Systems, 21*(2), 135–146.

Goles, T., & Hirschheim, R. (2000). The paradigm is dead, the paradiagm is dead...long live the paradigm: The legacy of Burrell and Morgan. *The International Journal of Management Science, 28*(3), 249–268.

Golinelli, G. M. (2010). *Viable systems approach: Governing business dynamics*. Padova: Cedam.

Gordijn, J. ., & Tan, Y.-H. . (2005). A design methodology for modeling trustworthy value webs. *International Journal of Electronic Commerce, 9*(3), 31–48.

Gordijn, J., & Akkermans, J. M. (2003). Value-based requirements engineering: Exploring innovative e-commerce ideas. *Requirements Engineering, 8*(2), 114–134.

Govind, R., Chatterjee, R., & Mittal, V. (2008). Timely access to health care: Customer-focused resource allocation in a hospital network. *International Journal of Research in Marketing, 25*(4), 294–300.

Gregor, S. (2006). The nature of theory in information systems. *MIS Quarterly, 30*(3), 611–642.

Gregor, S., & Hevner, A. R. (2013). Positioning and presenting design science research for maximum impact. *MIS Quarterly, 37*(2).

Gregor, S., & Jones, D. (2007). The anatomy of a design theory. *Journal of the Association for Information Systems, 8*(5), 312–335.

Grönroos, C., & Ojasalo, K. (2004). Service productivity: Towards a conceptualization of the transformation of inputs into economic results in services. *Journal of Business Research, 57*(4), 414–423.

Grönroos, C., & Ojasalo, K. (2015). Service productivity as mutual learning. *International Journal of Quality and Service Sciences, 7*(2/3), 296–311.

Gummesson, E. (1987). Lip service - a neglected area in service marketing. *The Journal of Services Marketing, 1*(1), 19–23.

Gummesson, E. (1994). Service management: An evaluation and the future. *International Journal of Service Industry Management, 5*(1), 77–96.

Gummesson, E. (1998). Productivity, quality and relationship marketing in service operations. *International Journal of Contemporary Hospitality Management, 10*(1), 4–15.

Gummesson, E. (2007). Exit services marketing - enter service marketing. *Journal of Customer Behaviour, 6*(2), 113–141.

Gummesson, E. (2008). Extending the service-dominant logic: From customer centricity to balanced centricity. *Journal of the Academy of Marketing Science, 36*(1), 15–17.

Gupta, S., Sharma, M., & Sunder M., V. (2016). Lean services: A systematic review. *International Journal of Productivity and Performance Management, 65*(8), 1025–1056.

Gustafsson, A., Ekdahl, F., & Edvardsson, B. (1999). Customer focused service development in practice: A case study at Scandinavian Airlines System (SAS). *International Journal of Service Industry Management, 10*(4), 344–358.

Hadid, W., Mansouri, S. A., & Gallear, D. (2016). Is lean service promising? A socio-technical perspective. *International Journal of Operations & Production Management, 36*(6), 618–642.

Hakanen, T., & Jaakkola, E. (2012). Co-creating customer-focused solutions within business networks: a service perspective. *Journal of Service Management, 23*(4), 593–611.

Halvorsrud, R., Haugstveit, I. M., & Pultier, A. (2016). Evaluation of a modelling language for customer journeys. In *2016 IEEE Symposium on Visual Langauges and Human-Centric Computing* (pp. 40–48).

Halvorsrud, R., Kvale, K., & Følstad, A. (2016). Improving service quality through customer journey analysis. *Journal of Service Theory and Practice, 26*(8), 840–876.

Halvorsrud, R., Lee, E., Haugstveit, I. M., & Følstad, A. (2014). Components of a visual language for service design. In *Proceedings of ServDes* (pp. 291–300). Lancaster.

Hammerschmidt, M., Falk, T., & Staat, M. (2012). Measuring and improving the performance of health service networks. *Journal of Service Research, 15*(3), 343–357.

Harvey, J. (2016). Professional service supply chains. *Journal of Operations Management, 42–43,* 52–61.

Helkkula, A., Kelleher, C., & Pihlstrom, M. (2012). Characterizing value as an experience: implications for service researchers and managers. *Journal of Service Research, 15*(1), 59–75.

Hevner, A. R., March, S. T., Park, J., & Ram, S. (2004). Design science in information systems research. *MIS Quarterly, 28*(1), 75–105.

Hillebrand, B., Driessen, P. H., & Koll, O. (2015). Stakeholder marketing: Theoretical foundations and required capabilities. *Journal of the Academy of Marketing Science, 43*(4), 411–428.

Horkoff, J., Barone, D., Jiang, L., Yu, E., Amyot, D., Borgida, A., & Mylopoulos, J. (2012). Strategic business modeling: Representation and reasoning. *Software & Systems Modeling, 13*(3), 1015–1041.

Hsu, C. (2011). Hyper-networking of customers, providers, and resources drives new service business designs: E-commerce and beyond. *Service Science, 3*(4), 325–337.

Hsu, C., & Spohrer, J. C. (2009). Improving service quality and productivity: Exploring the digital connections scaling model. *International Journal of Services Technology and Management, 11*(3), 272–292.

Huang, M., & Rust, R. T. (2013). IT-related service: A multidisciplinary perspective. *Journal of Service Research, 16*(3), 251–258.

Huang, M., & Rust, R. T. (2018). Artificial intelligence in service. *Journal of Service Research, 21*(2), 155–172.

Jaakkola, E., Helkkula, A., & Aarikka-Stenroos, L. (2015). Service experience co-creation: Conceptualization, implications, and future. *Journal of Service Management, 26*(2), 182–205.

Jacob, F., Bruns, K., & Sievert, J. (2013). Value in context: Eine ressourcendynamische Perspektive. In G. Schmitz (Ed.), *Theorie und Praxis des Dienstleistungsmarketings: Aktuelle Konzepte und Entwicklungen* (pp. 27–50). Wiesbaden: Springer.

Janeschek, S., Hottum, P., Kicherer, F., & Bienzeisler, B. (2013). The dynamics of service productivity and value creation: A service life cycle perspective. *The Service Industries Journal, 33*(3–4), 366–377.

Janzik, L. (2010). Contribution and Participation in Innovation Communities: a Classification of Incentives and Motives. *International Journal of Innovation and Technology Management, 7*(3), 247–262.

Johnes, P. (1988). Quality, capactiy and productivity in service industries. In R. Johnston (Ed.), *The Management of Service Operations: Proceedings of the Operations Management Association: 3. Annual Internat. Conference.* (pp. 309–321). Bedford & Berlin.

Johnson, H. M., Fruhling, A., & Fossum, M. (2016). An analysis of the work system framework for examining information exchange in a healthcare setting. *Communications of the Association for Information Systems, 39*, 73–95.

Johnston, R., & Jones, P. (2004). Service productivity: Towards understanding the relationship between operational and customer productivity. *International Journal of Productivity and Performance Management*, 53(3), 201–213.

Jones, P. (1988). Quality, capacity and productivity in service industries. *International Journal of Hospitality Management*, 7(2), 104–112.

Jordan, M. I., & Mitchell, T. M. (2015). Machine learning: Trends, perspectives, and prospects. *Science*, 349(6245), 255–260.

Karpen, I. O., Bove, L. L., & Lukas, B. a. (2012). Linking service-dominant logic and strategic business practice: A conceptual model of a service-dominant orientation. *Journal of Service Research*, 15(1), 21–38.

Kartseva, V., Gordijn, J., & Tan, Y.-H. (2005). Toward a modeling tool for designing control mechanisms for network organizations. *International Journal of Electronic Commerce*, 10(6), 57–84.

Kartseva, V., Hulstijn, J., Gordijn, J., & Tan, Y.-H. (2010). Control patterns in a health-care network. *European Journal of Information Systems*, 19(3), 320–343.

Kazemzadeh, Y., Milton, S. K., & Johnson, L. W. (2015a). A comparison of concepts in service blueprinting and process-chain-network (PCN). *International Journal of Business and Management*, 10(4), 13–25.

Kazemzadeh, Y., Milton, S. K., & Johnson, L. W. (2015b). Process chain network (PCN) and business process modeling notation (BPMN): A comparison of concepts. *Journal of Management and Strategy*, 6(1), 88–99.

Ketokivi, M., & Choi, T. (2014). Renaissance of case research as a scientific method. *Journal of Operations Management*, 32(5), 232–240.

Kieliszewski, C. A., Maglio, P. P., & Cefkin, M. (2012). On modeling value constellations to understand complex service system interactions. *European Management Journal*, 30(5), 438–450.

King, N. (2004). Using templates in the thematic analysis of text. In C. Cassell & G. Symon (Eds.), *Essential guide to qualitative methods in organizational research* (pp. 256–270). London: Sage.

Kleinaltenkamp, M. (1997). Integrativität als Kern einer umfassenden Leistungslehre. In K. Backhaus, B. Günter, M. Kleinaltenkamp, W. Plinke, & H. Raffée (Eds.), *Marktleistungs und Wettbewerb: Strategische und operative Perspektiven der marktorientierten Leistungsgestaltung* (pp. 83–115). Wiesbaden: Gabler.

Kleinaltenkamp, M., & Haase, M. (1999). Externe Faktoren in der Theorie der

Unternehmung. In H. Albach, E. Eymann, A. Luhmer, & M. Steven (Eds.), *Die Theorie der Unternehmung in Forschung und Praxis* (pp. 167–194). Berlin: Springer.

Klingner, S., Pravemann, S., & Becker, M. (2015). Service productivity in different industries – an empirical investigation. *Benchmarking: An International Journal, 22*(2), 238–253.

Kroll-Smith, S., Gunter, V., & Laska, S. (2000). Theoretical stances and environmental debates: Reconciling the physical and the symbolic. *The American Sociologist, 31*(1), 44–61.

Larivière, B., Bowen, D., Andreassen, T. W., Kunz, W., Sirianni, N. J., Voss, C., ... De Keyser, A. (2016). "Service Encounter 2.0": An investigation into the roles of technology, employees and customers. *Journal of Business Research, 79*, 238–246.

Lehmann, C. (2019). *Exploring service productivity: Studies in the German airport industry.* Wiesbaden: Springer Gabler.

Lehmann, C., & Möslein, K. M. (2014). Service productivity at airports. In *Driving service productivity: Value creation through innovation* (pp. 95–110).

Lessard, L. (2015). Modeling value cocreation processes and outcomes in knowledge-intensive business services engagements. *Service Science, 7*(3), 181–195.

Levitt, T. (1972). Production-line approach to service. *Harvard Business Review, 50*(5), 41–52.

Lewis, M. A., & Brown, A. D. (2012). How different is professionals ervice operations management. *Journal of Operations Management, 30*(1/2), 1–11.

Liedtka, J. (2015). Perspective: Linking design thinking with innovation outcomes through cognitive bias reduction. *Journal of Product Innovation Management, 32*(6), 925–938.

Liker, J. K., & Morgan, J. M. (2006). The Toyota way in services: The case of Lean product development. *Academy of Management Perspectives, 20*(2), 5–20.

Lillrank, P. (2009). Service processes. In G. Salvendy & W. Karwowski (Eds.), *Introduction to service engineering* (pp. 338–364). Hoboken, NJ: John Wiley & Sons.

Lim, C.-H., & Kim, K.-J. (2014). Information service blueprint: A service blueprinting framework for information-intensive services. *Service Science, 6*(4), 296–312.

Little, M. M., & Dean, A. M. (2006). Links between service climate, employee commitment and employees' service quality capability. *Managing Service Quality: An International Journal, 16*(5), 460–476.

Liu, H., Liu, L., & Liu, N. (2013). Risk evaluation approaches in failure mode and effects analysis : A literature review. *Expert Systems With Applications, 40*(2), 828–838.

Liu, S., & Lin, Y. (2006). *Grey information: Theory and practical applications.* London: Springer.

Lovelock, C. H., & Gummesson, E. (2004). Whither services marketing? In search of a new paradigm and fresh perspectives. *Journal of Service Research, 7*(1), 20–41.

Lovelock, C. H., & Young, R. F. (1979). Look to consumers to increase productivity. *Harvard Business Review, 57*(3), 168–178.

Maglio, P., Srinivasan, S., Kreulen, J., & Spohrer, J. (2006). Service systems, service scientists, SSME, and innovation. *Communications of the ACM, 49*(7), 81–85.

Maleri, R. (1997). *Grundlagen der Dienstleistungsproduktion.* Berlin: Springer.

Manchanda, P., Rossi, P. E., & Chintagunta, P. K. (2004). Response modeling with nonrandom marketing-mix variables. *Journal of Marketing Research, 41*(4), 467–478.

March, S. T., & Smith, G. F. (1995). Design and natural science research on information technology. *Decision Support Systems, 15*(4), 251–266.

March, S. T., & Storey, V. C. (2008). Design science in the information systems discipline: An introduction to the special issue on design science research. *MIS Quarterly, 32*(4), 725–730.

Marinova, D., Ruyter, K. De, & Huang, M. (2017). Getting smart: Learning from frontline interactions. *Journal of Service Research, 20*(1), 29–42.

Maroto-Sánchez, A. (2012). Productivity in the services sector: Conventional and current explanations. *The Service Industries Journal, 32*(5), 719–746.

Marshall, R. J. (1991). A review of methods for the statistical analysis of spatial patterns of disease. *Journal of the Royal Statistical Society, 154*(3), 421–441.

Matthias, O., & Brown, S. (2016). Implementing operations strategy through Lean processes within health care: The example of NHS in the UK. *International Journal of Operations & Production Management, 36*(11), 1435–1457.

McQuater, R. E., Scurr, C. H., Dale, B. G., & Hillman, P. G. (1995). Using quality tools and techniques successfully. *The TQM Magazine, 7*(6), 37–42.

Meyer, M. H., & DeTore, A. (1999). Product development for services. *Academy of Management Perspectives, 13*(3), 64–76.

Meyer, M. H., Jekowsky, E., & Crance, F. G. (2007). Applying platform design to improve the integration of patient services across the continuum of care. *Managing Service Quality An International Journal, 17*(1), 23–40.

Meyer, M. H., & Leonard, A. (1997). *The power of product platforms.* New York, NY: The Free Press.

Miles, M. B., Huberman, A. M., & Saldana, J. (2013). *Qualitative data analysis* (3rd ed.). Thousand Oaks: Sage.

Milton, S. K., & Johnson, L. W. (2012). Service blueprinting and BPM: A comparison. *Managing Service Quality: An International Journal, 22*(6), 606–621.

Misterek, S. D. A., Dooley, K. J., & Anderson, J. C. (1992). Productivity as a performance measure. *International Journal of Operations & Production Management, 12*(1), 29–45.

Mitchell, V.-W., & Greatorex, M. (1993). Risk perception and reduction in the purchase of consumer services. *The Services Industries Journal, 13*(4), 179–200.

Moeller, S. (2008). Customer integration: A key to an implementation perspective of service provision. *Journal of Service Research, 11*(2), 197–210.

Morris, K. C., Schlenoff, C., & Srinivasan, V. (2017). A remarkable resurgence of artificial intelligence and its impact on automation and autonomy. *IEEE Transactions on Automation Science and Engineering, 14*(2), 407–409.

Narayanan, S., Manchanda, P., & Chintagunta, P. K. (2005). Temporal differences in the role of marketing communication in new product categories. *Journal of Marketing Research, 42*(3), 278–290.

Neslin, S. A., Thomas, J. S., & Verhoef, P. C. (2006). Challenges and opportunities in multichannel customer management. *Journal of Service Research, 9*(2), 95–112.

Ng, I., Parry, G., Smith, L., Maull, R., & Briscoe, G. (2012). Transitioning from a goods-dominant to a service-dominant logic: Visualising the value proposition of Rolls-Royce. *Journal of Service Management, 23*(3), 416–439.

O'Shaughnessy, J., & O'Shaughnessy, N. J. (2009). The service-dominant perspective: A backward step? *European Journal of Marketing, 43*(5/6), 784–793.

O'Shaughnessy, J., & O'Shaughnessy, N. J. (2011). Service-dominant logic: A rejoinder to Lusch and Vargo's reply. *European Journal of Marketing, 45*(7/8), 1310–1318.

OECD. (2015). *The future of productivity.* Paris. Retrieved from https://dx.doi.org/10.1787/9789264248533-en

OECD. (2017). *Economic policy reforms 2017: Going for growth*. Paris. Retrieved from http://dx.doi.org/10.1787/growth-2017-en

Ostrom, A. L., Bitner, M. J., Brown, S. W., Burkhard, K. A., Goul, M., Smith-Daniels, V., ... Rabinovich, E. (2010). Moving forward and making a difference: Research priorities for the science of service. *Journal of Service Research, 13*(1), 4–36.

Ostrom, A. L., Parasuraman, A., Bowen, D. E., Patricio, L., & Voss, C. A. (2015). Service research priorities in a rapidly changing context. *Journal of Service Research, 18*(2), 127–159.

Oxford-Dictionaries. (n.d.). Definition of approach in English. Retrieved June 11, 2016, from http://www.oxforddictionaries.com/definition/english/approach

Parasuraman, A. (2002). Service quality and productivity : a synergistic perspective. *Managing Service Quality, 12*(1), 6–9.

Parasuraman, A. (2010). Service productivity, quality and innovation: Implications for service-design practice and research. *International Journal of Quality and Service Sciences, 2*(3), 277–286.

Parasuraman, A., Zeithaml, V. A., & Berry, L. L. (1988). SERVQUAL: A multiple-item scale for measuring consumer perceptions of service quality. *Journal of Retailing, 64*(1), 12–40.

Patrício, L., Falcão e Cunha, J., & Fisk, R. P. (2009). Requirements engineering for multi-channel services: The SEB method and its application to a multi-channel bank. *Requirements Engineering, 14*(3), 209–227.

Patrício, L., Fisk, R. P., & Falcão e Cunha, J. (2008). Designing multi-interface service experiences: The service experience blueprint. *Journal of Service Research, 10*(4), 318–334.

Patrício, L., Fisk, R. P., Falcão e Cunha, J., & Constantine, L. (2011). Multilevel service design: From customer value constellation to service experience blueprinting. *Journal of Service Research, 14*(2), 180–200.

Peffers, K., Rothenberger, M., Tuunanen, T., & Vaezi, R. (2012). Design science research evaluation. In K. Peffers, M. Rothenberger, & B. Kuechler (Eds.), *DESRIST 2012* (pp. 398–410). Berlin: Springer.

Peffers, K., Tuunanen, T., Rothenberger, M. A., & Chatterjee, S. (2007). A design science research methodology for information systems research. *Journal of Management Information Systems, 24*(3), 45–78.

Pena, R. M. (2011). *The nonprofit outcomes toolbox: A complete guide to program effectiveness, performance measurment and results.* New York: John Wiley & Sons.

Philips. (2017). *Schiphol airport opts for circular lighting: A responsible choice.* Retrieved from http://images.philips.com/is/content/PhilipsConsumer/PDFDownloads/Global/C ase-studies/CSLI20170418_001-UPD-en_AA-Case-Study-LaaS-Schiphol.pdf

Pine, J. B. I. (1999). *Mass customization.* Boston, Ma: Harvard Business School Press.

Pinho, N., Beirão, G., Patrício, L., & Fisk, R. P. (2014). Understanding value co-creation in complex services with many actors. *Journal of Service Management, 25*(4), 470–492.

Posselt, T., & Roth, A. (2017). Microfoundations of Organizational Competence for Servitization. *Journal of Competences, Strategy & Management, 9*(January), 85–107.

Prat, N., Comyn-Wattiau, I., & Akoka, J. (2015). A taxonomy of evaluation methods for information systems artifacts. *Journal of Management Information Systems, 32*(3), 229–267.

Preece, J., Roger, Y., & Sharp, H. (2002). *Beyond human-computer interaction.* New York: John Wiley & Sons.

Pritchard, R. D. (1990). *Measuring and improving organizational productivity: A practical guide.* New York: Praeger.

Pritchard, R. D., & Ashwood, E. L. (2008). *Managing motivation: A manager's guide to diagnosing and improving motivation.* New York: Erlbaum / Psychology Press.

Pritchard, R. D., Harrell, M. M., DiazGranados, D., & Guzman, M. J. (2008). The productivity measurement and enhancement system: A meta-analysis. *The Journal of Applied Psychology, 93*(3), 540–567.

Pritchard, R. D., Weaver, S. J., & Ashwood, E. L. (2012). *Evidence-based productivity improvement: A practical guide to the productivity measurement and enhancement system (ProMES).* New York: Routledge.

Puente, J., Pino, R., Priore, P., & de la Fuente, D. (2002). A decision support system for applying failure mode and effects analysis. *International Journal of Quality & Reliability Management, 19*(2), 137–150.

Pullman, M. E., & Thompson, G. (2003). Strategies for integrating capacity with demand in service networks. *Journal of Service Research, 5*(3), 169–183.

Quero, M. J., & Ventrua, R. (2015). The role of balanced centricity in the Spanish creative industries adopting a crowd-funding organisational model. *Journal of Service*

Theory and Practice, 25(2), 122–139.

Radnor, Z., & Osborne, S. P. (2013). Lean: A failed theory for public services? *Public Management Review, 15*(2), 265–287.

Recker, J., & Alter, S. (2012). Using the work system method with freshman information systems students. *Journal of Information Technology Education, 11*(1), 1–24.

Recker, J., Muehlen, M., Erickson, J., Indulska, M., Erickson, J., & Indulska, M. (2009). Measuring method complexity: UML versus BPMN. In *Proceedings of the 15th Americas Conference on Information Systems*. San Francisco.

Reijers, H. A., & Mansa, S. L. (2005). Best practices in business process redesign: An overview and qualitative evaluation of sucessful redesign heuristics. *Omega, 33*(4), 283–306.

Ross, T. ., Booker, J. M., & Parkinson, W. J. (2002). *Fuzzy logic and probability applications*. Philadelphia, PA.: ASA-SIAM.

Roth, A., Fritzsche, A., Jonas, J., Danzinger, F., & Möslein, K. M. (2014). Interaktive Kunden als Herausforderung: Die Fallstudie „JOSEPHS® – Die Service-Manufaktur". *HMD Praxis Der Wirtschaftsinformatik*, 1–13.

Russell, J. (2016). Think labs raises $125m to put its free-to-use smartphone in more hotel rooms worldwide. Retrieved December 29, 2016, from https://techcrunch.com/2016/09/28/tink-labs-handy-125-millon/

Rust, R. T., & Huang, M.-H. (2012). Optimizing Service Productivity. *Journal of Marketing, 76*(2), 47–66.

Sahay, B. S. (2006). Multi-factor productivity measurment model for service organisation. *International Journal of Productivity and Performance Management, 54*(1), 7–22.

Sametinger, J. (1997). *Software engineering with reusable components*. Berlin: Springer.

Sampson, S. E. (2001). *Understanding service businesses: Applying principles of the unified services theory*. (2nd ed.). New York: John Wiley & Sons.

Sampson, S. E. (2010). The unified service theory: A paradigm for service science. In M. Paul P., C. A. Kieliszewski, & and J. C. Spohrer (Eds.), *Handbook of Service Science* (pp. 107–131). New York: Springer.

Sampson, S. E. (2012). Visualizing service operations. *Journal of Service Research, 15*(2), 182–198.

Sampson, S. E. (2015). *Essentials of service design and innovation* (4th ed.). Provo: CreateSpace Independent Publishing Platform.

Sampson, S. E., & Froehle, C. (2006). Foundations and implications of a proposed unified services theory. *Production and Operations Management, 15*(2), 329–343.

Sampson, S. E., Menor, L. J., & Bone, S. A. (2010). Why we need a service logic: A comparative review. *Journal of Applied Management and Entrepreneurship, 15*(3), 17–32.

Sampson, S. E., Schmidt, G., Gardner, J. W., & Van Orden, J. (2015). Process coordination within a health care service supply network. *Journal of Business Logistics, 36*(4), 355–373.

Scerri, M., & Agarwal, R. (2018). Service enterprise productivity in action: measuring service productivity. *Journal of Service Theory and Practice, 28*(4), 524–551.

Schembri, S. (2006). Rationalizing service logic, or understanding services as experience? *Marketing Theory, 6*(3), 381–392.

Segelström, F. (2013). *Stakeholder engagement for service design.* Linköping University.

Sein, M. K., Henfridsson, O., Rossi, M., & Lindgren, R. (2011). Action design research. *MIS Quarterly, 35*(1), 37–56.

Sekhon, H., Yalley, A. A., Roy, S. K., & Shergill, G. S. (2016). A cross-country study of service productivity. *Service Industries Journal, 36*(5–6).

Sharma, R. K., Kumar, D., & Kumar, P. (2005). Systematic failure mode effect analysis (FMEA) using fuzzy linguistic modelling. *International Journal of Quality & Reliability Management, 22*(9), 986–1004.

Shostack, G. L. (1977). Breaking free from product marketing. *Journal of Marketing, 41*(2), 73–80.

Shostack, G. L. (1982). How to design a service. *European Journal of Marketing, 16*(1), 49–63.

Shostack, G. L. (1984). Designing services that deliver. *Harvard Business Review, 62*(1), 133–139.

Simar, L. (2003). Detecting outliers in frontier models: A simple approach. *Journal of Productivity Analysis, 20*(3), 391–424.

Simar, L., & Wilson, P. W. (1998). Sensitivity analysis of efficiency scores: How to bootstrap in nonparametric frontier models. *Management Science, 44*(1), 49–61.

Simon, H. A. (1996). *The sciences of the artifical*. Cambridge, MA: The MIT Press.

Smith, A. (1776). *The wealth of nations* (Reprint). Chicago: University of Chicago Press.

Sonnenberg, C., & vom Brocke, J. (2012). Design science research evaluation. In K. Peffers, M. Rothenberger, & B. Kuechler (Eds.), *DESRIST 2012, LNCS 7286* (pp. 381–397). Berlin, Heidelberg: Springer.

Spohrer, J., & Kwan, S. K. (2009). Service science, management, engineering, and design (SSMED): An emerging discipline - Outline & references. *International Journal of Information Systems in the Service Sector, 1*(3), 1–31.

Spohrer, J., Maglio, P. P., Bailey, J., & Gruhl, D. (2007). Steps towards a science of service systems. *Computer, 40*(1), 71–77.

Staats, B. R., Brunner, D. J., & Upton, D. M. (2011). Lean principles, learning, and knowledge work: Evidence from a software services provider. *Journal of Operations Management, 29*(5), 376–390.

Staats, B. R., & Upton, D. M. (2011). Lean knowledge work. *Harvard Business Review, 89*(10), 100–110.

Starr, M. K. (1965). Modular production - a new concept. *Harvard Business Review, 43*(6), 131–142.

Stauss, B. (2005). A pyrrhic victory: The implications of an unlimited broadening of the concept of services. *Managing Service Quality, 15*(3), 219–229.

Stickdorn, M., Frischhut, B., & Schmid, J. S. (2014). Mobile ethnography: A pioneering research approach for customer-centered destination management. *Tourism Analysis, 19*(4), 491–503.

Stickdorn, M., & Schneider, J. (2011). *This is service design thinking: Basics, Tools and Cases*. Amsterdam: BIS Publishers.

Storbacka, K., Brodie, R. J., Böhmann, T., Maglio, P. P., & Nenonen, S. (2016). Actor engagement as a microfoundation for value co-creation. *Journal of Business Research, 69*(8), 3008–3017.

Suprenant, C. F., & Solomon, M. R. (1987). Predictability and personalization in the service encounter. *Journal of Marketing, 51*(4), 86–96.

Svensson, G. (2001). The quality of bi-directional service quality in dyadic service encounters. *Journal of Services Marketing, 15*(5), 357–378.

Svensson, G. (2002). A triadic network approach to service quality. *Journal of Services*

Marketing, 16(2), 158–179.

Syltevik, S., Karamperidis, S., Antony, J., & Taheri, B. (2018). Lean for airport services: A systematic literature review and agenda for future research. *International Journal of Quality & Reliability Management, 35*(1), 34–49.

Tan, W. C., Haas, P. J., Mak, R. L., Kielizewski, C. A., Selinger, P., Maglio, P. P., & Li, Y. (2012). Splash: A platform for analysis and simulation of health. In *IHI'12 - Proceedings of the 2nd ACM SIGHIT International Health Informatics Symposium* (pp. 543–552).

Tan, Y., Hofman, W., Gordijn, J., & Hulstijn, J. (2011). A framework for the design of service systems. In H. Demirkan, J. C. Spohrer, & V. Krishna (Eds.), *Service Systems Implementation* (pp. 51–74). New York: Springer.

Tangen, S. (2005). Demystifying productivity and performance. *International Journal of Productivity and Performance Management, 54*(1), 34–46.

Tax, S. S., McCutcheon, D., & Wilkinson, I. F. (2013). The service delivery network (SDN): A customer-centric perspective of the customer journey. *Journal of Service Research, 16*(4), 454–470.

Teece, D. J. (2007). Explicating dynamic capabilities: The nature and microfoundations of (sustainable) enterprise performance. *Strategic Management Journal, 28*(13), 1319–1350.

Teixeira, J. G., Patrício, L., Huang, K.-H., Fisk, R. P., Nóbrega, L., & Constantine, L. (2017). The MINDS method: Integrating management and interaction design perspectives for service design. *Journal of Service Research, 20*(3), 240–258.

Teixeira, J. G., Patrício, L., Nunes, N. J., Nóbrega, L., Fisk, R. P., & Constantine, L. (2012). Customer experience modeling: From customer experience to service design. *Journal of Service Management, 23*(3), 362–376.

Tranfield, D., Denver, D., & Smart, P. (2003). Towards a methodology for developing evidence-informed management knowledge by means of systematic review. *British Journal of Management, 14*(3), 207–222.

Trischler, J., & Zehrer, A. (2012). Service design: Suggesting a qualitative multistep approach for analyzing and examining theme park experiences. *Journal of Vavation Marketing, 18*(1), 57–71.

Truex, D., Alter, S., & Long, C. (2010). System analysis for everyone else: Empowering business professionals through a systems analysis method that fits their needs. In *Proceedings of the 18th European Conference on Information Systems*. Pretoria.

Tsoukalas, L. H., & Uhrig, R. (1997). *Fuzzy and neural approaches in engineering*. New York: Wiley.

Van de Ven, A. H. (2007). *Engaged scholarship: A guide for organizational and social research*. Oxford: Oxford University Press.

Van de Ven, A. H., & Johnson, P. E. (2006). Knowledge for theory and practice. *Academy of Management Review, 31*(4), 802–821.

van der Wiele, T., Hesselink, M., & van Iwaarden, J. (2005). Mystery shopping: A tool to develop insight into customer service provision. *Total Quality Management & Business Excellence, 16*(4), 529–541.

van der Wiele, T., van Iwaarden, J., Dale, B. G., & Williams, R. (2006). A comparison of five modern improvement approaches. *International Journal of Productivity and Quality Management, 1*(4), 363–378.

Van Looy, B., Gemmel, P., Desmet, S., Van Dierdonck, R., & Serneels, S. (1998). Dealing with productivity and quality indicators in a service environment: Some field experiences. *International Journal of Service Industry Management, 9*(4), 359–376.

Vandermerwe, S., & Rada, J. (1988). Servitization of business: Adding value by adding services. *European Management Journal, 6*(4), 314–324.

Vargo, S. L. (2008). Customer integration and value creation: Paradigmatic traps and perspectives. *Journal of Service Research, 11*(2), 211–215.

Vargo, S. L., & Lusch, R. F. (2004a). Evolving to a new dominant logic for marketing. *Journal of Marketing, 68*(1), 1–17.

Vargo, S. L., & Lusch, R. F. (2004b). The four service marketing myths: Reminants of a goods-based, manufacturing model. *Journal of Service Research, 6*(4), 324–335.

Vargo, S. L., & Lusch, R. F. (2008). Service-dominant logic: Continuing the evolution. *Journal of the Academy of Marketing Science, 36*(1), 1–10.

Vargo, S. L., & Lusch, R. F. (2011). It's all B2B...and beyond: Toward a systems perspective of the market. *Industrial Marketing Management, 40*(2), 181–187.

Vargo, S. L., & Lusch, R. F. (2017). Service-dominant logic 2025. *International Journal of Research in Marketing, 34*(1), 46–67.

Vargo, S. L., Maglio, P. P., & Akaka, M. A. (2008). On value and value co-creation: A service systems and service logic perspective. *European Management Journal, 26*(3), 145–152.

Venable, J., Pries-Heje, J., & Baskerville, R. (2016). FEDS: A framework for evaluation in design science research. *European Journal of Information Systems, 25*(1), 77–89.

Verleye, K., Jaakkola, E., Hodgkinson, I. R., Gyuchan, T. J., Odekerken- Schröder, G., & Quist, J. (2017). What causes imbalance in complex service networks? Evidence from a public health service. *Journal of Service Management, 28*(1), 34–56.

Voorhees, C. M., Fombelle, P. W., Gregoire, Y., Bone, S., Gustafsson, A., Sousa, R., & Walkowiak, T. (2017). Service encounters, experiences and the customer journey: Defining the field and a call to expand our lens. *Journal of Business Research, 79,* 269–280.

Voss, C., Tsikriktsis, N., & Frohlich, M. (2002). Case research in operations management. *International Journal of Operations & Production Management, 22*(2), 195–219.

Vuorinen, I., Järvinen, R., & Lehtinen, U. (1998). Content and measurement of productivity in the service sector: A conceptual analysis with an illustrative case from the insurance business. *International Journal of Service Industry Management, 9*(4), 377–396.

Walker, G., & Weber, D. (1984). A transaction cost approach to make-or-buy decisions. *Administrative Science Quarterly, 29*(3), 373–391.

Walsh, A. G., Walgenbach, P., Evanschitzky, H., & Schaarschmidt, M. (2016). Service productivity: What stops service firms from measuring it ? *Journal of Organisational Transformation & Social Change, 13*(1), 5–25.

Webster, J., & Watson, R. T. (2002). Analyzing the past to prepare for the future: Writing a literature review. *MIS Quarterly, 26*(2), xiii–xxiii.

Wheeler, L., & Reis, H. T. (1991). Self-recording of everyday life events. origins, types, and uses. *Journal of Personality, 59*(3), 339–354.

Wickham, M., & Woods, M. (2005). Reflecting on the strategic use of CAQDAS to manage and report on the qualitative research process. *The Qualitative Report, 10*(4), 687–702.

Wilson, A., Zeithaml, V. A., Bitner, M. J., & Gremler, D. D. (2012). *Service marketing: integrating customer focus across the firm.* Berkshire: McGraw Hill.

Witell, L., Kristensson, P., Gustafsson, A., & Löfgren, M. (2011). Idea generation: Customer co-creation versus traditional market research techniques. *Journal of Service Management, 22*(2), 140–159.

World Bank. (n.d.). Employment in services (% of total employment). Retrieved March

19, 2018, from http://data.worldbank.org/indicator/SL.SRV.EMPL.ZS

Wynstra, F., Spring, M., & Schoenherr, T. (2015). Service triads: A research agenda for buyer–supplier–customer triads in business services. *Journal of Operations Management, 35,* 1–20.

Yalley, A. A., & Sekhon, H. S. (2014). Service production process: Implications for service productivity. *International Journal of Productivity and Performance Management, 63*(8), 1012–1030.

Yin, R. K. (2014). *Case study research: Design and methods.* Thousand Oaks, CA: SAGE Publications.

Yu, E. S. (2002). Agent-oriented modelling: Software versus the world. In W. M.J., G. Weiß, & P. Ciancarini (Eds.), *Agent-Oriented Software Engineering II (Lecture Notes in Computer Science)* (Vol. 2222, pp. 206–225). Berlin: Springer.

Yu, E. S. (2009). Social modeling and i*. In A. T. Borgida, V. Chaudhri, P. Giorgini, & E. Yu (Eds.), *Conceptual Modeling: Foundations and Applications. Lecture Notes in Computer Science.* (Vol. 5600, pp. 99–121). Berlin: Springer.

Zanella, A., Member, S., Bui, N., Castellani, A., Vangelista, L., Member, S., & Zorzi, M. (2014). Internet of Things for Smart Cities. *IEEE Internet of Things Journal, 1*(1), 22–32.

Zeithaml, V. A. (1981). How consumer evaluation processes differ between goods and services. In J. H. Donnelly & W. R. George (Eds.), *The Marketing of Services, Proceedings of the 1981 National Services Conference* (pp. 186–190). Chicago: American Marketing Association.

Zeithaml, V. A., Parasuraman, A., & Berry, L. L. (1985). Problems and strategies in services marketing. *Journal of Marketing, 49*(2), 33–46.

Zhang, Y. U. N., & Bartels, R. (1998). The effect of sample size on the mean efficiency in DEA with an application to electricity distribution in Australia, Sweden and New Zealand. *Journal of Productivity Analysis, 9*(3), 187–204.

Zomerdijk, L. G., & Voss, C. A. (2010). Service design for experience-centric services. *Journal of Service Research, 13*(1), 67–82.

Appendix

© Springer Fachmedien Wiesbaden GmbH, part of Springer Nature 2020
C. F. Daiberl, *Driving Networked Service Productivity*, Markt- und
Unternehmensentwicklung Markets and Organisations,
https://doi.org/10.1007/978-3-658-29580-6

Appendix A: Author's work relevant to this dissertation

Conference contributions relevant to this dissertation are listed in chronological order below. The first author was primarily accountable for research design, data collection, and analysis. However, the guidance and support of the co-authors played an important role for the quality of the contributions. The dissertation builds upon and extends these contributions. Still, some parts remained verbatim and unchanged.

Daiberl, C. F. (2015). A proposed method for enhancing service interaction productivity: The case of eMobilisten.de. Paper presented and discussed at the 8th *Service Operations Management Forum*. Nuremberg, Germany.

Daiberl, C. F., Roth, A., & Möslein, K. M. (2016). Approaches for enhancing productivity of networked service delivery: A review and assessment. Paper presented and discussed at the 26th *Annual RESER Conference*. Naples, Italy.

Daiberl, C. F., Roth, A., & Möslein, K. M. (2016). Conceptualizing productivity within a service network: The case of JOSEPHS®. Paper presented and discussed at the 23rd *EurOMA Conference*. Trondheim, Norway.

Daiberl, C. F., Roth, A., & Möslein, K. M. (2016). Towards perceived service interaction productivity: A proposed conceptual model. Paper published in the *Proceedings of the 2nd KSS Research Workshop*. Karlsruhe, Germany.

Daiberl, C. F., Naik, H., & Roth, A. (2018). Proposing the NSPIRE technique: Improving productivity of networked service delivery. Paper presented and discussed at the *R&D Management Conference 2018*. Milan, Italy.

The following forthcoming book chapter co-authored by Angela Roth synthesizes key findings of this dissertation to inform decision makers of open innovation laboratories.

Daiberl, C. F., & Roth, A. (Forthcoming). Driving service productivity of an open innovation lab. In A. Fritzsche., J. M. Jonas, A. Roth, & K. M. Möslein (Eds.), *Innovating in the open lab*. Oldenbourg: De Gruyer.

Earlier stages of this dissertation have been presented and discussed at the following research and doctoral colloquia. As the respective papers served as the foundations for the conference contributions detailed above, some parts remained verbatim and unchanged.

Daiberl, C. F. (2015). Understanding service productivity from an interaction perspective. A proposed conceptual model. Paper presented and discussed at the *10th Research Colloquium on Innovation & Value Creation*, Leipzig, Germany.

Daiberl, C. F. (2016). Identifying failure and innovation modes for driving networked service productivity. Paper presented and discussed at the *11th Research Colloquium on Innovation & Value Creation*, Linz, Austria.

Daiberl, C. F. (2017). The DNSP technique: Driving productivity of networked service delivery. Paper presented and discussed at the *12th Research Colloquium on Innovation & Value Creation*. Hamburg, Germany.

Daiberl, C. F. (2017). Driving networked service productivity. Dissertation proposal presented and discussed at the *Doctoral colloquium of the European Academy of Management Conference 2017*. Glasgow, Scotland.

The following journal article co-authored by Sascha J. Oks, Angela Roth, Kathrin M. Möslein, and Steven Alter provided inspiration for the development of NSPIRET. In particular, it revealed the potentials of harnessing work system theory for the systematic improvement of networked service delivery.

Daiberl, C. F., Oks, S. J., Roth, A., Möslein, K. M., & Alter, S. (2019). Design principles for establishing a multi-sided open innovation platform: Lessons learned from an action research study in the medical technology industry. *Electronic Markets*. In Press.

Appendix B: Research proposal for the literature review

1 Working title

"Approaches for Enhancing Service Productivity: A Review and Assessment"

Keywords: Service Productivity, Service Networks, Systematic Review

2 Intended outlet

- RESER 2016 Conference as a leading conference for service research
- Call: 1. Service Ecosystems: strategy and management issues, Sub-theme: Service networks and service ecosystems
- Deadline for Abstracts: April 30, 2016

3 Objectives of the study

This study aims to contribute to a better theoretical as well as operational understanding of how to enhance productivity in the context of networked service delivery. Given the heterogeneity of existing approaches for enhancing service productivity, a high-level classification scheme is developed fostering an integrated understanding for both scholars and practitioners. Moreover, as common approaches typically address service productivity from a monadic or dyadic perspective, a structured literature review is conducted. All in all, the following questions are addressed:

- *How can approaches for the enhancement of service productivity be classified?*

- *Which systematic approaches are discussed in service research for the improvement of service productivity from a network perspective and what are their application-oriented qualities?*

4 Method

In order to create evidence-informed knowledge for academics and practitioners, a systematic literature review following followed the overall procedure of Tranfield, Denver, and Smart (2003) and harnessing the advice of Webster and Watson (2002) and Wickham and Woods (2005) is proposed. For this purpose, initially, a scoping study is conducted in order to in order to delimit the subject area, identify relevant keywords, outlets as well as inclusion and exclusion criteria. After this, the actual review is conducted. In this stage, the final sets of keywords and search strings are built based on the insights from the scoping study as well as the discussions with the researchers involved in this study.

For the main search the database Business Source Complete (via EBSCO Host) as it covers the relevant subject area. As this study aims to contribute to service research, all leading, peer-reviewed, service-specific journals are considered for the keyword search. In order to ensure that the best quality evidence is investigated, VHB JOURQUAL ranking will be applied and journals are only considered if they are ranked A-C in VHB JOURQUAL3. This list is extended based on the insights of the scoping study. Moreover, the approaches for productivity management published in the service productivity toolbox are considered. The toolbox represents a collection of best practice approaches which were either used, reflected upon or developed in the context of the funding priority *"productivity of services"* of the German Ministry of Education and Research. The latter comprised 33 sponsored research projects with a funding volume of 41,54 million EUR and lasted from August 2009 to September 2015. Thus, it presents a database of approaches considered practically relevant by the participating institutions. As proposed by Wickham and Woods (2005), in order to foster efficient and effective analysis, key information is extracted using computer-aided qualitative data analysis software MAXQDA 12.

5 Expected results

The study aims to foster scholarly and managerial understanding concerning existing and empirically assessed approaches for systematically enhancing service productivity.

- For scholars, results shall provide a descriptive and thematic analysis of empirical studies on enhancing service productivity. Reviewing and comparing results from different research streams shall lead to a better understanding of the heterogeneous field and help to identify undergirding qualities for driving service productivity throughout the service productivity life cycle.

- Analyzing results from a network perspective shall provide theoretical insights and inspire future research for developing systematic approaches to drive service productivity in the context of networked service provision

- For practitioners the review shall create an empirically-based knowledge base concerning systematic approaches for driving service productivity. By doing so, best practices, limitations as well as potentials for integrating different approaches throughout the service life cycle shall be shared. By doing so, managers should be enabled to inform their decisions with scientific evidence. Additionally, it shall raise their awareness of the necessity to look beyond a dyadic perspective on managing service productivity.

Appendix C: Review protocol

1 Research problem and significance

Enhancing service productivity is considered a key research priority to advance the service field (Ostrom et al., 2015). Whereas the topic of service productivity has been discussed for decades, its general conception is still largely manufacturing-based and lacks behind scientific progress in service management (Yalley & Sekhon, 2014). Literature highlights that service processes increasingly integrate resources of and create outcomes for multiple entities (Sampson, 2012; Tax et al., 2013; Wynstra, Spring, & Schoenherr, 2015). However, it remains unclear how to operationally increase productivity within service networks. In order to reflect on the status quo, this study aims to systematically review existing research on methods for driving service productivity and discuss implications for networked service delivery.

2 Notes for conducting the review

Search for articles that describe systematic approaches (e.g., tools, technique, systems, or strategic approaches) for driving productivity of new/established service offerings (addresses both effectiveness and efficiency considerations).

a) Inclusion and exclusion criteria

- Approaches should have a managerial focus and not focus on a macro-economic perspective on service productivity.
- Approaches should present a systematic that informs the improvement of service efficiency and/or effectiveness from a network perspective (i.e., consider the role of the customer and two or more providers for service delivery).
- Approaches discussed should be applicable to different settings of networked service delivery and not only present a solution to very specific domains (e.g., optimization of call-center networks).
- Contributions should be application-oriented (i.e., describe how to apply a particular approach).
- Contributions should be written in English or German language and published in scientific outlets.

b) Where the search is conducted

- Business Source Complete
- Google Scholar (forward and backward search)
- Productivity Toolbox via www.serviceproductivity.de
- Final list of Journals considered see Part III, Table 2, p. 51

c) Keywords for the search in Business Source Complete via Ebsco-Host

Search in title (TI), abstract (AB). or author supplied keywords (KW)

"servic*" +

1ˢᵗ set of keywords (network-related terms)

TI (net* or syste* or tria*) OR AB (net* or syste* or tria*) OR KW (net* or syste* or tria*)

2ⁿᵈ set of keywords (productivity-related terms)

TI (productiv*, effectiv*, efficienc*, qual*, perfor*, experienc*, valu*) OR AB (productiv*, effectiv*, efficienc*, qual*, perfor*, experienc*, valu*) OR KW (productiv*, effectiv*, efficienc*, qual*, perfor*, experienc*, valu*)

3ʳᵈ set of keywords (improvement-related terms)

TI (enhanc*, improv*, increas*, optimi*, manag*, desig*, enginee*, innovat*, develo*, driv*, rais*, gai*) OR AB (enhanc*, improv*, increas*, optimi*, manag*, desig*, enginee*, innovat*, develo*, driv*, rais*, gai*) OR KW (enhanc*, improv*, increas*, optimi*, manag*, desig*, enginee*, innovat*, develo*, driv*, rais*, gai*)

4ᵗʰ set of keywords (systematic-related terms)

TI (metho*, tool, system, approach, instrument, procedure, framework, technique, process, strategy) OR AB (metho*, tool, system, approach, instrument, procedure, framework, technique, process, strategy) OR KW (metho*, tool, system, approach, instrument, procedure, framework, technique, process, strategy).

3. Number of core and related contributions identified

Description	# Contributions
Application of keywords in Business Source Complete via Ebsco Host	934
Manual review in "Journal of Service Theory and Practice", "Service Science" and "Service Productivity Toolbox"	244
Identified core contributions after key-word based and manual review	17
Identified contributions via forward and backward search	64
Core contributions after forward and backward search	19
Related contributions	62
Final set of core and related contributions	81

Appendix D: Interview guide for exploratory case study

Note that several interviews were conducted as part of collaborative research projects. Thus, the focus and content of interviews as well as the order of questions varied. In the following, only the questions relevant to the exploratory case study (Part IV) are depicted. The questions were translated from German.

Subject area	Main questions (depending on setting and interviewee)
Personal	*eMobilizer & OI-Lab:* • What is your position at the firm/organization? *(Focal provider, Org. customers; Org. co-providers)* • How were/are you involved in eMobilizer/OI-Lab? *(Focal provider, Customers; Org. co-providers)* • What is your profession? *(Ind. customers/co-providers)* • Do you have experiences with similar services? *(Ind. customers, Org. customers; Ind. co-providers)*
Objectives & Expectations	*eMobilizer:* • Why does your employer participate in eMobilizer? *(Focal providers, Org. co-providers)* • What are the long-term objectives for your organization? *(Focal providers, Org. co-providers)* • What was your first impression/expectation what can be done on the eMobilizer platform? *(Ind. customers/co-providers)* • Why did you register on the eMobilizer platform? *(Ind. customers/co-providers)* • What did you expect from using the eMobilizer platform? *(Ind. customers/co-providers)* *OI-Lab:* • What are/were your objectives for using/in the context of OI-Lab? *(Focal provider; Org. customer)* • What benefits did you expect in advance? *(Org. customer)* • Have the objectives [for using OI-Lab] changed over time? If yes, why? *(Org. customer)* • Why did you come to OI-Lab? *(Ind. co-provider)* • What was your first impression/expectation what can be done at OI-Lab? *(Ind. co-provider)* [After introduction to the "standard" OI-Lab process] • Did you have any expectations concerning the process steps? *(Org. customer)*

Subject area	Main questions (depending on setting and interviewee)
Inputs & interactions (Efficiency-related)	*eMobilizer:* • What is the role of your employer for eMobilizer [which resources did your organization contribute?] *(Focal providers, Org. co-providers)* • With which partners were/are you in regular contact with? Why? *(Focal providers, Org. co-providers)* • Were/are the roles/activities of the different partners [i.e., providers] clearly defined and communicated? *(Focal provider, Org. co-providers)* • How efficient are the interactions with the different project partners [i.e., providers]? Why? Has efficiency changed over time? *(Focal provider, Org. co-providers)* • How did you learn about eMobilizer? *(Ind. customers/co-providers)* • How do you rate the interactions on the platform? *(Ind. customers, Ind. co-providers)* • How do you rate your personal effort for using the eMobilizer platform? *(Ind. customers/co-providers)* *OI-Lab:* • What activities do you regularly conduct? Who is involved? *(Focal provider)* • Are there activities that require particular high effort for you or the customer? *(Focal provider)* • How do you rate the efficiency of the different process phases of OI-Lab? *(Focal provider)* • How has the process worked out for you [which resources did your organization contribute]? *(Org. customer)* • Have you collaborated with other actors [besides the focal provider of OI-Lab]? Why and how? *(Org. customer)* • Which roles did the above mentioned actors play [which resources did they contribute]? *(Org. customer)* • How efficient were interactions with the different actors throughout the overall process? Why? Has efficiency changed over time? *(Org. customer)* • How do you rate the opportunities to interact at OI-Lab? *(Ind. co-provider)* • How do you rate the time expenditure for contributing to OI-Lab? *(Ind. co-provider)*

Subject area	Main questions (depending on setting and interviewee)
	eMobilizer:
	• How well have your objectives/expectations been met to date? Why? *(Focal providers; Ind. customers; Org. co-providers; Ind. co-providers)*
	• Were you able to draw a personal benefit from using eMobilizer? If yes, which? *(Ind. customers, Ind. co-providers)*
	• Have you experienced any learning in the context of using/contributing to the eMobilizer platform? *(Focal providers; Ind. customers; Org. co-providers; Ind. co-providers)*
	OI-Lab:
Outcomes (Effectiveness-related)	• How do you rate the effectiveness of the different process phases of OI-Lab? *(Focal provider)*
	• Have you experienced any learning in the context of using/contributing to OI-Lab? *(Focal providers; Ind. customers; Org. co-providers; Ind. co-providers)*
	• How well have your expectations concerning the process steps been met? *(Org. customer)*
	• How satisfied were you with the results of using OI-Lab? Why? *(Org. customer)*
	• How would you rate the success of using OI-Lab? How do you define success? *(Org. customers)*
	• Were there any side-effects? *(Org. customers)*
	• How do you feel after experiencing OI-Lab? *(Ind. co-providers)*
	• Would you revisit OI-Lab/recommend it to others? *(Ind. co-providers)*

Subject area	Main questions (depending on setting and interviewee)
Drivers & related resistances	*eMobilizer:* • Which factors have a particular positive/negative influence on efficiency of interactions/meeting of objectives? *(Focal providers, Org. co-providers)* • Can you remember any particular challenges in the context of contributing to eMobilizer? *(Focal providers, Org. co-providers)* • Which measures could improve efficiency/the degree of goal attainment? *(Focal provider, ind. customers; Org. co-providers: Ind. co-providers)* • Did you encounter any challenges for using the eMobilizer platform? *(Ind. customers/ co-providers)* • Is there anything that should be changed/could be improved for the future? *(Ind. customers/co-providers* *OI-Lab:* • Are there activities that are particularly challenging [i.e., unclear, difficult, problematic] for you or the customer? *(Focal provider)* • Which factors had a particular positive/negative influence on interactions/ results? *(Org. customer; Ind. co-providers)* • Can you remember any particular challenges/inefficient interactions with other actors? *(Org. customer)* Is there anything that should be changed/could be improved for the future? *(Org. customer; Ind. co-providers)*
General	*eMobilizer & OI-Lab:* How could productivity/effectiveness/efficiency be measured in this particular context? *(Focal provider; Org. co-providers; Org. customers)*

Appendix E: Interview guide for DSR study

Like in the context of the exploratory case study, several interviews for evaluating NSPIRET were conducted as part of collaborative research projects. Thus, the focus and content of interviews as well as the order of questions varied. In the following, only the questions relevant to the DSR study (Part V) are depicted. The questions were translated from German.

Subject area	Main questions (depending on setting and interviewee)
	Beta version
Requirements	• How useful do you think it is that the various actors contributing to OI-Lab are integrated into an iterative productivity improvement process? *(Focal provider)* • What insights would you like to gain from the improvement process in order to ensure utility? *(Focal provider)* • What are the most important potentials and challenges when using a digital, web-based feedback tool? *(Focal provider)* • How should a web-based feedback tool be designed to foster use on site? What are required contents and functionalities? *(Focal provider)*
Effectiveness	*Alpha version* • In retrospect, how well could potentials for increasing productivity (i.e., existing problems or ideas for further development) be identified through the use of NSPIRET? Can it be improved? How? *(Focal providers)* • In retrospect, how well could these potentials be evaluated? Can it be improved? How? *(Focal providers)* • In retrospect, how well could this potential be realized? Can it be improved? How? *(Focal providers)* *Beta version of NSPIRET:* • In retrospect, how well could opportunities for increasing productivity (i.e., existing problems or ideas for further development) be identified through the use of NSPIRET? Can it be improved? How? *(Focal provider)* • In retrospect, how well could these opportunities be evaluated? Can it be improved? How? *(Focal provider)* • In retrospect, how well could these opportunities be realized? Can it be improved? How? *(Focal provider)*

Subject area	Main questions (depending on setting and interviewee)
Effectiveness	• In retrospect, how well could the various productivity perspectives be taken into account by means of using NSPIRET? Can it be improved? How? *(Focal provider)* • In retrospect, is there anything particularly that needs to be considered for successfully implementing NSPIRET? Can it be improved? How? *(Focal provider)* • In retrospect, did using NSPIRET support you to establish an iterative productivity improvement process? Can it be improved? How? *(Focal provider)*
Utility	*Alpha version of NSPIRET* • In retrospect, how would you rate the utility of applying NSPRIET in the context of eMobilizer? What were the main insights/benefits/challenges? Can it be improved? How? *(Focal providers; Org. co-provider)* *Beta version of NSPIRET:* • Considering its objectives, how would you generally rate the utility of NSPIRET? Can it be improved? How? *(Focal provider)* • In retrospect, how would you rate the utility of the on-site deployment at OI-Lab? What were the main insights/benefits/challenges? Can it be improved? How? *(Focal provider)* • Considering its objective, do you think that the effort for applying NSPRIET is appropriate? Why? *(Focal provider)* • How high would you describe your personal effort required to carry out your task in the context of NSPIRET? Can your personal effort be reduced? How? *(Focal provider)* • How beneficial do you consider the feedback tool [i.e., the NSPIRET Shoutbox]? Can it be improved? How? *(Focal provider; Org. customers; Ind. co-providers)* • How much effort is it to use the feedback tool [i.e., the NSPIRET Shoutbox]? Anything particularly complicated? Can the effort be reduced? How? *(Focal provider; Org. customers; Ind. co-providers)* • Considering the objective, do you think that the effort for using the feedback tool [i.e., the NSPIRET Shoutbox] is appropriate? Please explain. *(Focal provider; Org. customers; Ind. co-providers)*

Subject area	Main questions (depending on setting and interviewee)
	Alpha version of NSPIRET
	• How understandable are the objectives/steps of NSPIRET? Can it be improved? How? *(Focal providers; Org. co-providers)* • How understandable are the contents of the different artifacts of NSPIRET? Can it be improved? How? *(Focal providers; Ind. customers; Org. co-providers)*
	Beta version
Understandability	• How understandable is the function of the different artifacts? Can it be improved? How? *(Focal provider)* • How understandable is the interaction of the different artifacts? Can it be improved? How? *(Focal provider)* • How understandable are the contents of the different artifacts? Can it be improved? How? *(Focal provider)* • How understandable are the questions of the feedback tool [i.e., the NSPIRET Shoutbox]? Can it be improved? How? *(Focal provider; Org. customers; Ind. co-providers)* • How understandable do you find the navigation within the feedback tool [i.e., the NSPIRET Shoutbox]? Can it be improved? How? *(Focal provider; Org. customers; Ind. co-providers)*
Operational feasibility	*Beta version of NSPIRET:* • To what extent are the different artifacts of NSPIRET already being used in your daily work? Please explain. *(Focal provider)* • Do you believe that the different artifacts of NSPIRET are already designed to be used by you and your employees in the long run? If not, what needs to be changed? *(Focal provider)* • In retrospect, which aspects play a special role in the implementation of NSPIRET in order to foster use in daily operations? *(Focal provider)* • How well does using the feedback tool [i.e., the NSPIRET Shoutbox] fit into a visit at OI-Lab? Can it be improved? How? *(Ind. co-providers)* • Do you like using a tablet for giving feedback or would you prefer another channel? *(Ind. co-providers)* • Would you reuse the feedback tool [i.e., the NSPIRET Shoutbox] throughout your next visit at OI-Lab/in the future in case you identify any problems or you have an innovative idea? If not, what needs to be changed? *(Customers; Ind. co-providers)*
General	*Alpha & beta version of NSPIRET:* • Do you have any further feedback concerning NSPIRET? *(Focal provider; Org. customers; Ind. co-providers)*

Appendix F: Feedback tablet positioned at OI-Lab

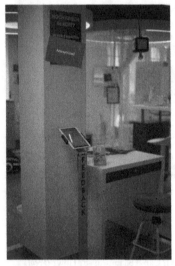 

Source: Photo taken by Eva Redelbach. Print with permission.

Printed in the United States
By Bookmasters